SKINWALKER™

written by
Nunzio DeFilippis & Christina Weir

pencilled by
Brian Hurtt

digital finishes and lettering by
Arthur Dela Cruz

cover and main chapter breaks by
Durwin Talon

secondary chapter breaks by
Brian Hurtt

Introduction by
Greg Rucka

book design by
Keith Wood

edited by
Jamie S. Rich

Published by Oni Press, Inc.

Joe Nozemack, publisher

James Lucas Jones, associate editor

This collects issues 1-4 of the Oni Press comics series *Skinwalker*.

ONI PRESS, INC.
6336 SE Milwaukie Avenue, PMB30
Portland, OR 97202
USA

www.onipress.com

First edition: March 2003
ISBN 1-929998-45-7

1 3 5 7 9 10 8 6 4 2

PRINTED IN CANADA.

iNtroduction By Greg Rucka

In the end, then, this is about collaboration. This is how comics thrive, this is what elevates them, this is what makes them truly magic. You write a novel, you're in it by yourself, for the long haul. You may get an editor near the final lap, but ultimately, that editor has very little to do with the process, with the creation. You write a screenplay, you're on your own, and God forbid you sell the thing and then Mister Director gets his grubby little mitts on it and tells you, and the studio, and the producers, that he actually can write it so much better, and that's just before the actor gets involved, and by the time you're done, you say, hey, I wrote this...

...they just stare at you as if you've peed in their coffee.

There is no medium that relies and thrives on artistic collaboration as much as comics. And I would argue—and probably be stoned to death in some quarters for the statement—that the best comics ever produced are the results of collaborative efforts... rather, say, than the efforts of that rarest of beasts, the Writer-Artist. But for every Art Spiegelman and the tired refrain of *Maus*, I can offer my own tired rendition of Moore and Gibbons and *The Watchmen*. For every Frank Miller, I'm quick to shout the name Klaus Janson.

We are a collaborative medium. At its worst, it's a seven-car pile-up on the BQE translated to the printed page.

At its best, it's magical.

You hold what is, truly, a magical collaboration.

Nunzio DeFilippis and I go back to the fall of 1987 and a freshman year at Vassar College, and a midnight meeting in a bathroom (make of that what you will). He is, perhaps, my dearest friend in the entirety of my known universe. He is a righteous man, a passionate man, and a man who can take me from zero to livid in all of three seconds; he's a fighter, and he never does anything half-assed. He is demanding, not solely of himself and the people around him, but of the world, and he is like that *every fucking day* of his life.

That's a hard road to travel, harder still when you believe in the strength of your convictions, and the need to speak out when it is far easier, and far more comfortable, to remain silent.

Christina Weir and I go back not quite as far, and with many more detours, but none that involved midnight liaisons in collegiate bathrooms. She is, genuinely, the living breathing walking talking example of a still water that runs deep. She lulls you with a smile and a nod and her silence, and then the steel trap closes, and the intellect strikes, and it's devastating, because smarts alone do not a writer make. She has the heart to back it up. She plays nice, sure... but she'll give as good as she gets. Christina Weir is not a force to be trifled with.

Nunzio and Christina are partners, in every sense of the word. They live together, they love together, they despair together... and they write together, which, by default, includes the aforementioned. And they fight over each word, each comma, each scene, each motivation. There are partner teams that split the work, taking the story and cracking it into pieces, parceling out duties, and then stitching sections back together to make a whole.

They don't work like that. They sit there, in front of the keyboard, together, and

one types and the other talks, and then the other talks, and one types, and they storm around the room and shout at each other and then calm down and type some more and then delete it and get fed-up and watch *Angel* on video and try it again... and again... and again, until they have it *right*.

That's not just magical, that's a damn miracle.

And still, it's not enough, it's less than nothing, because in this medium the words don't exist outside the image. You don't have a comic unless you have the artists to back it. You don't have the heat of Navajo Country or the claustrophobic terror of a skinned body in a hogan unless you've got someone on the pencils and on the inks who can drive that devastatingly home.

Ladies and Gentlemen, Brian Hurtt and Arthur De La Cruz, and if you don't believe in magic, look again at Ann Adakai and the fact that you have *never before* seen a Navajo woman on a comic book page who looked like... a Navajo woman.

Suspense thrives on subtlety, and this story, for all of its potential horror trappings, is one of suspense. What Hurtt does with posture, with expression, with sheer power of visual storytelling, is the engine of this story. And if Brian gets to claim the part of the goddamn Pratt & Whitney PW305As, then Arthur must be credited as every other flight surface on this Learjet of a story. Without his finishes, you've got a fuselage that goes down in a flaming wreck.

But with all of them together... you get a hell of a ride, and a promise of things to come.

And that's my last point, really, because what makes *Skinwalker* all the more remarkable is its timing, not in the Big Wide World, but in the careers of the four major players of the work. Each of them is relatively new to the form, in the way that every overnight success has twenty years of back-breaking labor to show for it. If this is truly to be seen in any way as a freshman effort, then the promise of what is yet to come, from each of these talents...

...like I said, man.

Magic.

Greg Rucka lives and writes in Portland, Oregon, and has never actually been on a Learjet.

CHAPTER 1

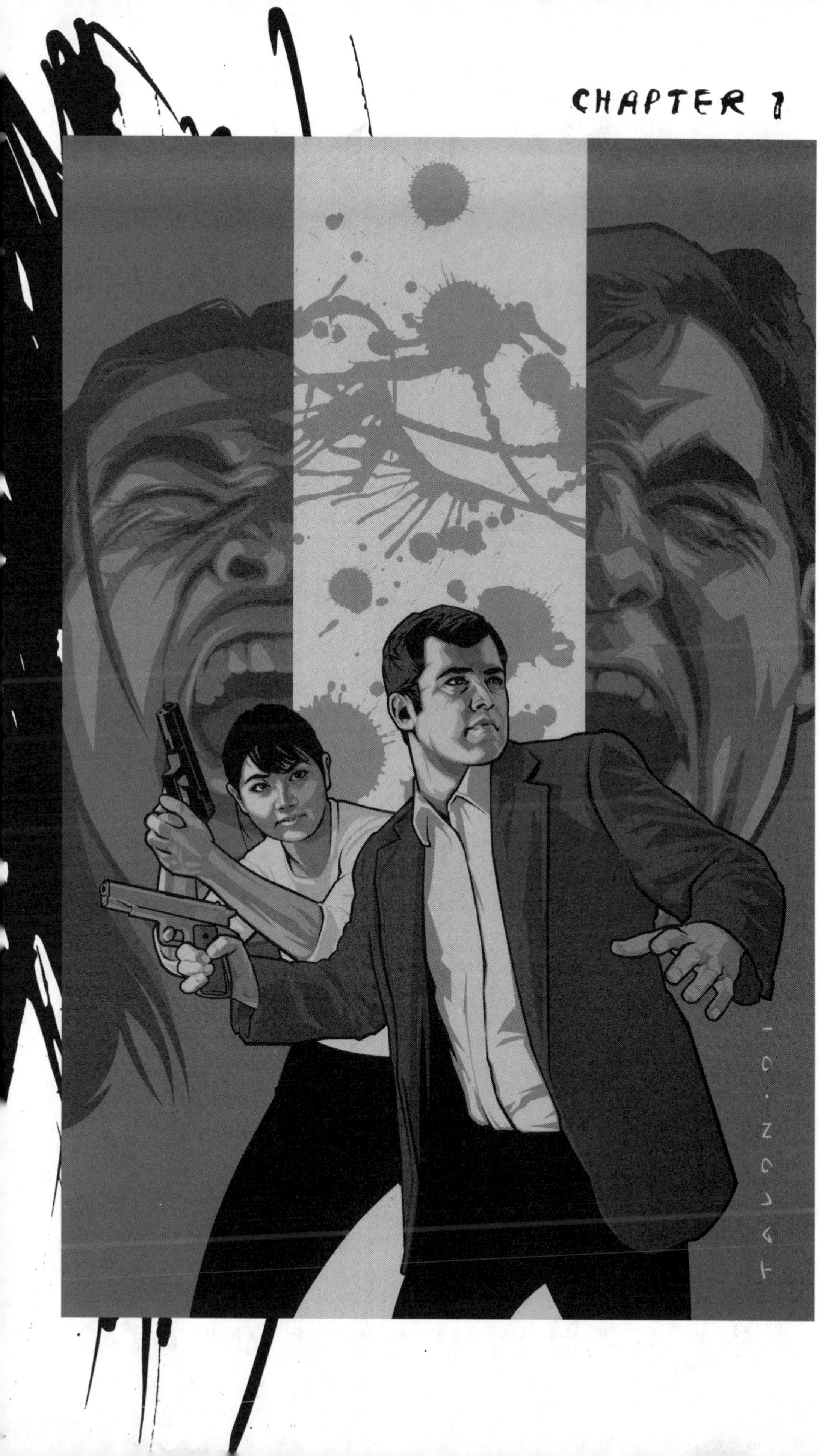

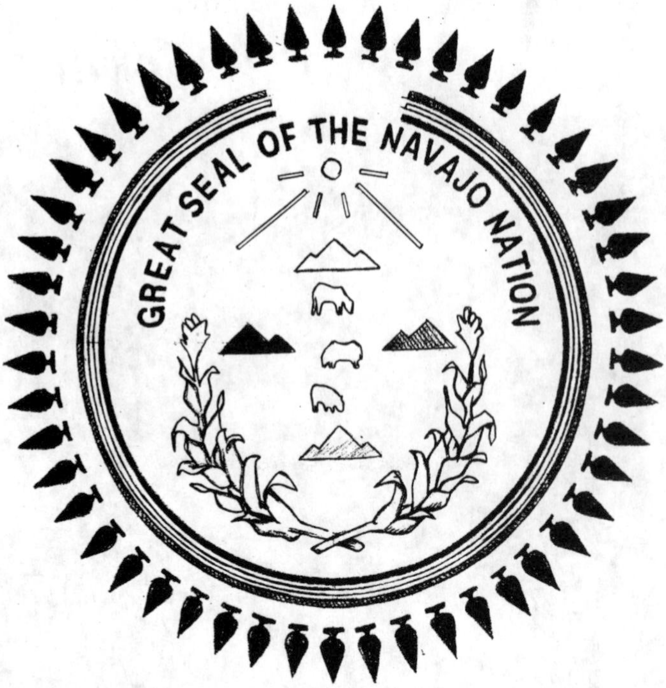
GREAT SEAL OF THE NAVAJO NATION

The Great Seal of the Navajo Nation, designed by John Claw, Jr., from Many Farms, Arizona, was officially accepted by the Navajo Tribal Council on January 18, 1952, by Resolution CJ-9-52.

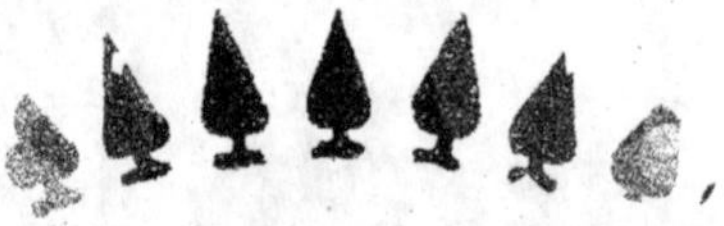

Fifty outward pointing arrowheads form the outer edge of the seal. They symbolize the Tribe's protection within the fifty states.

These three bands of the rainbow represent the sovereignty of the Navajo Nation. The outside line is blue, the middle yellow, and the inside red. The opening at the top is considered the east.

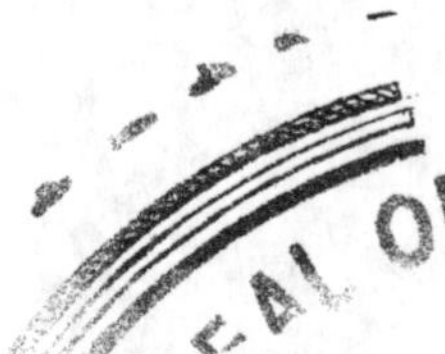

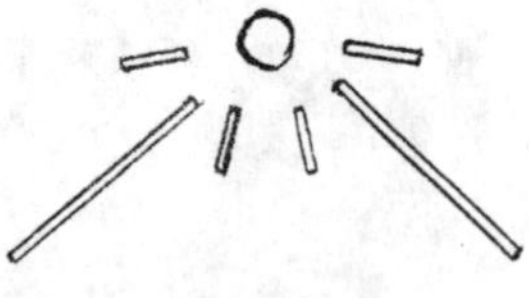

The Yellow Sun shines from the east on the four mountains sacred to the Navajo.

These holy mountains mark the boundaries of the Navajo land. Located at the cardinal points, they are in their ceremonial colors: White in the East representing White Shell Woman; Blue in the South representing Turqoise Woman; Yellow to the West representing Abalone Woman; and Black to the North representing Jet Woman.

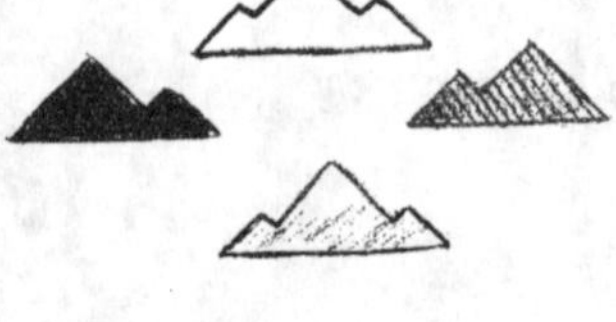

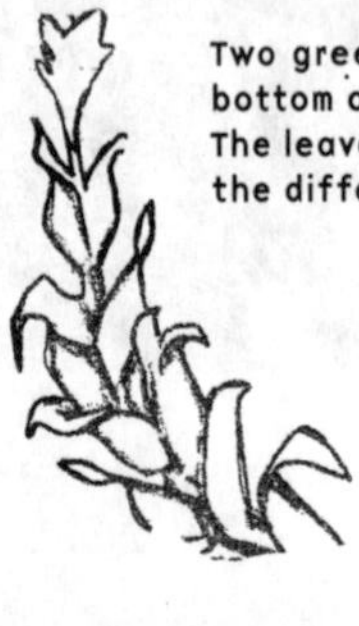

Two green corn plants, symbolic as the sustainer of Navajo Life, decorate the bottom of the Seal, with their tips of yellow pollen used in many Navajo ceremonies. The leaves that come off the corn stalk are the different paths one can take and the different levels of knowledge.

Directly between the top and the bottom mountain is a horse, a cow, and a sheep. These animals represent life and the traditional Navajo livestock economy.

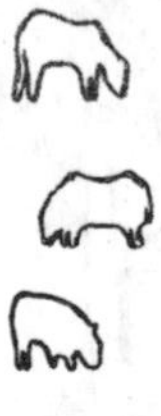

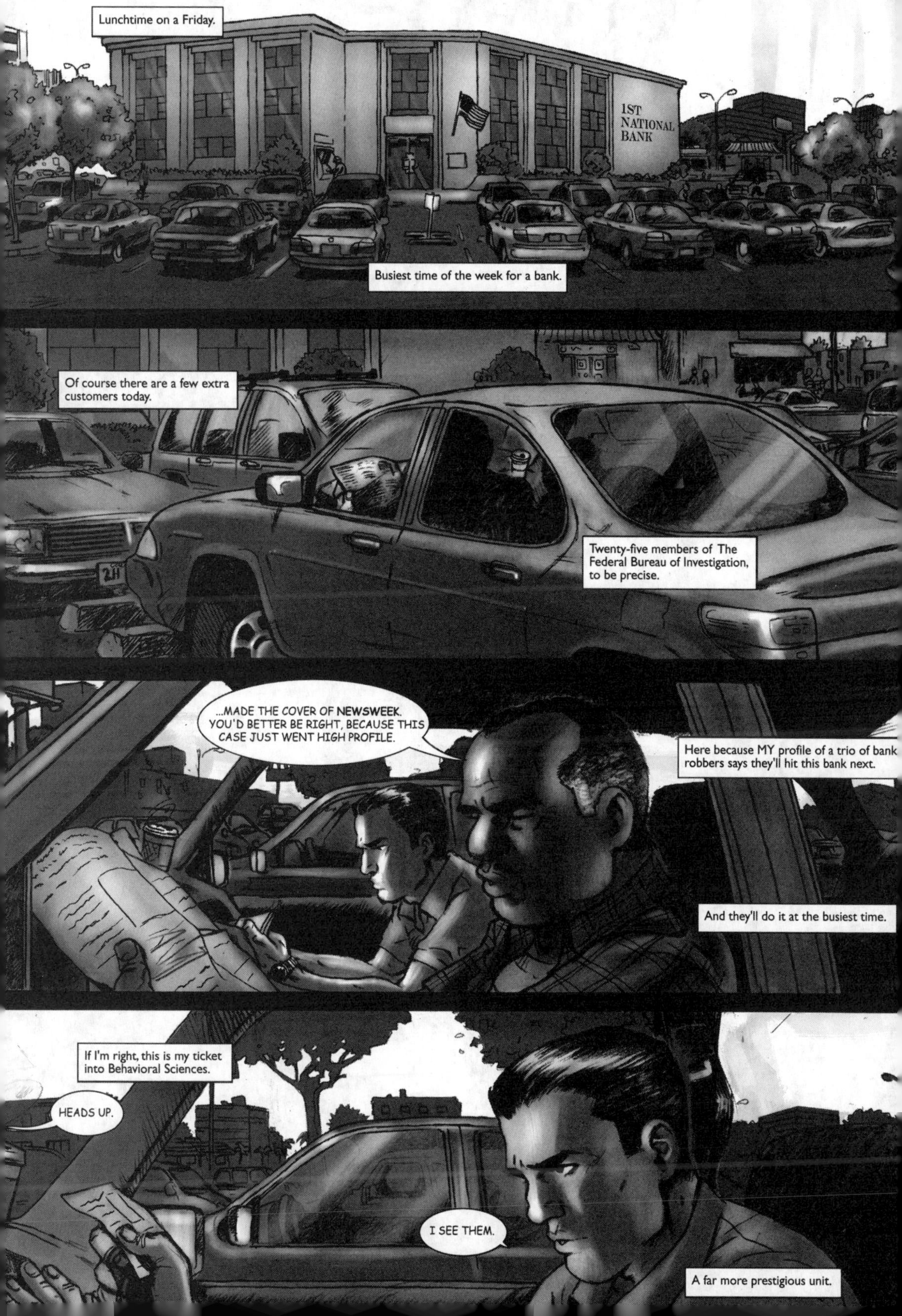

Lunchtime on a Friday.
1ST NATIONAL BANK
Busiest time of the week for a bank.
Of course there are a few extra customers today.
Twenty-five members of The Federal Bureau of Investigation, to be precise.
...MADE THE COVER OF NEWSWEEK. YOU'D BETTER BE RIGHT, BECAUSE THIS CASE JUST WENT HIGH PROFILE.
Here because MY profile of a trio of bank robbers says they'll hit this bank next.
And they'll do it at the busiest time.
If I'm right, this is my ticket into Behavioral Sciences.
HEADS UP.
I SEE THEM.
A far more prestigious unit.

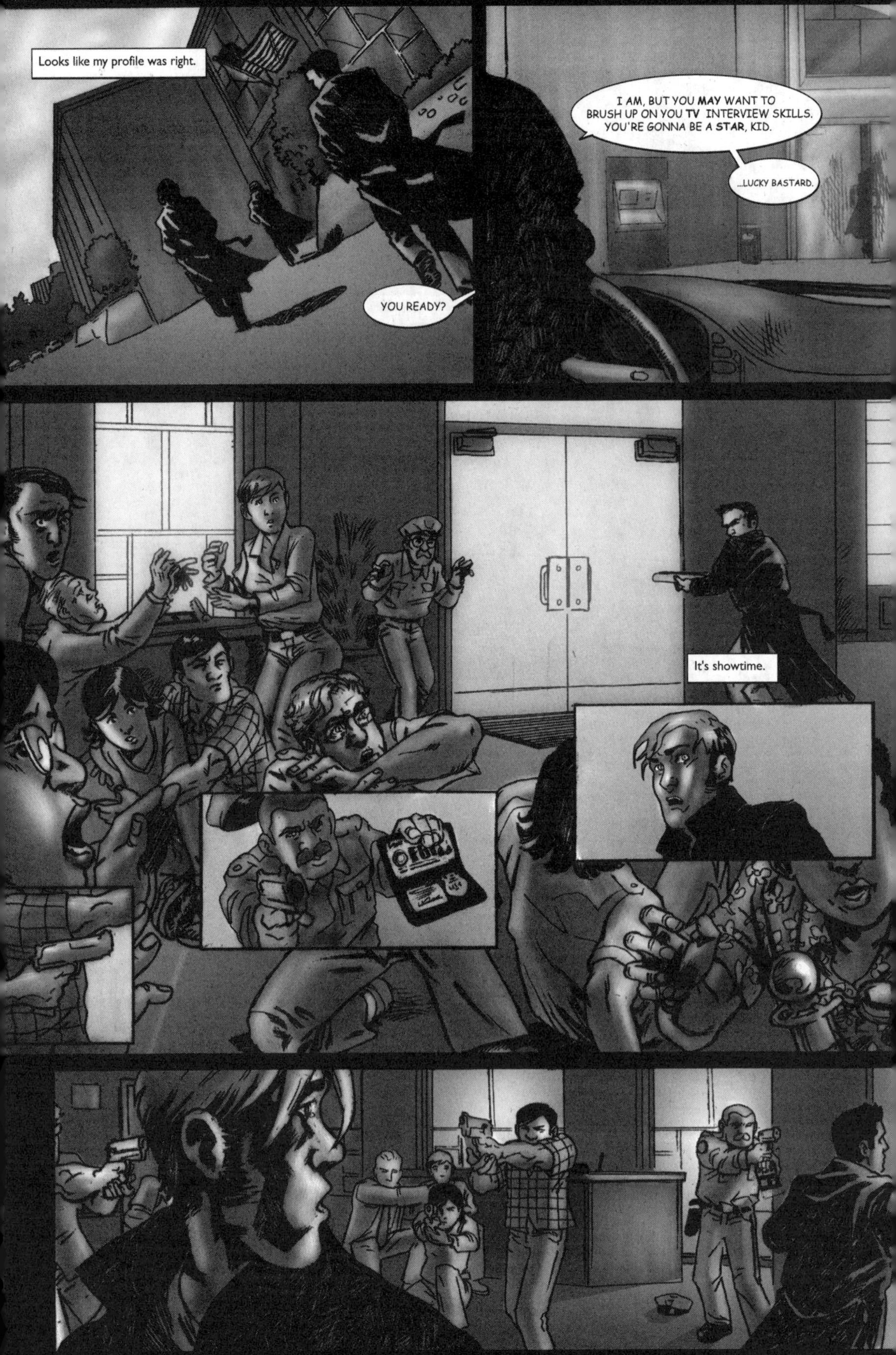
Looks like my profile was right.
YOU READY?
I AM, BUT YOU MAY WANT TO BRUSH UP ON YOU TV INTERVIEW SKILLS. YOU'RE GONNA BE A STAR, KID.
...LUCKY BASTARD.
It's showtime.

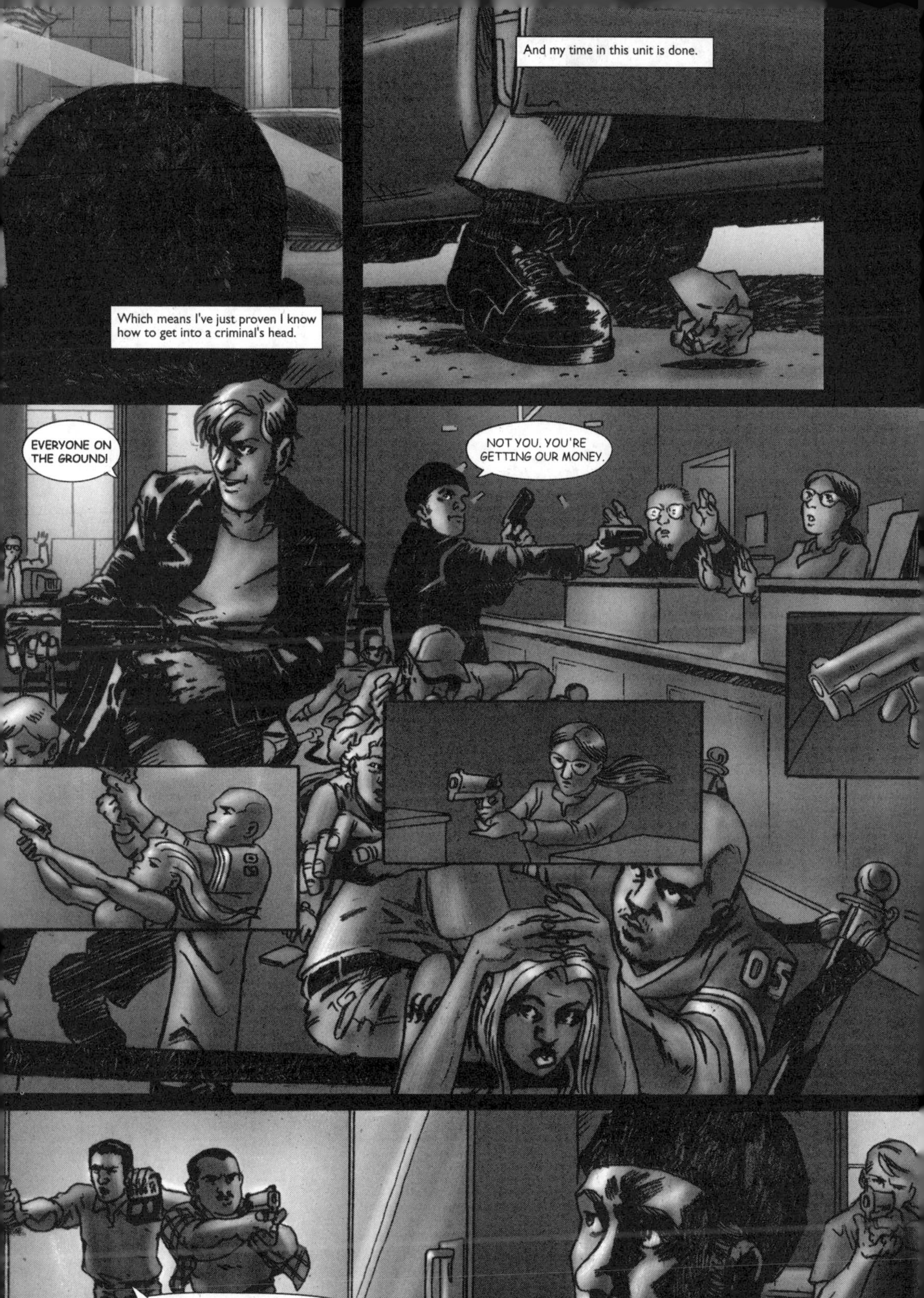

Which means I've just proven I know how to get into a criminal's head.
And my time in this unit is done.
EVERYONE ON THE GROUND!
NOT YOU. YOU'RE GETTING OUR MONEY.
I'M AGENT GREGORY HAWORTH OF THE FEDERAL BUREAU OF INVESTIGATIONS.
AND YOU ARE UNDER ARREST!

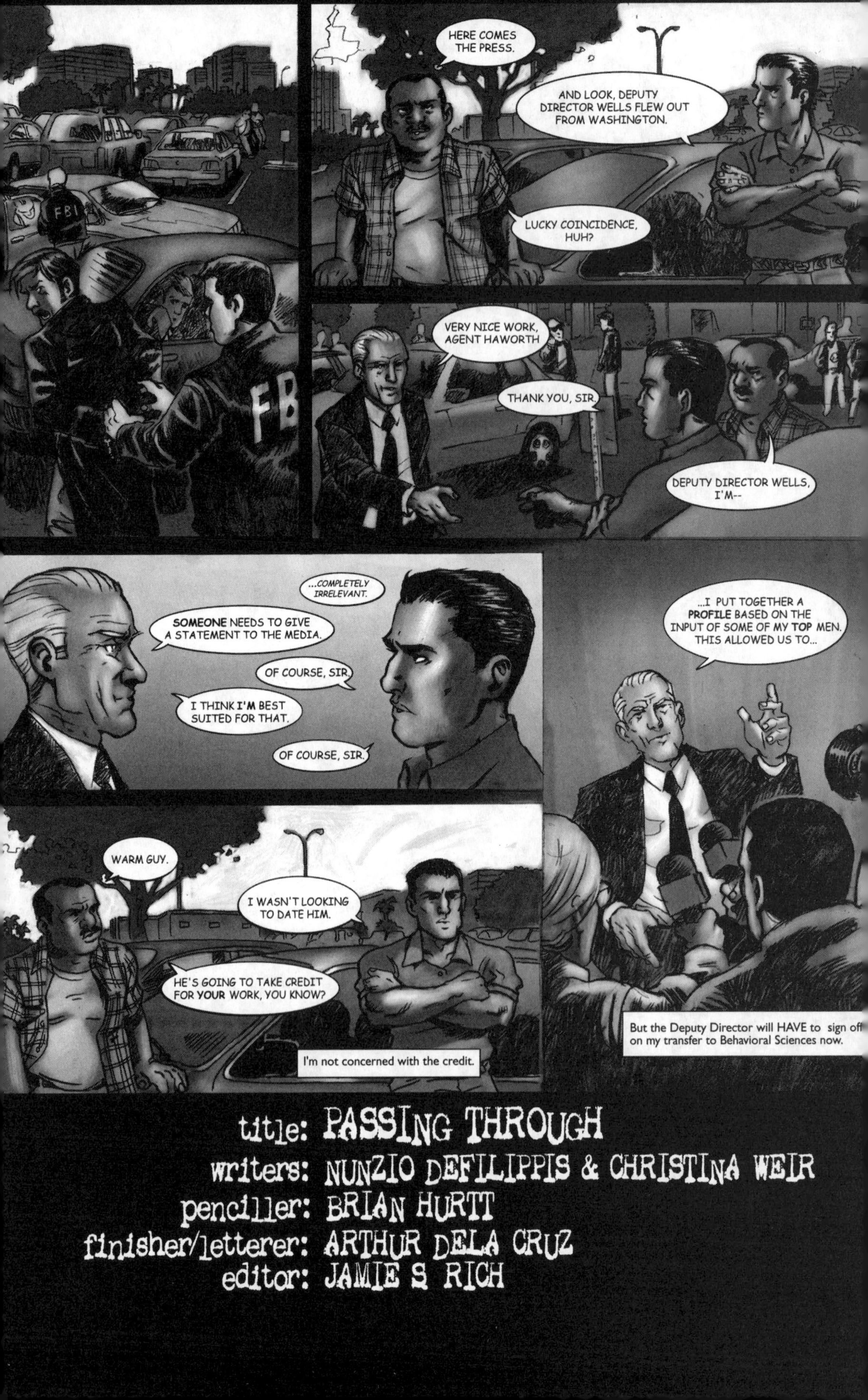
HERE COMES THE PRESS.
AND LOOK, DEPUTY DIRECTOR WELLS FLEW OUT FROM WASHINGTON.
LUCKY COINCIDENCE, HUH?
VERY NICE WORK, AGENT HAWORTH
THANK YOU, SIR.
DEPUTY DIRECTOR WELLS, I'M--
...COMPLETELY IRRELEVANT.
SOMEONE NEEDS TO GIVE A STATEMENT TO THE MEDIA.
OF COURSE, SIR.
I THINK I'M BEST SUITED FOR THAT.
OF COURSE, SIR.
WARM GUY.
I WASN'T LOOKING TO DATE HIM.
HE'S GOING TO TAKE CREDIT FOR YOUR WORK, YOU KNOW?
I'm not concerned with the credit.
...I PUT TOGETHER A PROFILE BASED ON THE INPUT OF SOME OF MY TOP MEN. THIS ALLOWED US TO...
But the Deputy Director will HAVE to sign off on my transfer to Behavioral Sciences now.

title: PASSING THROUGH
writers: NUNZIO DEFILIPPIS & CHRISTINA WEIR
penciller: BRIAN HURTT
finisher/letterer: ARTHUR DELA CRUZ
editor: JAMIE S RICH

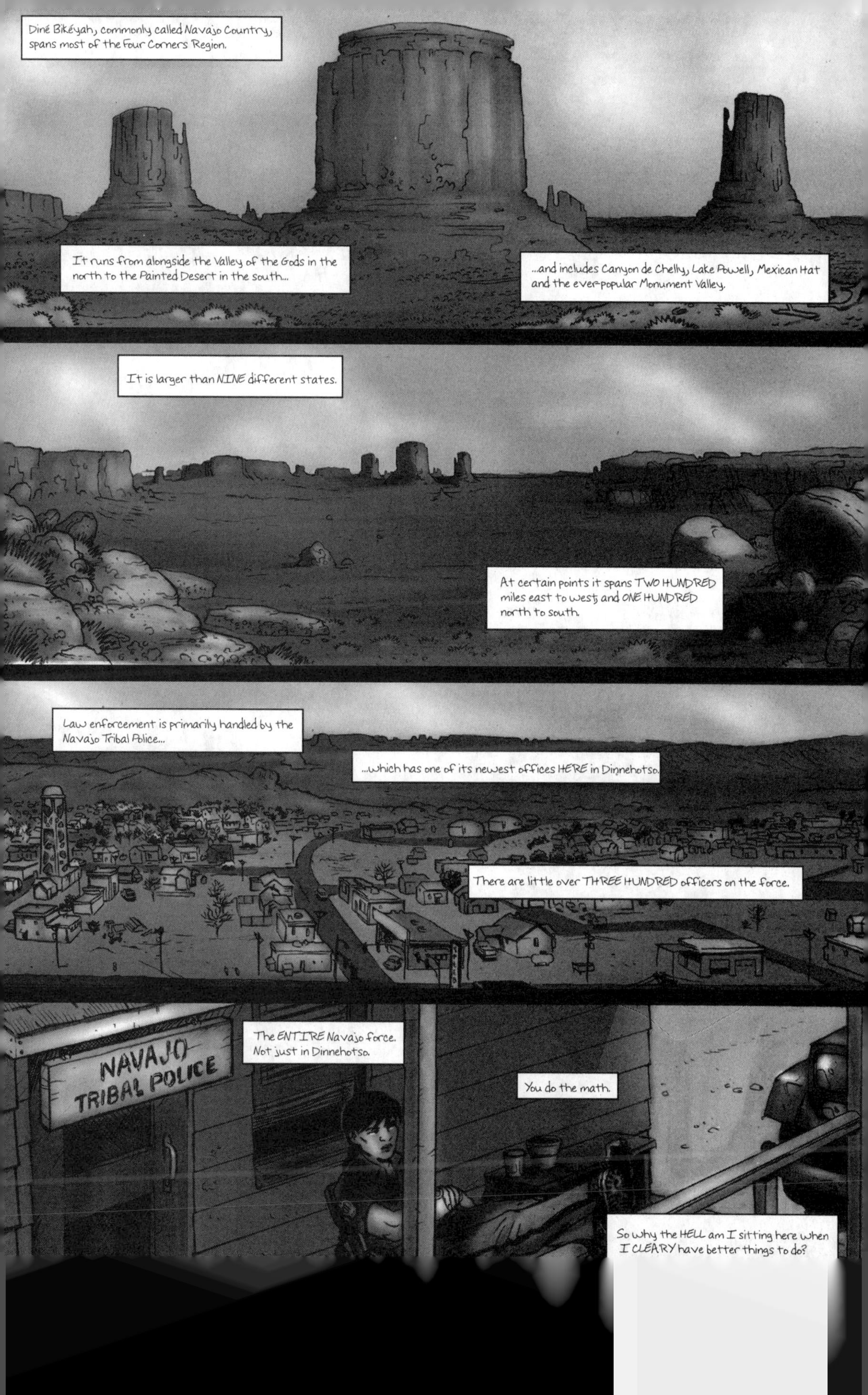
Diné Bikéyah, commonly called Navajo Country, spans most of the Four Corners Region.
It runs from alongside the Valley of the Gods in the north to the Painted Desert in the south...
...and includes Canyon de Chelly, Lake Powell, Mexican Hat and the ever-popular Monument Valley.
It is larger than NINE different states.
At certain points it spans TWO HUNDRED miles east to west, and ONE HUNDRED north to south.
Law enforcement is primarily handled by the Navajo Tribal Police...
...which has one of its newest offices HERE in Dinnehotso.
There are little over THREE HUNDRED officers on the force.
NAVAJO TRIBAL POLICE
The ENTIRE Navajo force. Not just in Dinnehotso.
You do the math.
So why the HELL am I sitting here when I CLEARY have better things to do?

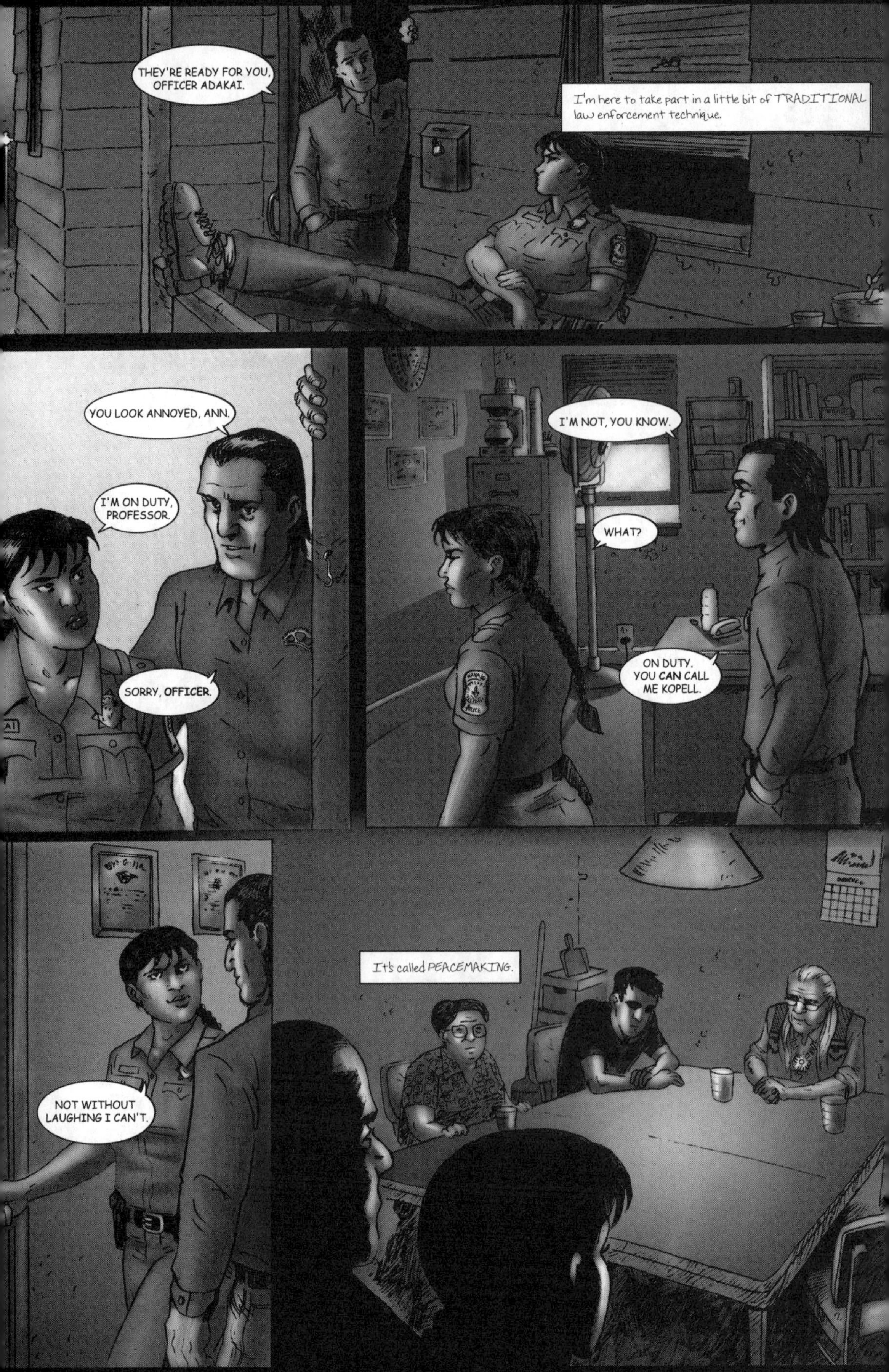
THEY'RE READY FOR YOU, OFFICER ADAKAI.
I'm here to take part in a little bit of TRADITIONAL law enforcement technique.
YOU LOOK ANNOYED, ANN.
I'M ON DUTY, PROFESSOR.
SORRY, OFFICER.
I'M NOT, YOU KNOW.
WHAT?
ON DUTY. YOU CAN CALL ME KOPELL.
NOT WITHOUT LAUGHING I CAN'T.
It's called PEACEMAKING.

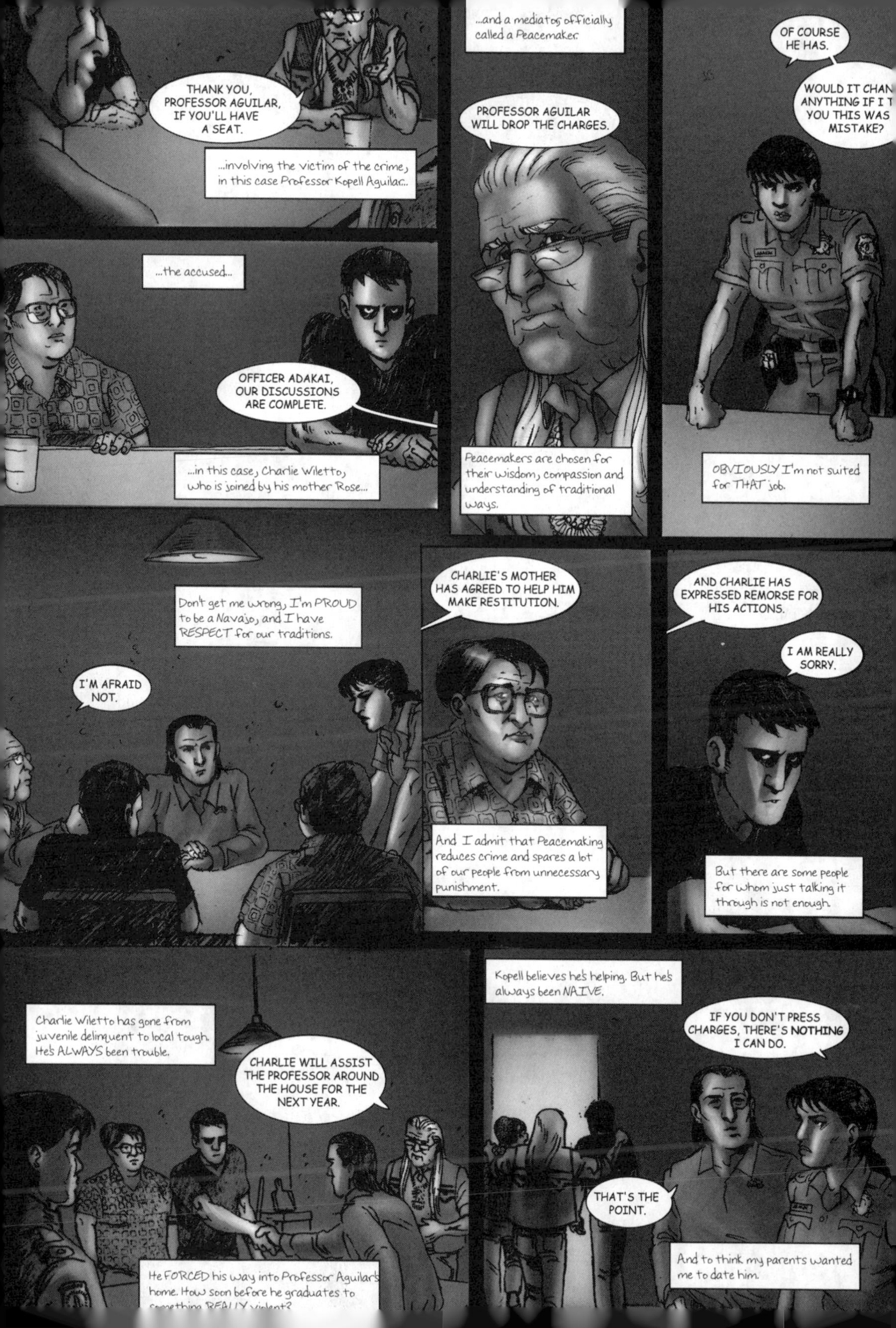
THANK YOU, PROFESSOR AGUILAR, IF YOU'LL HAVE A SEAT.
...involving the victim of the crime, in this case Professor Kopell Aguilar...
...the accused...
OFFICER ADAKAI, OUR DISCUSSIONS ARE COMPLETE.
...in this case, Charlie Wiletto, who is joined by his mother Rose...
...and a mediator officially called a Peacemaker.
PROFESSOR AGUILAR WILL DROP THE CHARGES.
Peacemakers are chosen for their wisdom, compassion and understanding of traditional ways.
OF COURSE HE HAS.
WOULD IT CHAN ANYTHING IF I T YOU THIS WAS MISTAKE?
OBVIOUSLY I'm not suited for THAT job.
Don't get me wrong, I'm PROUD to be a Navajo, and I have RESPECT for our traditions.
I'M AFRAID NOT.
CHARLIE'S MOTHER HAS AGREED TO HELP HIM MAKE RESTITUTION.
And I admit that Peacemaking reduces crime and spares a lot of our people from unnecessary punishment.
AND CHARLIE HAS EXPRESSED REMORSE FOR HIS ACTIONS.
I AM REALLY SORRY.
But there are some people for whom just talking it through is not enough.
Charlie Wiletto has gone from juvenile delinquent to local tough. He's ALWAYS been trouble.
CHARLIE WILL ASSIST THE PROFESSOR AROUND THE HOUSE FOR THE NEXT YEAR.
He FORCED his way into Professor Aguilar's home. How soon before he graduates to something REALLY violent?
Kopell believes he's helping. But he's always been NAIVE.
IF YOU DON'T PRESS CHARGES, THERE'S NOTHING I CAN DO.
THAT'S THE POINT.
And to think my parents wanted me to date him.

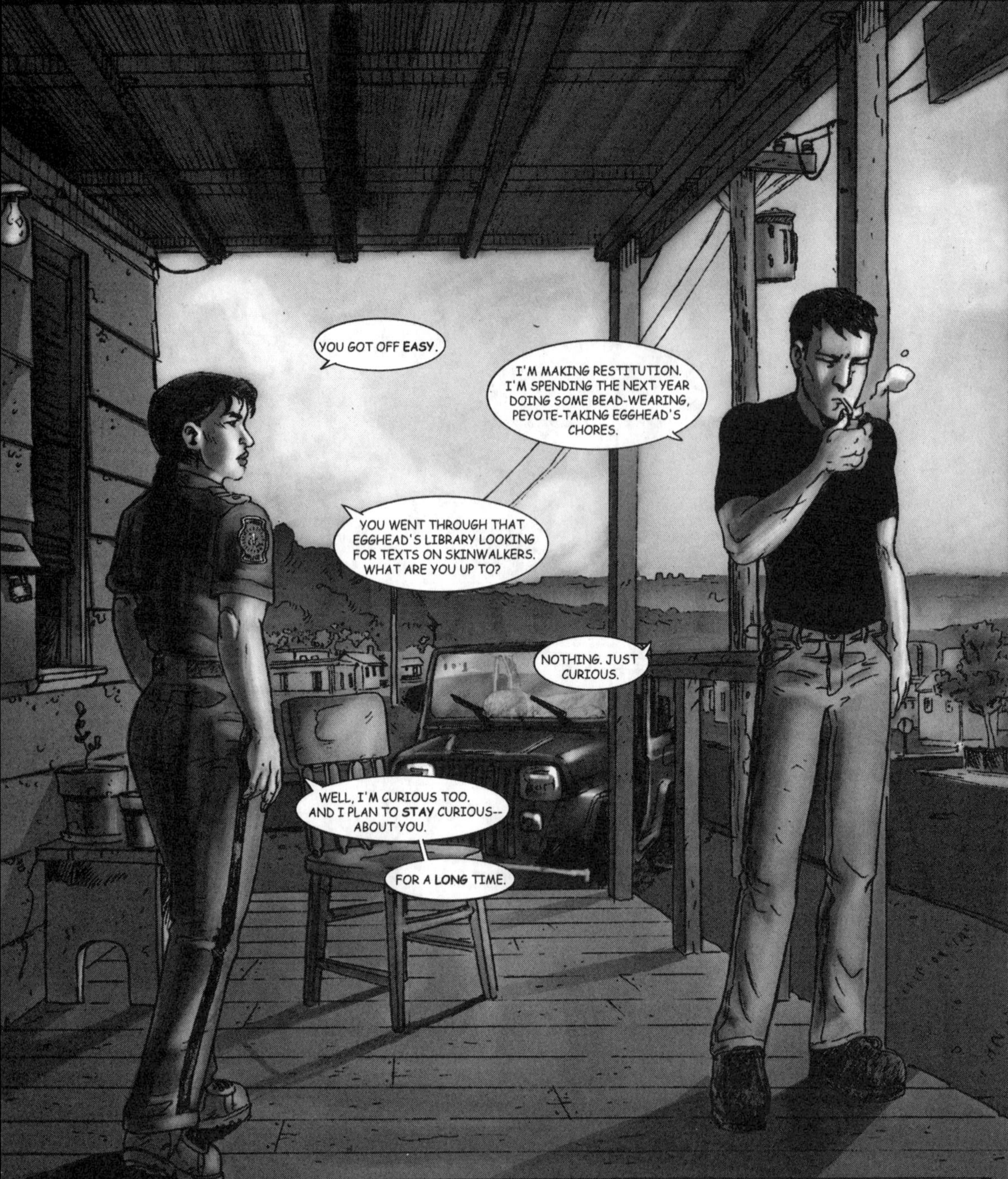
YOU GOT OFF EASY.
I'M MAKING RESTITUTION. I'M SPENDING THE NEXT YEAR DOING SOME BEAD-WEARING, PEYOTE-TAKING EGGHEAD'S CHORES.
YOU WENT THROUGH THAT EGGHEAD'S LIBRARY LOOKING FOR TEXTS ON SKINWALKERS. WHAT ARE YOU UP TO?
NOTHING. JUST CURIOUS.
WELL, I'M CURIOUS TOO. AND I PLAN TO STAY CURIOUS-- ABOUT YOU.
FOR A LONG TIME.

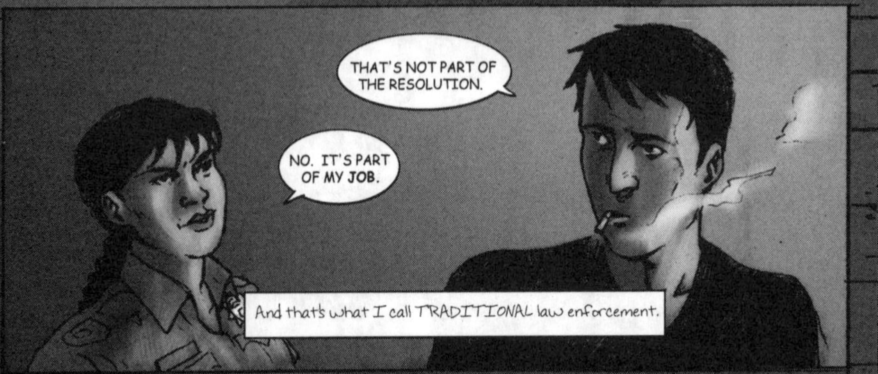
THAT'S NOT PART OF THE RESOLUTION.
NO. IT'S PART OF MY JOB.
And that's what I call TRADITIONAL law enforcement.

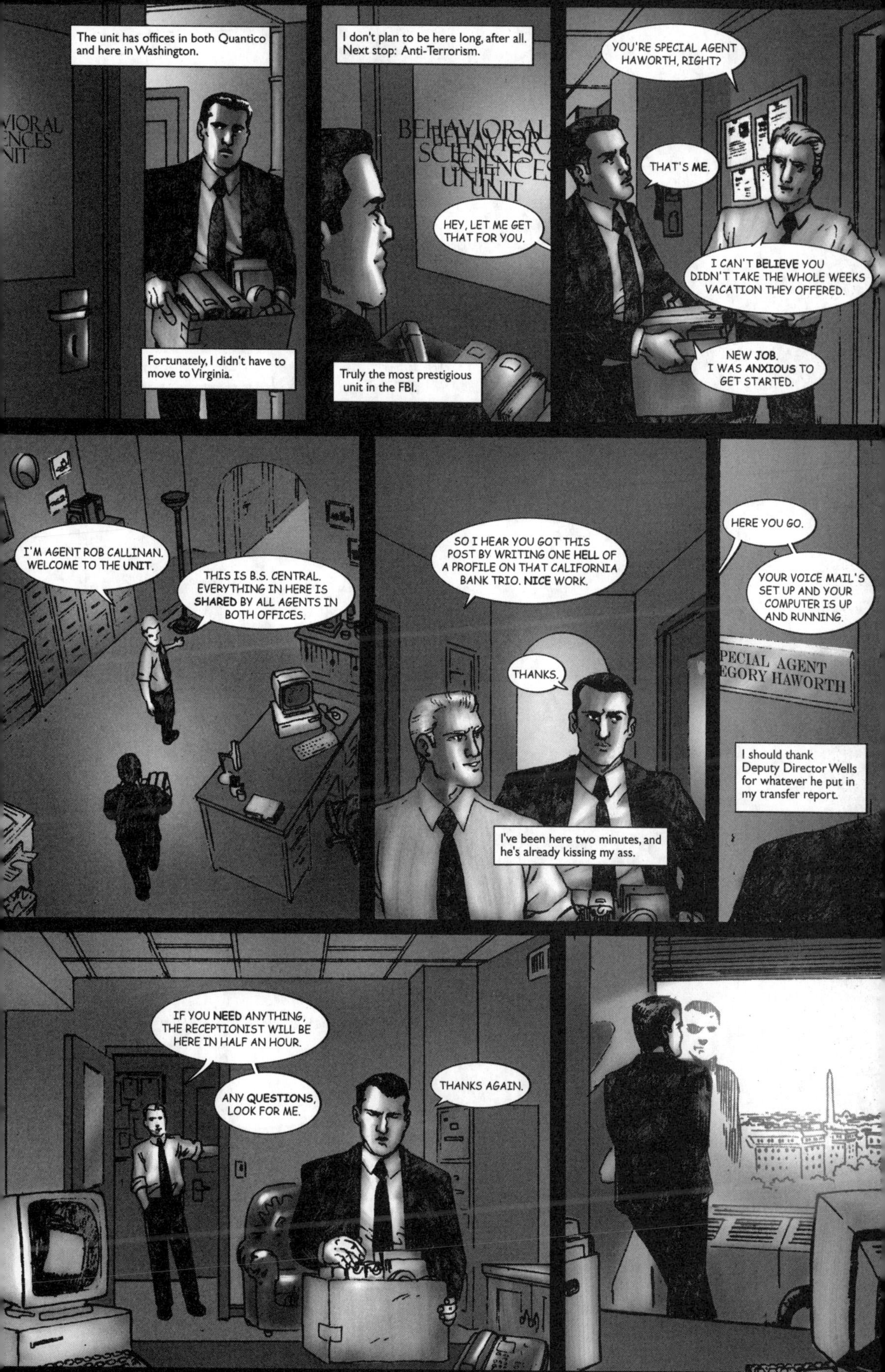
The unit has offices in both Quantico and here in Washington.
VIORAL
ENCES
NIT
Fortunately, I didn't have to move to Virginia.
I don't plan to be here long, after all. Next stop: Anti-Terrorism.
BEHAVIORAL SCIENCES UNIT
HEY, LET ME GET THAT FOR YOU.
Truly the most prestigious unit in the FBI.
YOU'RE SPECIAL AGENT HAWORTH, RIGHT?
THAT'S ME.
I CAN'T BELIEVE YOU DIDN'T TAKE THE WHOLE WEEKS VACATION THEY OFFERED.
NEW JOB. I WAS ANXIOUS TO GET STARTED.
I'M AGENT ROB CALLINAN. WELCOME TO THE UNIT.
THIS IS B.S. CENTRAL. EVERYTHING IN HERE IS SHARED BY ALL AGENTS IN BOTH OFFICES.
SO I HEAR YOU GOT THIS POST BY WRITING ONE HELL OF A PROFILE ON THAT CALIFORNIA BANK TRIO. NICE WORK.
THANKS.
I've been here two minutes, and he's already kissing my ass.
HERE YOU GO.
YOUR VOICE MAIL'S SET UP AND YOUR COMPUTER IS UP AND RUNNING.
PECIAL AGENT
EGORY HAWORTH
I should thank Deputy Director Wells for whatever he put in my transfer report.
IF YOU NEED ANYTHING, THE RECEPTIONIST WILL BE HERE IN HALF AN HOUR.
ANY QUESTIONS, LOOK FOR ME.
THANKS AGAIN.

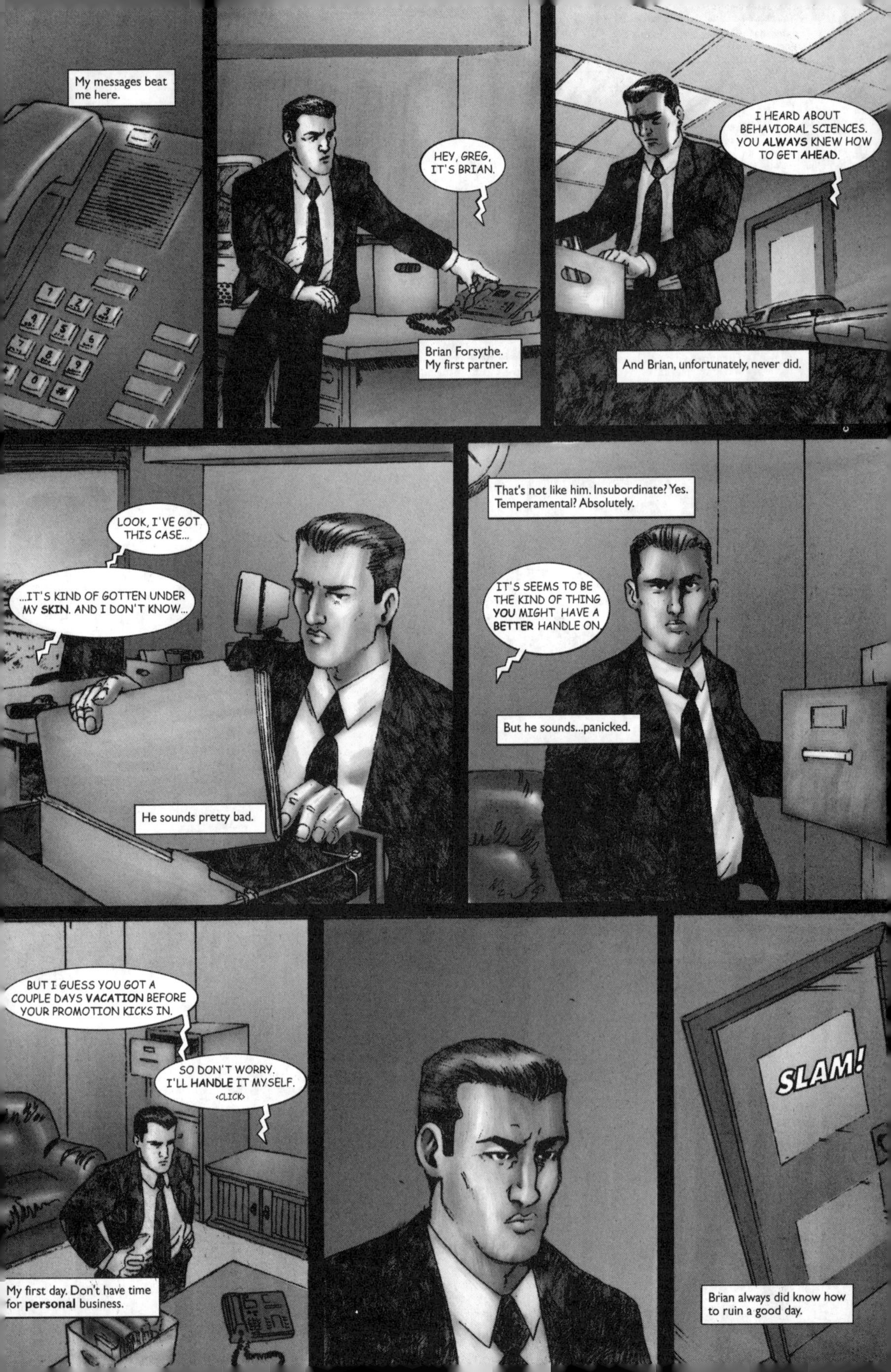
My messages beat me here.
HEY, GREG, IT'S BRIAN.
Brian Forsythe. My first partner.
I HEARD ABOUT BEHAVIORAL SCIENCES. YOU ALWAYS KNEW HOW TO GET AHEAD.
And Brian, unfortunately, never did.
LOOK, I'VE GOT THIS CASE...
...IT'S KIND OF GOTTEN UNDER MY SKIN. AND I DON'T KNOW...
He sounds pretty bad.
That's not like him. Insubordinate? Yes. Temperamental? Absolutely.
IT'S SEEMS TO BE THE KIND OF THING YOU MIGHT HAVE A BETTER HANDLE ON.
But he sounds...panicked.
BUT I GUESS YOU GOT A COUPLE DAYS VACATION BEFORE YOUR PROMOTION KICKS IN.
SO DON'T WORRY. I'LL HANDLE IT MYSELF. <CLICK>
My first day. Don't have time for personal business.
SLAM!
Brian always did know how to ruin a good day.

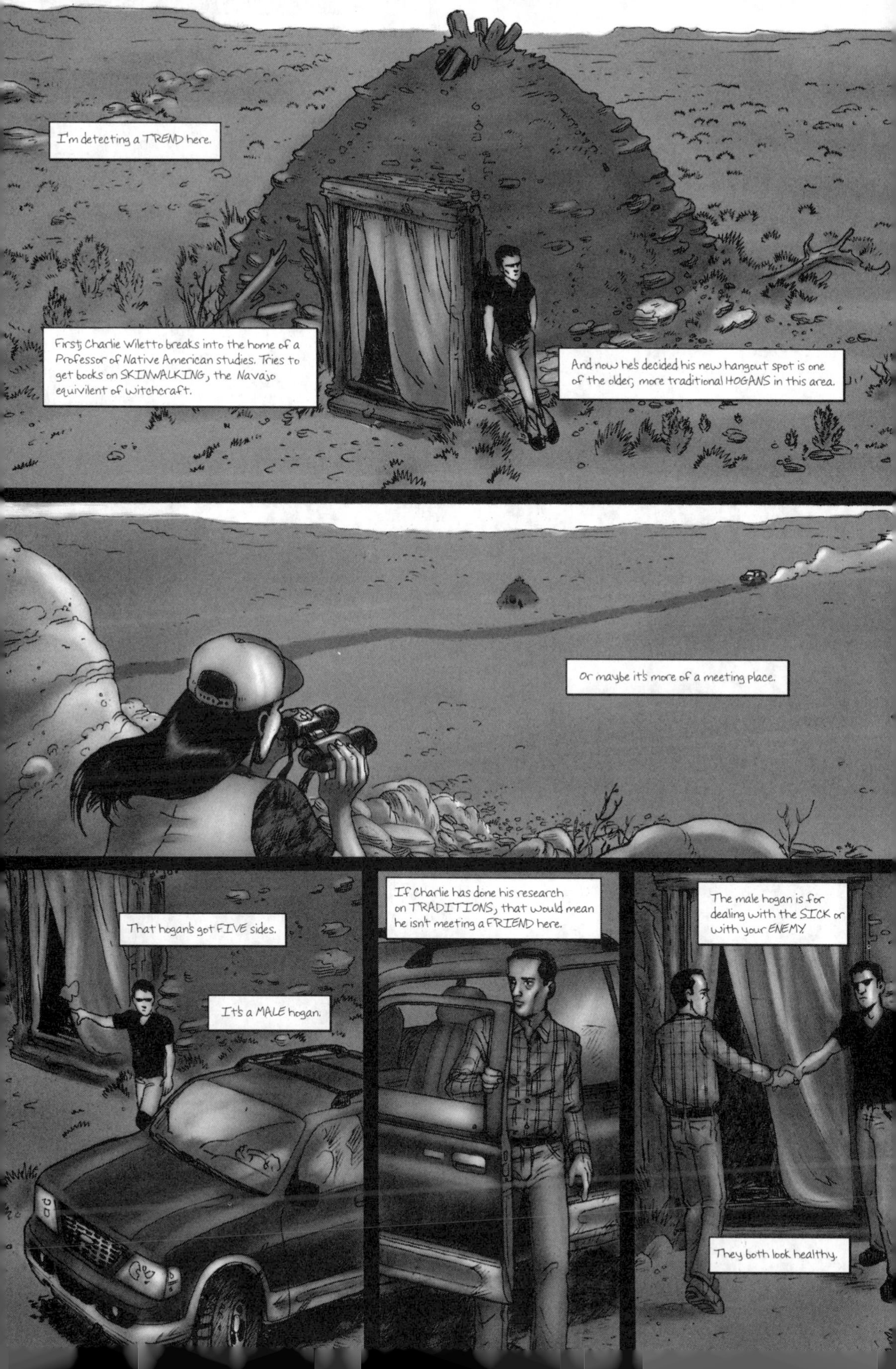
I'm detecting a TREND here.
First, Charlie Wiletto breaks into the home of a Professor of Native American studies. Tries to get books on SKINWALKING, the Navajo equivilent of witchcraft.
And now he's decided his new hangout spot is one of the older, more traditional HOGANS in this area.
Or maybe it's more of a meeting place.
That hogan's got FIVE sides.
It's a MALE hogan.
If Charlie has done his research on TRADITIONS, that would mean he isn't meeting a FRIEND here.
The male hogan is for dealing with the SICK or with your ENEMY.
They both look healthy.

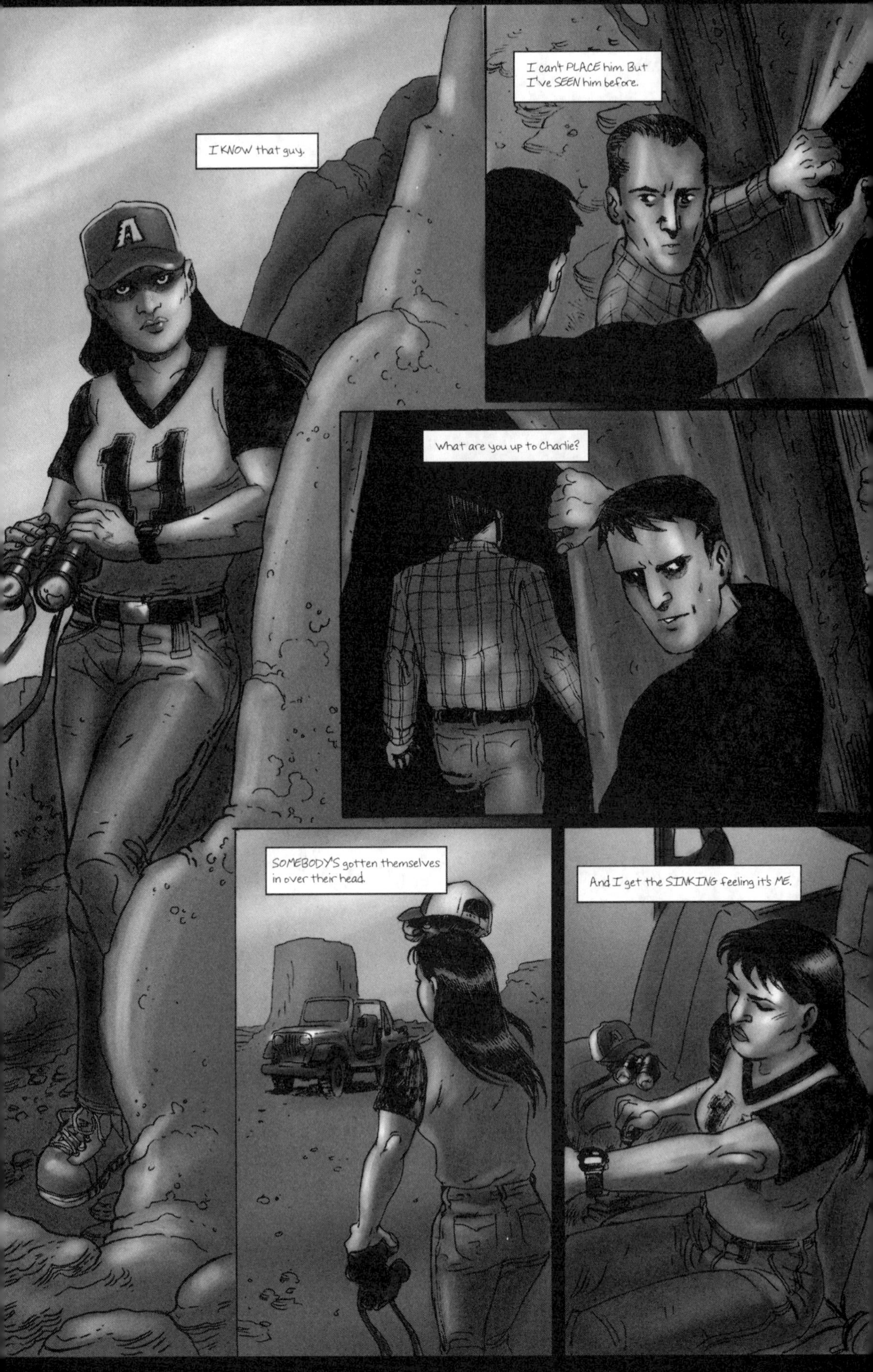

I KNOW that guy.
I can't PLACE him. But I've SEEN him before.
What are you up to Charlie?
SOMEBODY'S gotten themselves in over their head.
And I get the SINKING feeling it's ME.

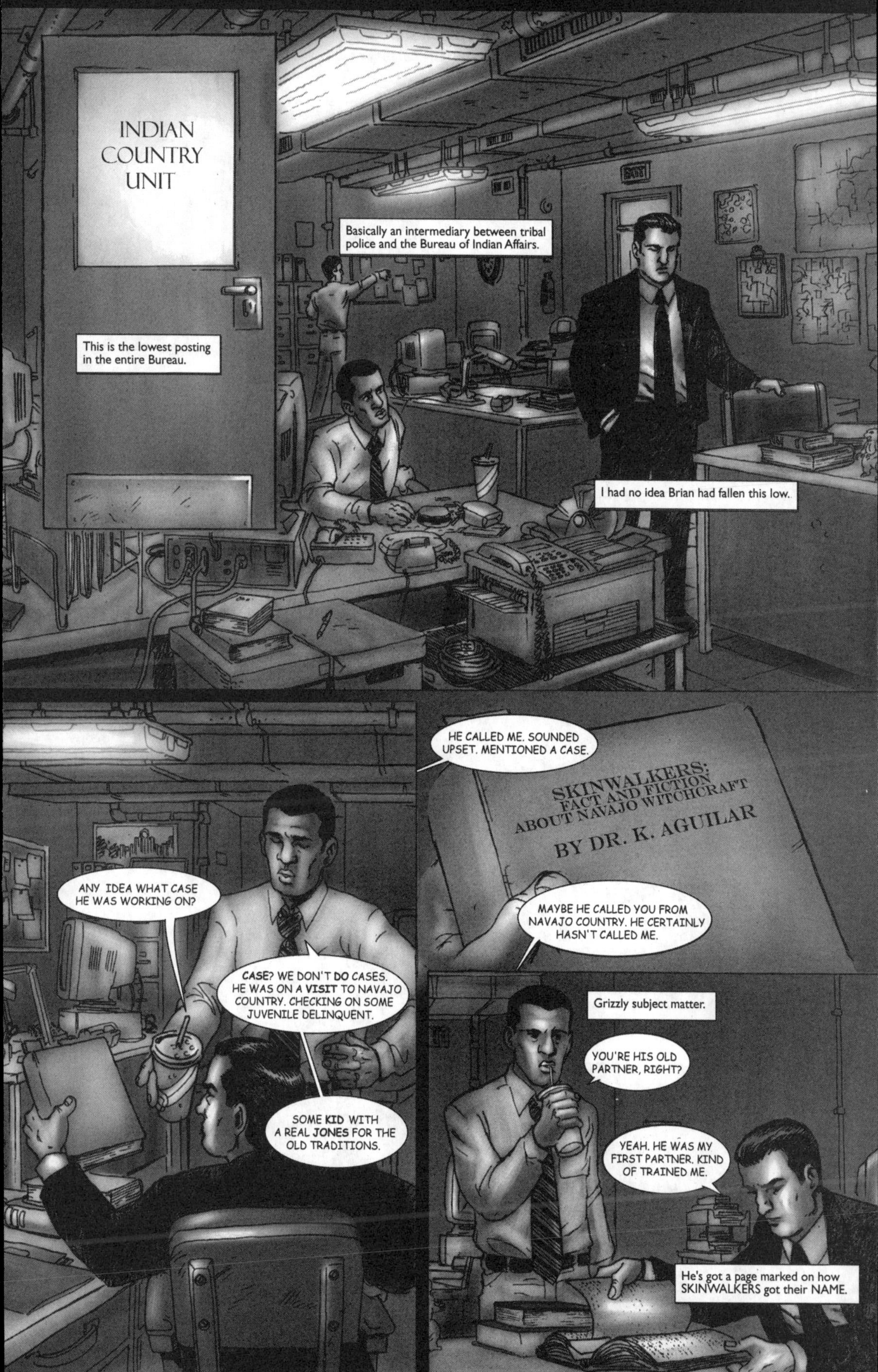
INDIAN COUNTRY UNIT
Basically an intermediary between tribal police and the Bureau of Indian Affairs.
This is the lowest posting in the entire Bureau.
I had no idea Brian had fallen this low.
ANY IDEA WHAT CASE HE WAS WORKING ON?
CASE? WE DON'T DO CASES. HE WAS ON A VISIT TO NAVAJO COUNTRY. CHECKING ON SOME JUVENILE DELINQUENT.
SOME KID WITH A REAL JONES FOR THE OLD TRADITIONS.
HE CALLED ME. SOUNDED UPSET. MENTIONED A CASE.
SKINWALKERS: FACT AND FICTION ABOUT NAVAJO WITCHCRAFT
BY DR. K. AGUILAR
MAYBE HE CALLED YOU FROM NAVAJO COUNTRY. HE CERTAINLY HASN'T CALLED ME.
Grizzly subject matter.
YOU'RE HIS OLD PARTNER, RIGHT?
YEAH. HE WAS MY FIRST PARTNER. KIND OF TRAINED ME.
He's got a page marked on how SKINWALKERS got their NAME.

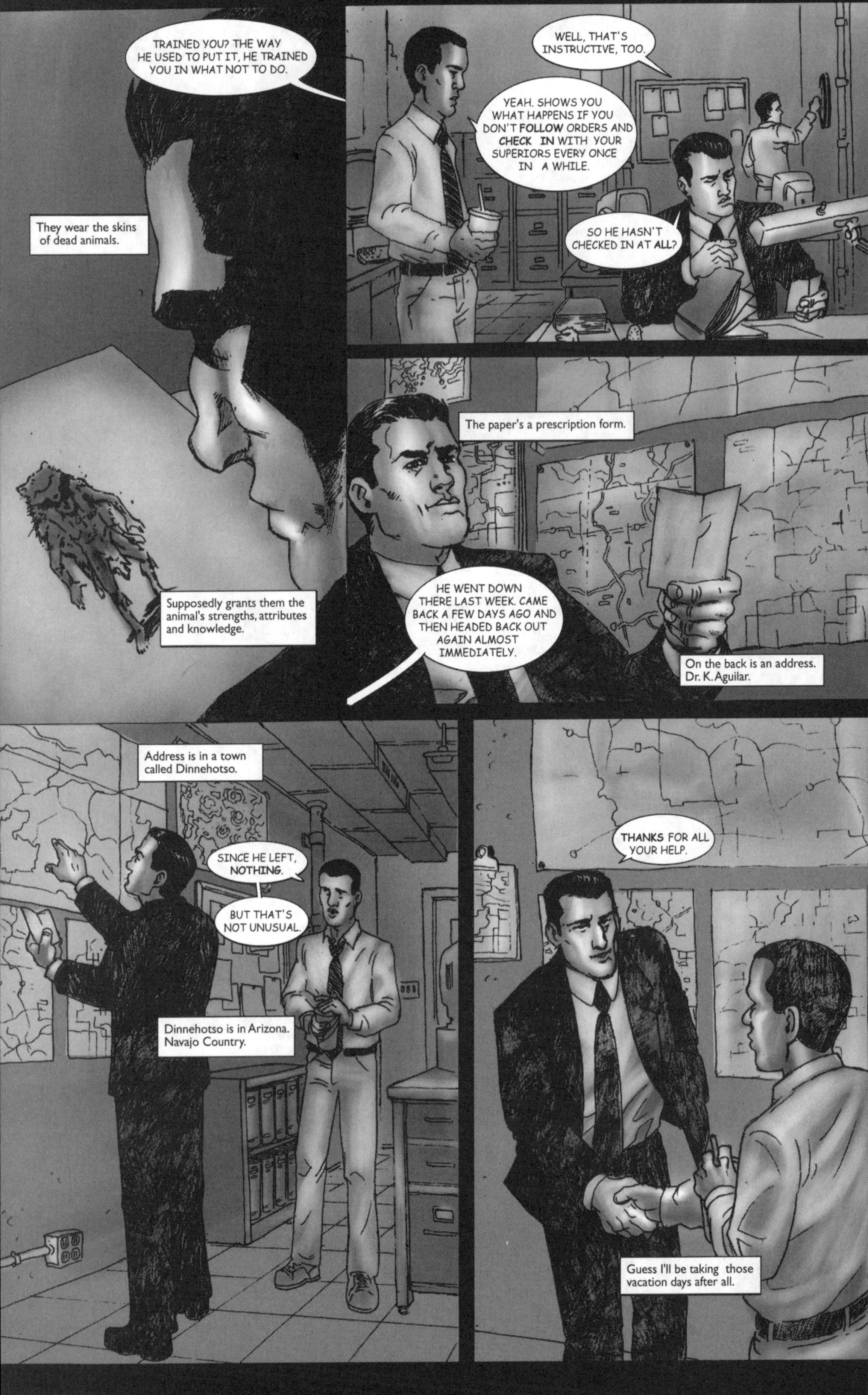
TRAINED YOU? THE WAY HE USED TO PUT IT, HE TRAINED YOU IN WHAT NOT TO DO.
They wear the skins of dead animals.
Supposedly grants them the animal's strengths, attributes and knowledge.
WELL, THAT'S INSTRUCTIVE, TOO.
YEAH. SHOWS YOU WHAT HAPPENS IF YOU DON'T FOLLOW ORDERS AND CHECK IN WITH YOUR SUPERIORS EVERY ONCE IN A WHILE.
SO HE HASN'T CHECKED IN AT ALL?
The paper's a prescription form.
HE WENT DOWN THERE LAST WEEK. CAME BACK A FEW DAYS AGO AND THEN HEADED BACK OUT AGAIN ALMOST IMMEDIATELY.
On the back is an address. Dr. K. Aguilar.
Address is in a town called Dinnehotso.
SINCE HE LEFT, NOTHING.
BUT THAT'S NOT UNUSUAL.
Dinnehotso is in Arizona. Navajo Country.
THANKS FOR ALL YOUR HELP.
Guess I'll be taking those vacation days after all.

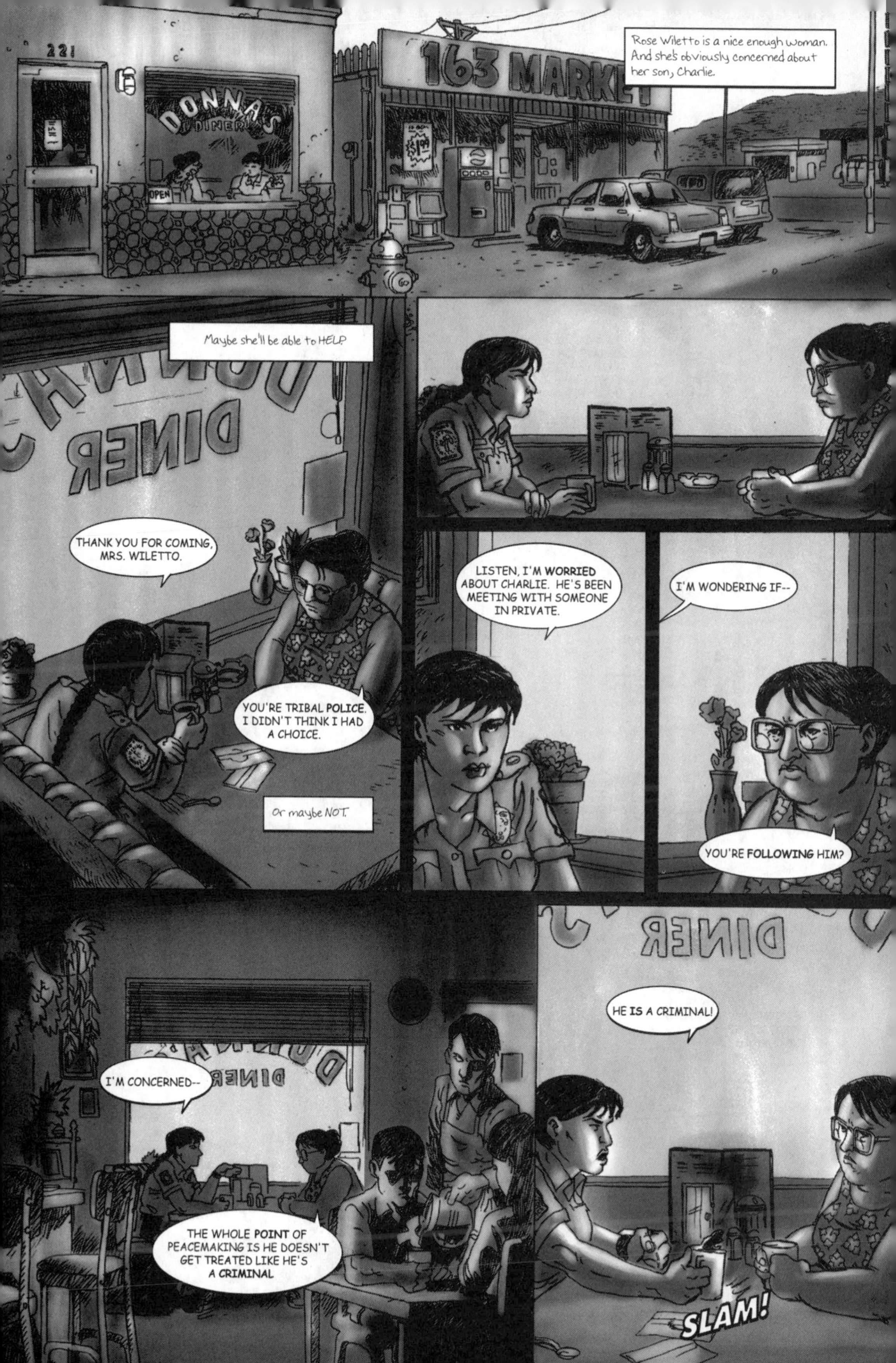

221
DONNA'S DINER
OPEN
163 MARKET
$1.99
Rose Wiletto is a nice enough woman. And she's obviously concerned about her son, Charlie.
Maybe she'll be able to HELP.
DONNA'S DINER
THANK YOU FOR COMING, MRS. WILETTO.
YOU'RE TRIBAL POLICE. I DIDN'T THINK I HAD A CHOICE.
Or maybe NOT.
LISTEN, I'M WORRIED ABOUT CHARLIE. HE'S BEEN MEETING WITH SOMEONE IN PRIVATE.
I'M WONDERING IF--
YOU'RE FOLLOWING HIM?
I'M CONCERNED--
THE WHOLE POINT OF PEACEMAKING IS HE DOESN'T GET TREATED LIKE HE'S A CRIMINAL
DINER
HE IS A CRIMINAL!
SLAM!

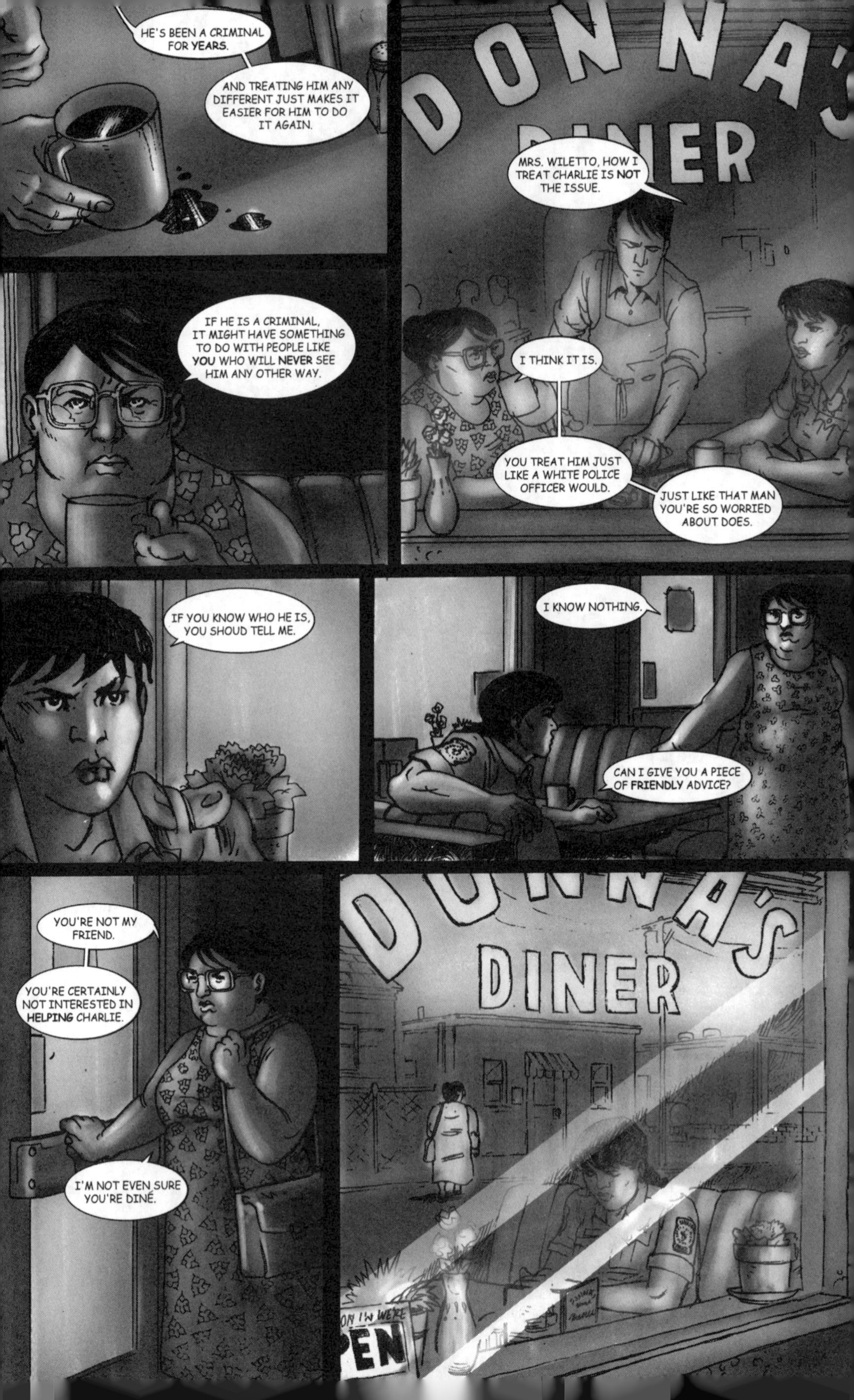
HE'S BEEN A CRIMINAL FOR YEARS.
AND TREATING HIM ANY DIFFERENT JUST MAKES IT EASIER FOR HIM TO DO IT AGAIN.
DONNA'S DINER
MRS. WILETTO, HOW I TREAT CHARLIE IS NOT THE ISSUE.
IF HE IS A CRIMINAL, IT MIGHT HAVE SOMETHING TO DO WITH PEOPLE LIKE YOU WHO WILL NEVER SEE HIM ANY OTHER WAY.
I THINK IT IS.
YOU TREAT HIM JUST LIKE A WHITE POLICE OFFICER WOULD.
JUST LIKE THAT MAN YOU'RE SO WORRIED ABOUT DOES.
IF YOU KNOW WHO HE IS, YOU SHOUD TELL ME.
I KNOW NOTHING.
CAN I GIVE YOU A PIECE OF FRIENDLY ADVICE?
YOU'RE NOT MY FRIEND.
YOU'RE CERTAINLY NOT INTERESTED IN HELPING CHARLIE.
I'M NOT EVEN SURE YOU'RE DINÉ.
DONNA'S DINER
PEN

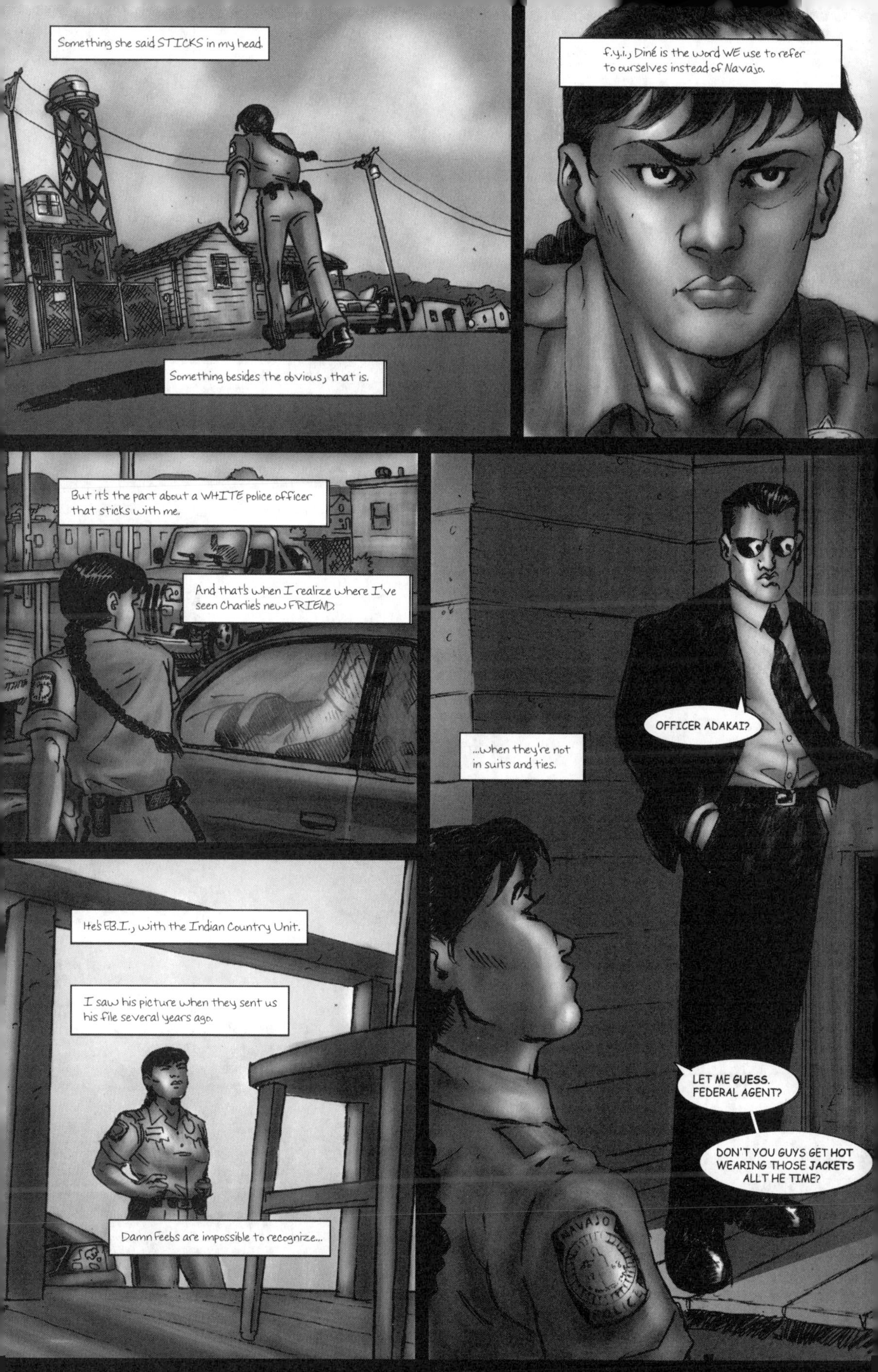

Something she said STICKS in my head.
Something besides the obvious, that is.
f.y.i., Diné is the word WE use to refer to ourselves instead of Navajo.
But it's the part about a WHITE police officer that sticks with me.
And that's when I realize where I've seen Charlie's new FRIEND.
He's F.B.I., with the Indian Country Unit.
I saw his picture when they sent us his file several years ago.
Damn Feebs are impossible to recognize...
...when they're not in suits and ties.
OFFICER ADAKAI?
LET ME GUESS. FEDERAL AGENT?
DON'T YOU GUYS GET HOT WEARING THOSE JACKETS ALLTHE TIME?
NAVAJO
POLICE

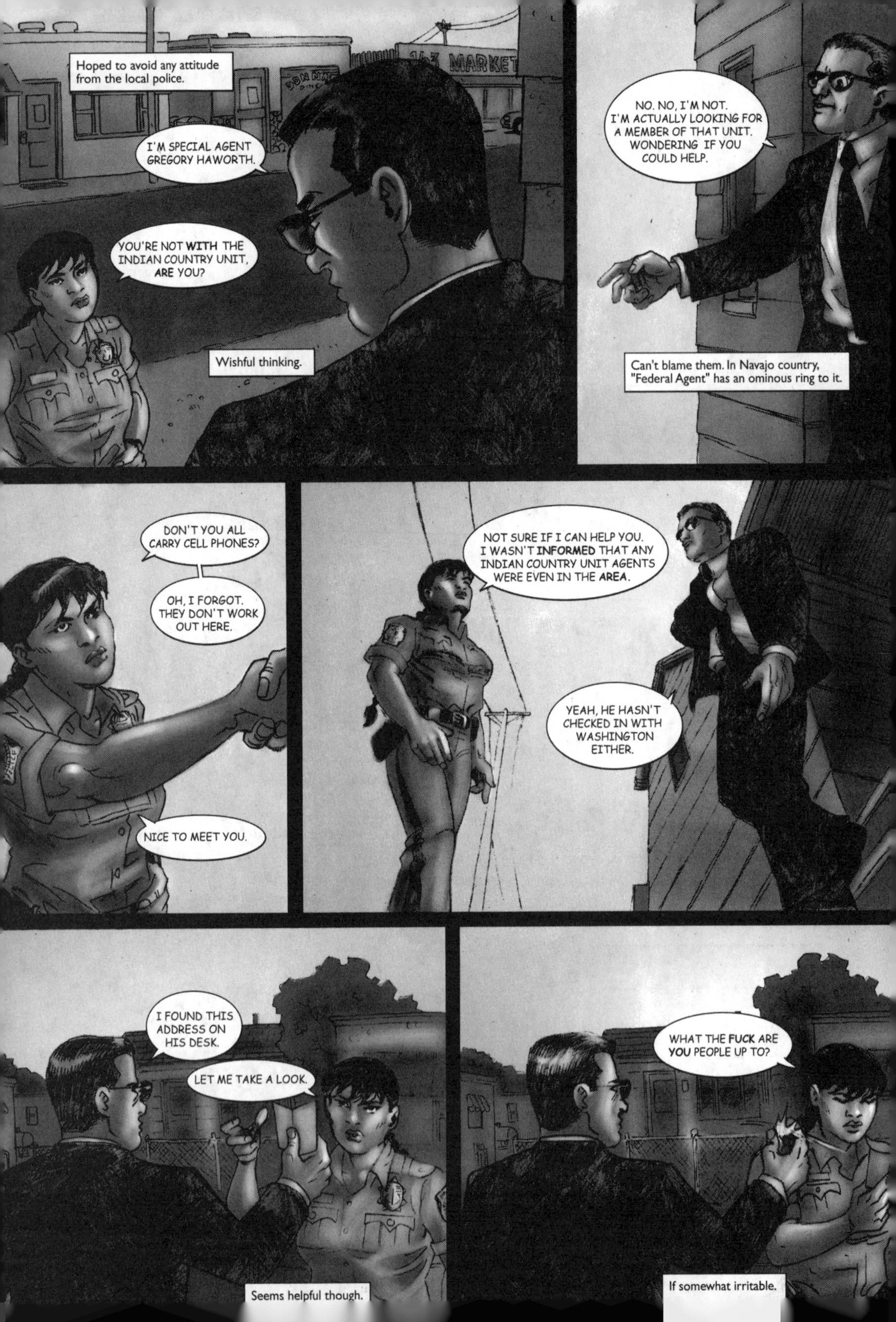
Hoped to avoid any attitude from the local police.
1&3 MARKET
I'M SPECIAL AGENT GREGORY HAWORTH.
YOU'RE NOT WITH THE INDIAN COUNTRY UNIT, ARE YOU?
Wishful thinking.
NO. NO, I'M NOT. I'M ACTUALLY LOOKING FOR A MEMBER OF THAT UNIT. WONDERING IF YOU COULD HELP.
Can't blame them. In Navajo country, "Federal Agent" has an ominous ring to it.
DON'T YOU ALL CARRY CELL PHONES?
OH, I FORGOT. THEY DON'T WORK OUT HERE.
NICE TO MEET YOU.
NOT SURE IF I CAN HELP YOU. I WASN'T INFORMED THAT ANY INDIAN COUNTRY UNIT AGENTS WERE EVEN IN THE AREA.
YEAH, HE HASN'T CHECKED IN WITH WASHINGTON EITHER.
I FOUND THIS ADDRESS ON HIS DESK.
LET ME TAKE A LOOK.
Seems helpful though.
WHAT THE FUCK ARE YOU PEOPLE UP TO?
If somewhat irritable.

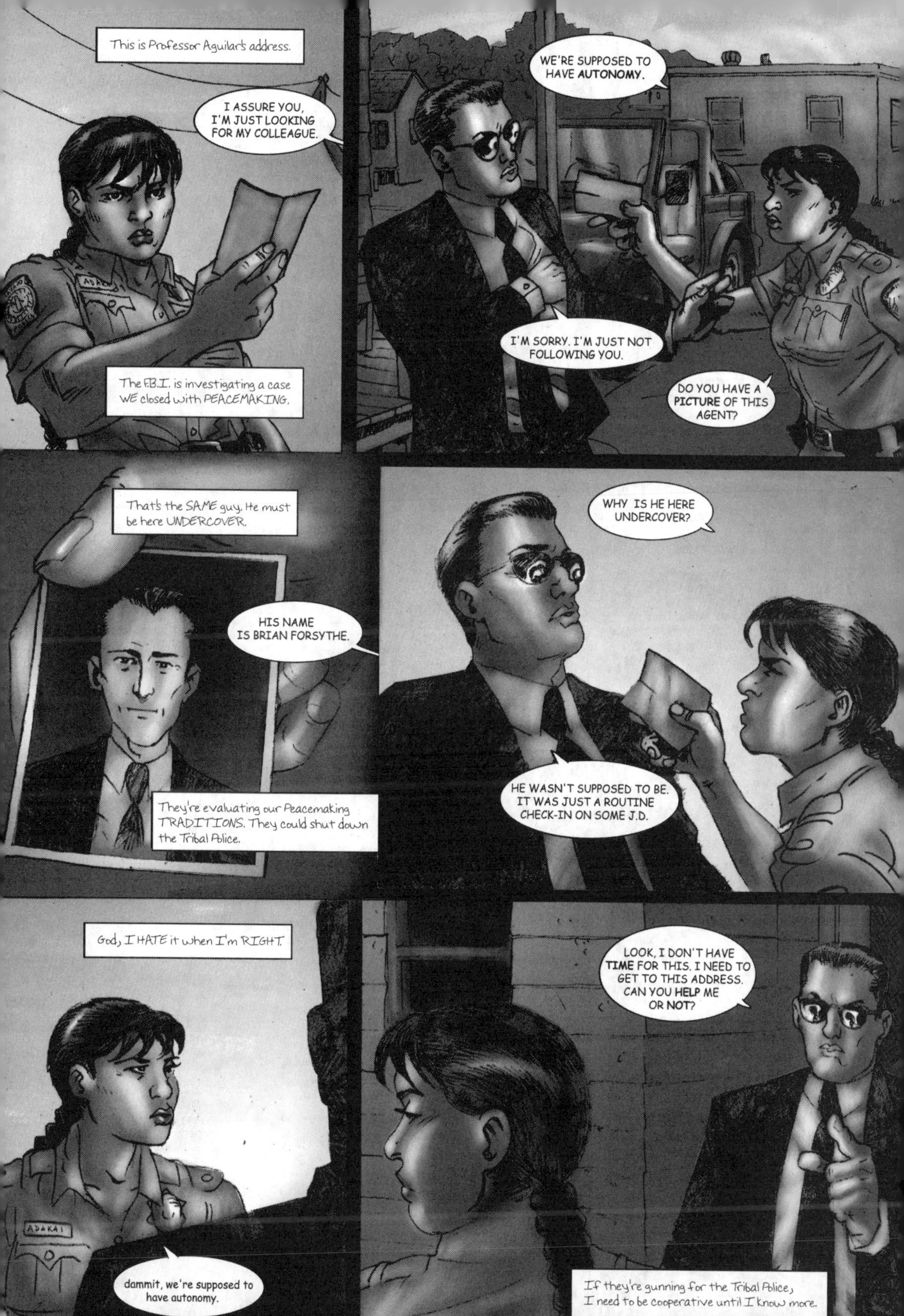
This is Professor Aguilar's address.
I ASSURE YOU, I'M JUST LOOKING FOR MY COLLEAGUE.
The F.B.I. is investigating a case WE closed with PEACEMAKING.
WE'RE SUPPOSED TO HAVE AUTONOMY.
I'M SORRY. I'M JUST NOT FOLLOWING YOU.
DO YOU HAVE A PICTURE OF THIS AGENT?
That's the SAME guy. He must be here UNDERCOVER.
HIS NAME IS BRIAN FORSYTHE.
They're evaluating our Peacemaking TRADITIONS. They could shut down the Tribal Police.
WHY IS HE HERE UNDERCOVER?
HE WASN'T SUPPOSED TO BE. IT WAS JUST A ROUTINE CHECK-IN ON SOME J.D.
God, I HATE it when I'm RIGHT.
ADAKAI
dammit, we're supposed to have autonomy.
LOOK, I DON'T HAVE TIME FOR THIS. I NEED TO GET TO THIS ADDRESS. CAN YOU HELP ME OR NOT?
If they're gunning for the Tribal Police, I need to be cooperative until I know more.

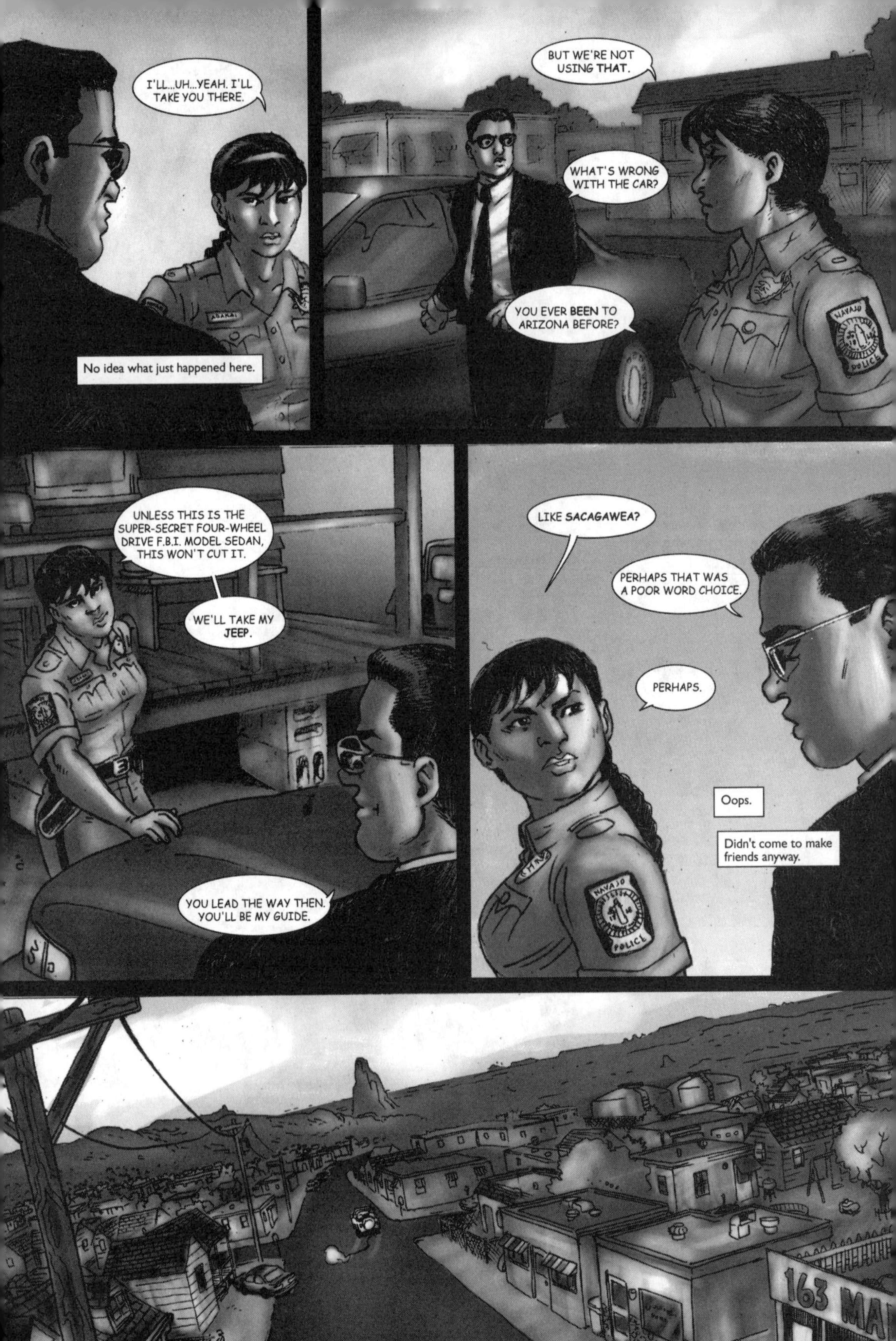

I'LL...UH...YEAH. I'LL TAKE YOU THERE.
No idea what just happened here.
BUT WE'RE NOT USING THAT.
WHAT'S WRONG WITH THE CAR?
YOU EVER BEEN TO ARIZONA BEFORE?
UNLESS THIS IS THE SUPER-SECRET FOUR-WHEEL DRIVE F.B.I. MODEL SEDAN, THIS WON'T CUT IT.
WE'LL TAKE MY JEEP.
YOU LEAD THE WAY THEN. YOU'LL BE MY GUIDE.
LIKE SACAGAWEA?
PERHAPS THAT WAS A POOR WORD CHOICE.
PERHAPS.
Oops.
Didn't come to make friends anyway.
NAVAJO POLICE
163 MA

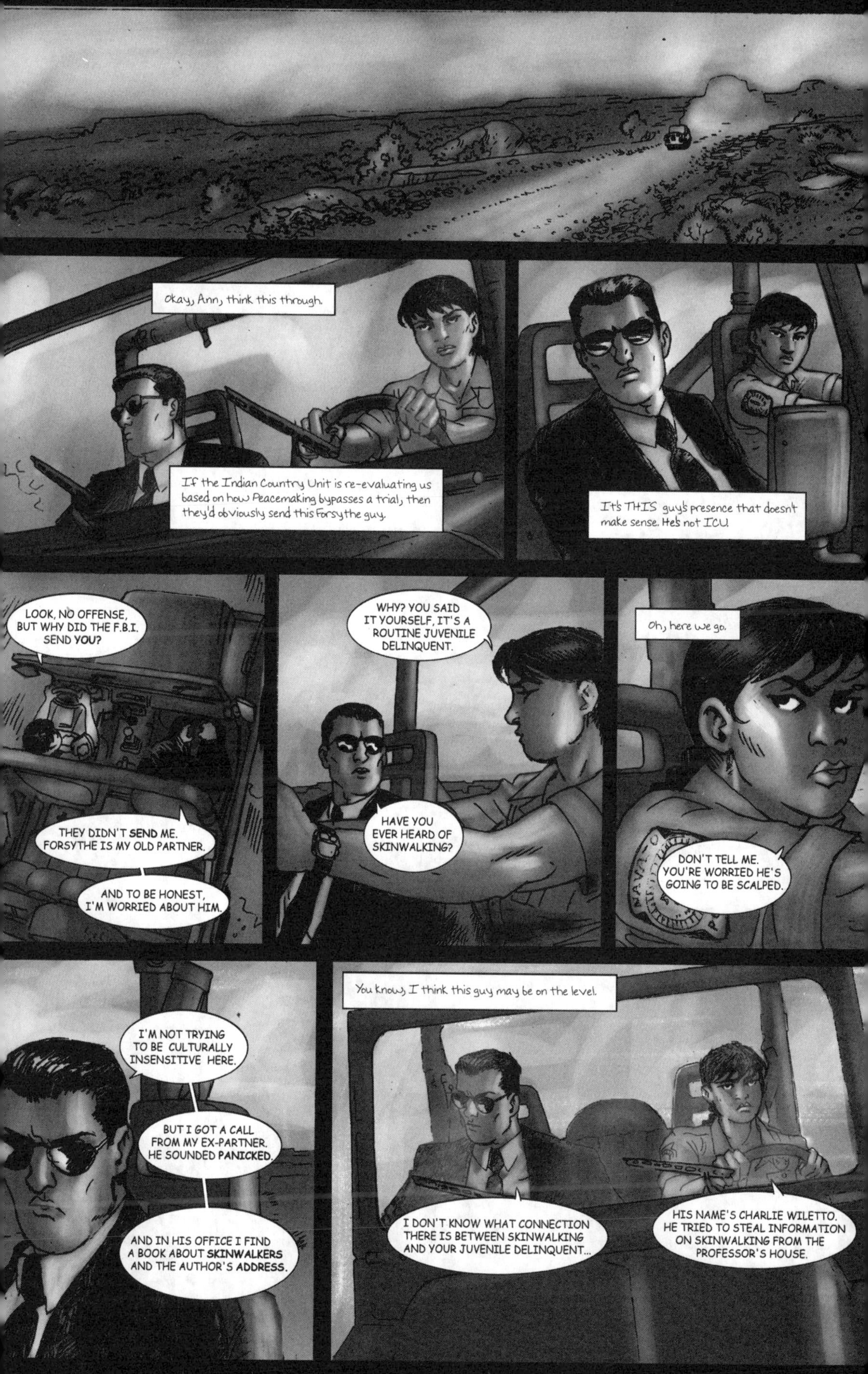
Okay, Ann, think this through.
If the Indian Country Unit is re-evaluating us based on how Peacemaking bypasses a trial, then they'd obviously send this Forsythe guy.
It's THIS guy's presence that doesn't make sense. He's not ICU.
LOOK, NO OFFENSE, BUT WHY DID THE F.B.I. SEND YOU?
THEY DIDN'T SEND ME. FORSYTHE IS MY OLD PARTNER.
AND TO BE HONEST, I'M WORRIED ABOUT HIM.
WHY? YOU SAID IT YOURSELF, IT'S A ROUTINE JUVENILE DELINQUENT.
HAVE YOU EVER HEARD OF SKINWALKING?
Oh, here we go.
DON'T TELL ME. YOU'RE WORRIED HE'S GOING TO BE SCALPED.
I'M NOT TRYING TO BE CULTURALLY INSENSITIVE HERE.
BUT I GOT A CALL FROM MY EX-PARTNER. HE SOUNDED PANICKED.
AND IN HIS OFFICE I FIND A BOOK ABOUT SKINWALKERS AND THE AUTHOR'S ADDRESS.
You know, I think this guy may be on the level.
I DON'T KNOW WHAT CONNECTION THERE IS BETWEEN SKINWALKING AND YOUR JUVENILE DELINQUENT...
HIS NAME'S CHARLIE WILETTO. HE TRIED TO STEAL INFORMATION ON SKINWALKING FROM THE PROFESSOR'S HOUSE.

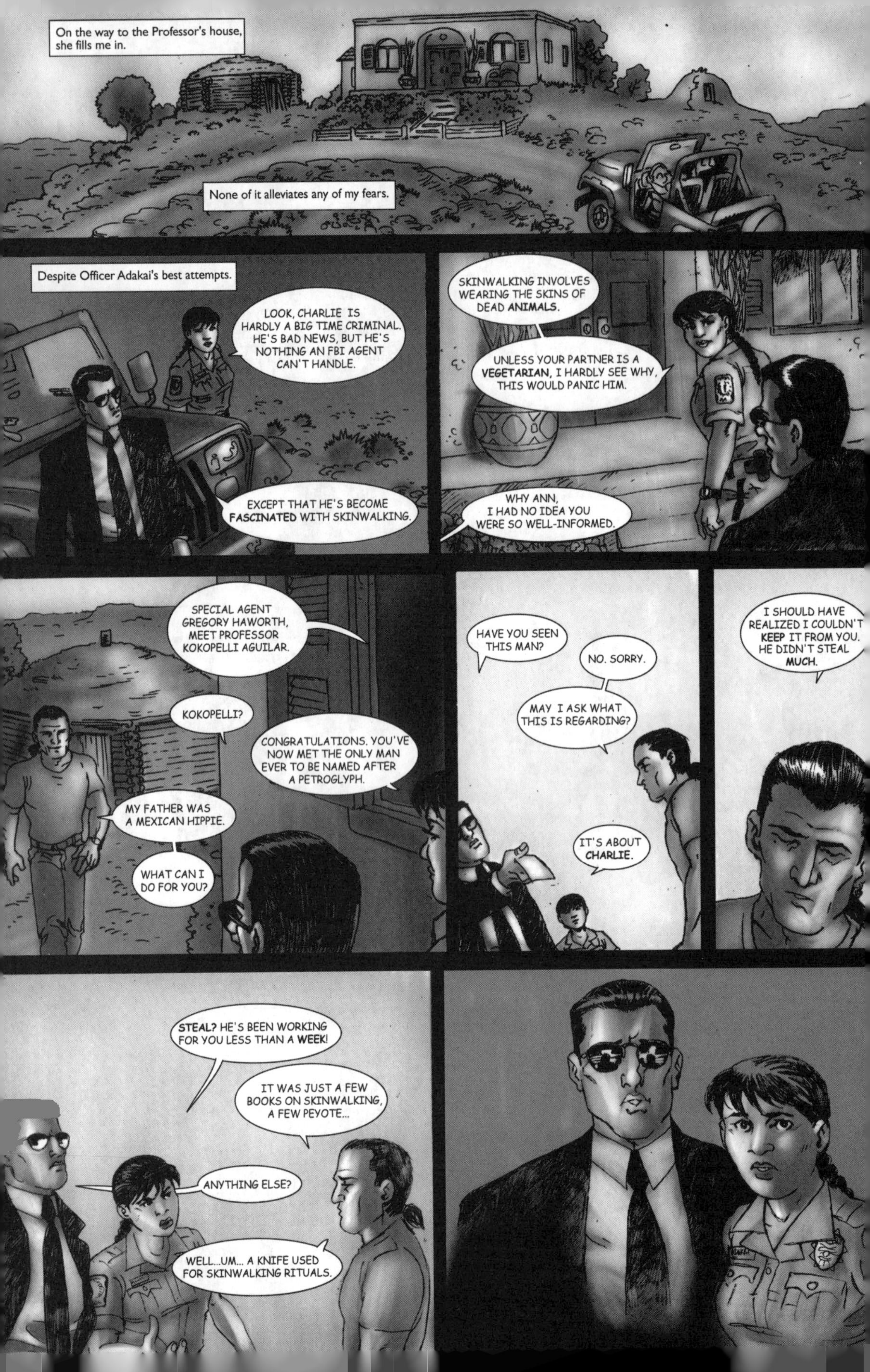
On the way to the Professor's house, she fills me in.
None of it alleviates any of my fears.
Despite Officer Adakai's best attempts.
LOOK, CHARLIE IS HARDLY A BIG TIME CRIMINAL. HE'S BAD NEWS, BUT HE'S NOTHING AN FBI AGENT CAN'T HANDLE.
EXCEPT THAT HE'S BECOME FASCINATED WITH SKINWALKING.
SKINWALKING INVOLVES WEARING THE SKINS OF DEAD ANIMALS.
UNLESS YOUR PARTNER IS A VEGETARIAN, I HARDLY SEE WHY, THIS WOULD PANIC HIM.
WHY ANN, I HAD NO IDEA YOU WERE SO WELL-INFORMED.
SPECIAL AGENT GREGORY HAWORTH, MEET PROFESSOR KOKOPELLI AGUILAR.
KOKOPELLI?
CONGRATULATIONS. YOU'VE NOW MET THE ONLY MAN EVER TO BE NAMED AFTER A PETROGLYPH.
MY FATHER WAS A MEXICAN HIPPIE.
WHAT CAN I DO FOR YOU?
HAVE YOU SEEN THIS MAN?
NO. SORRY.
MAY I ASK WHAT THIS IS REGARDING?
IT'S ABOUT CHARLIE.
I SHOULD HAVE REALIZED I COULDN'T KEEP IT FROM YOU. HE DIDN'T STEAL MUCH.
STEAL? HE'S BEEN WORKING FOR YOU LESS THAN A WEEK!
IT WAS JUST A FEW BOOKS ON SKINWALKING, A FEW PEYOTE...
ANYTHING ELSE?
WELL...UM... A KNIFE USED FOR SKINWALKING RITUALS.

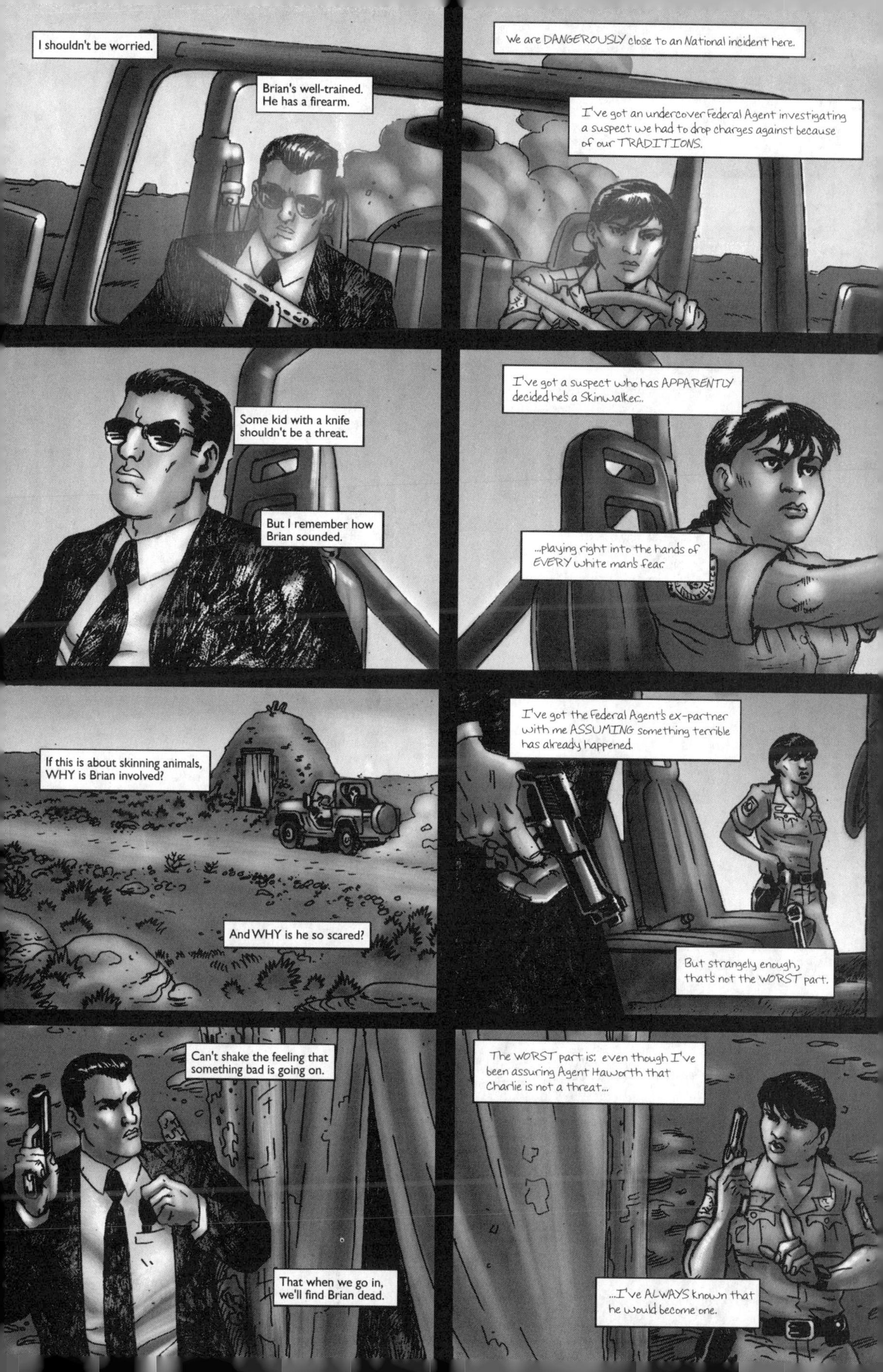
I shouldn't be worried.
Brian's well-trained. He has a firearm.
We are DANGEROUSLY close to an National incident here.
I've got an undercover Federal Agent investigating a suspect we had to drop charges against because of our TRADITIONS.
Some kid with a knife shouldn't be a threat.
But I remember how Brian sounded.
I've got a suspect who has APPARENTLY decided he's a Skinwalker...
...playing right into the hands of EVERY white man's fear.
If this is about skinning animals, WHY is Brian involved?
And WHY is he so scared?
I've got the Federal Agent's ex-partner with me ASSUMING something terrible has already happened.
But strangely enough, that's not the WORST part.
Can't shake the feeling that something bad is going on.
That when we go in, we'll find Brian dead.
The WORST part is: even though I've been assuring Agent Haworth that Charlie is not a threat...
...I've ALWAYS known that he would become one.

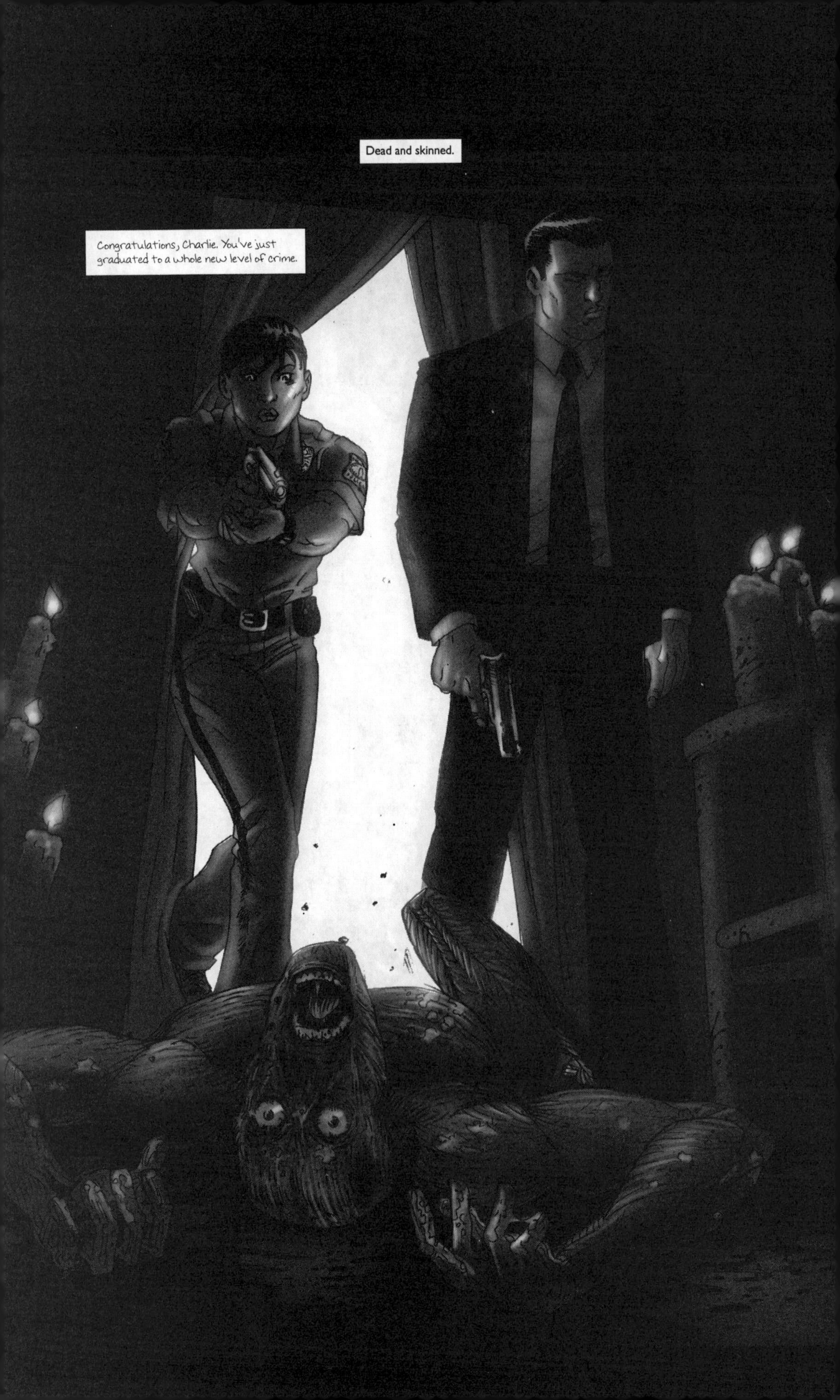
Dead and skinned.
Congratulations, Charlie. You've just graduated to a whole new level of crime.

CHAPTER 2

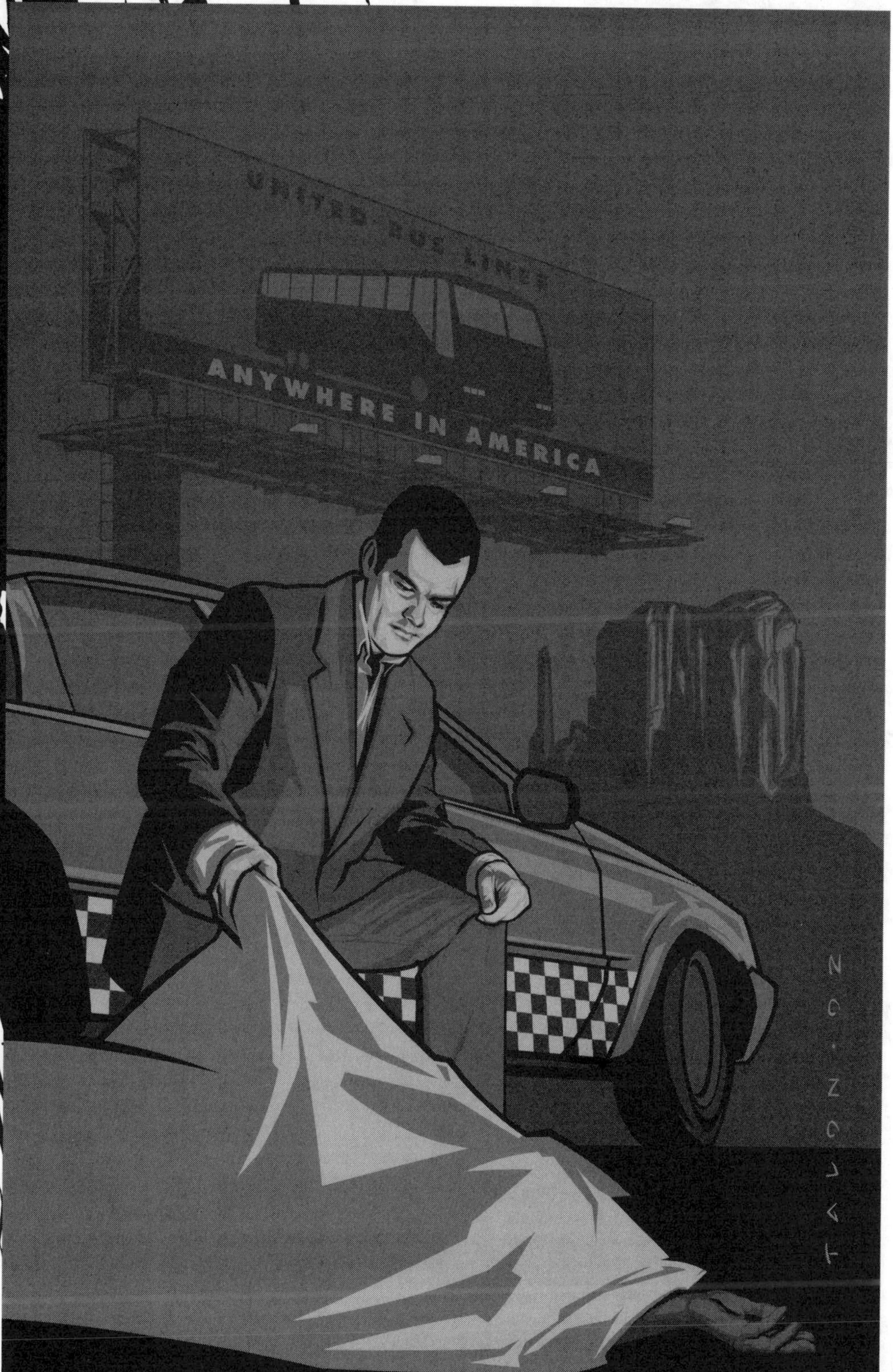
UNITED BUS LINES
ANYWHERE IN AMERICA

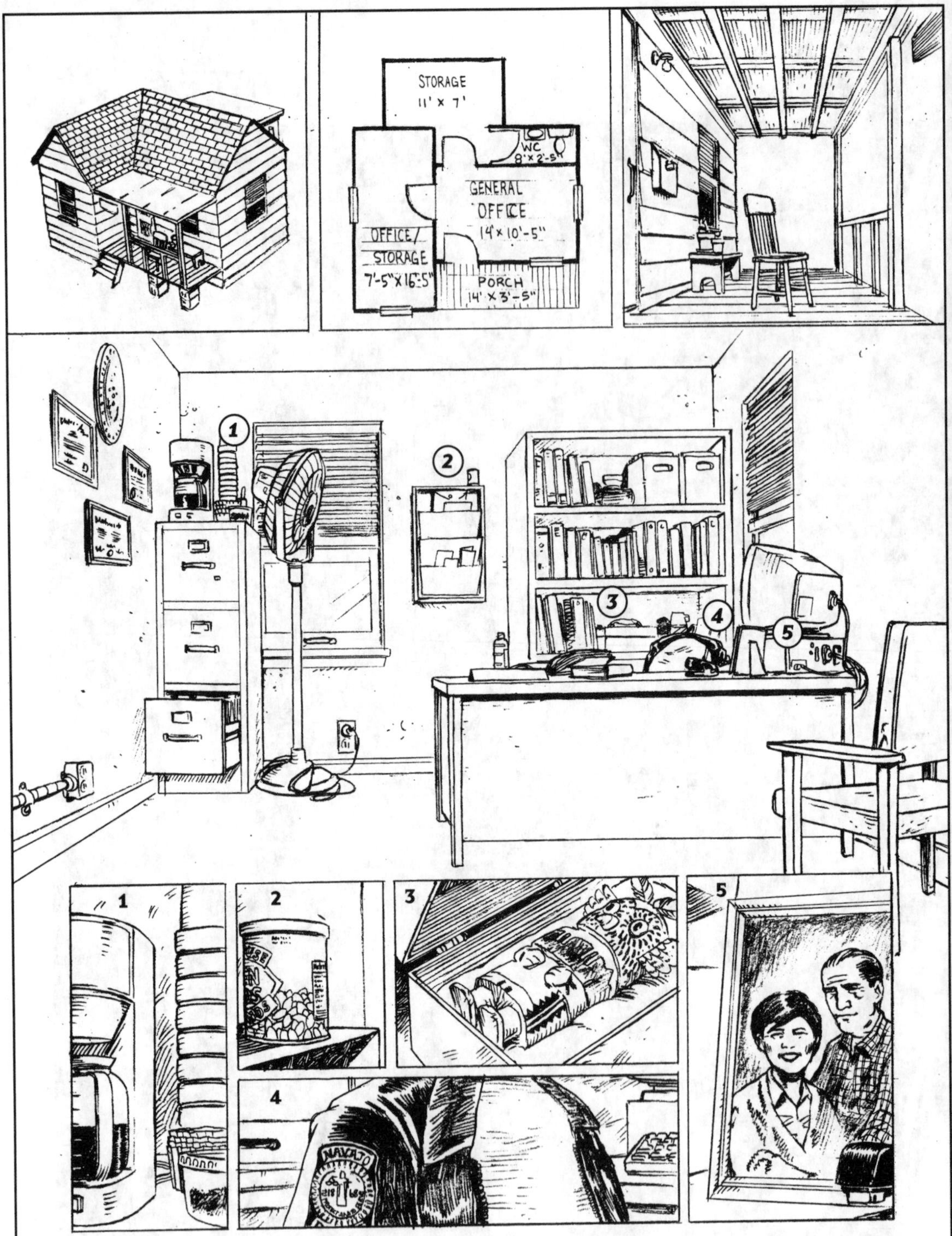
STORAGE
11' x 7'
WC
8' x 2'-5"
GENERAL
OFFICE
14' x 10'-5"
OFFICE/
STORAGE
7'-5" x 16'-5"
PORCH
14' x 3'-5"
1
2
3
4
5
NAVAJO

***(1)** the coffee pot belongs to Officer Adakai, not the Tribal Police. She is cranky until after her first cup of morning coffee. After that, she's slightly less cranky. Adakai does not drink custom blends, and gets her ground coffee beans from the local donut chain. **(2)** atop this mail rack, Officer Adakai usually keeps a can of Smokehouse Almonds, which is her favorite snack. **(3)** this tihu (or doll) of a Hopi kachina was given to Officer Adakai by Professor Aguilar a year and a half ago to decorate her office. It has sat in this box ever since. The tihu represents a kachina from the neighboring Hopi tribe. The Mongwu, the Great Horned Owl Kachina, is a warrior who disciplines the clowns when their behavior becomes too outrageous. Professor Aguilar thought this quite appropriate for Officer Adakai. **(4)** members of the Navajo Tribal Police are given official jackets, although the weather precludes wearing such jackets during the day. However, the jacket is vital at night in the desert. **(5)** a framed photo of Michael and Deana Adakai, Officer Adakai's parents, sits on her desk. Both were farmers who lived in Dinnehotso their whole lives. Deana died of cancer five years ago and Michael suffered a heart attack two years later. It is the one personal item she has used to decorate her office.*

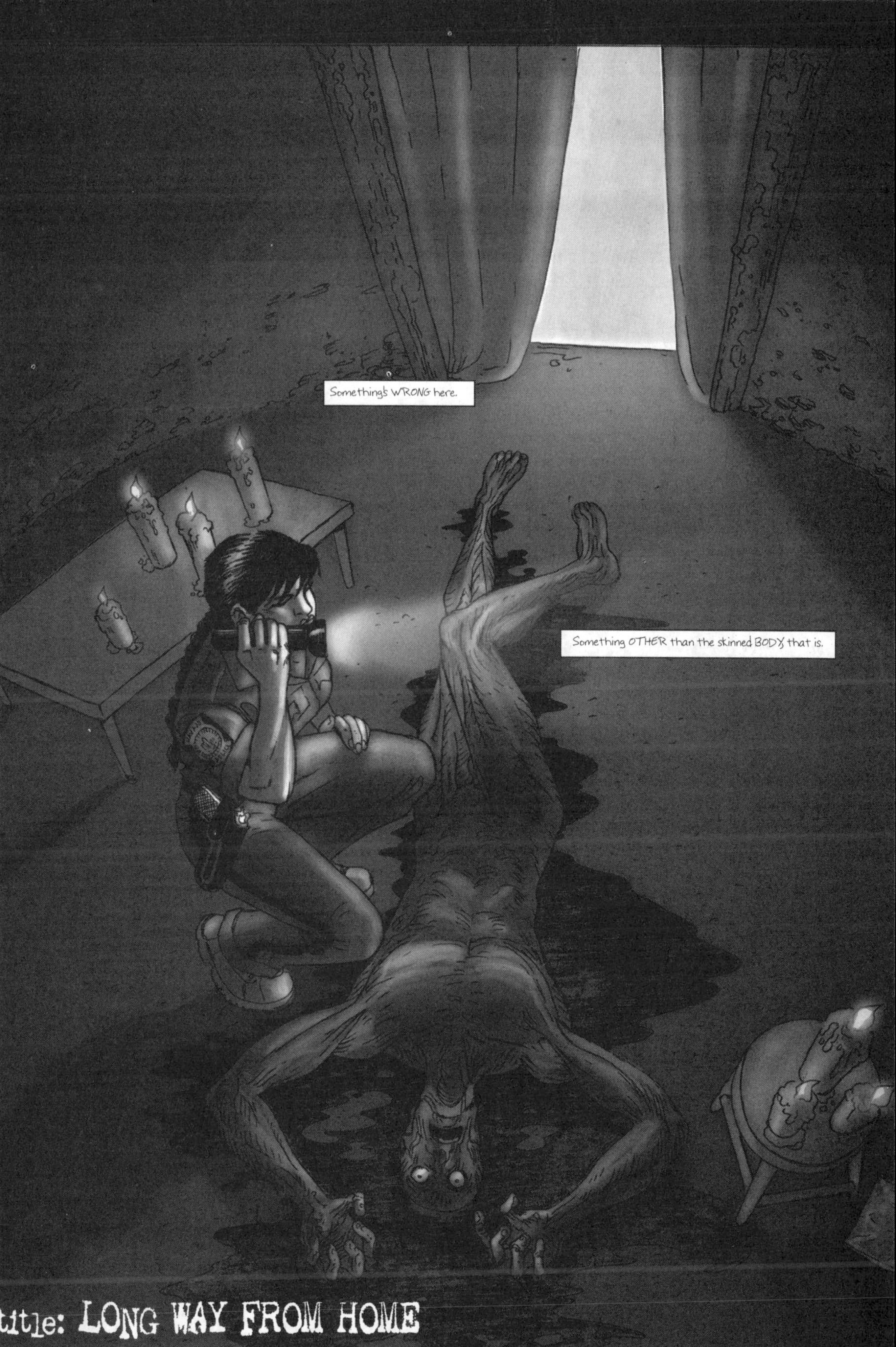
Something's WRONG here.
Something OTHER than the skinned BODY, that is.

title: LONG WAY FROM HOME

riters: NUNZIO DEFILIPPIS & CHRISTINA WEIR

penciller: BRIAN HURTT finisher/letterer: ARTHUR DELA CRUZ

editor: JAMIE S RICH

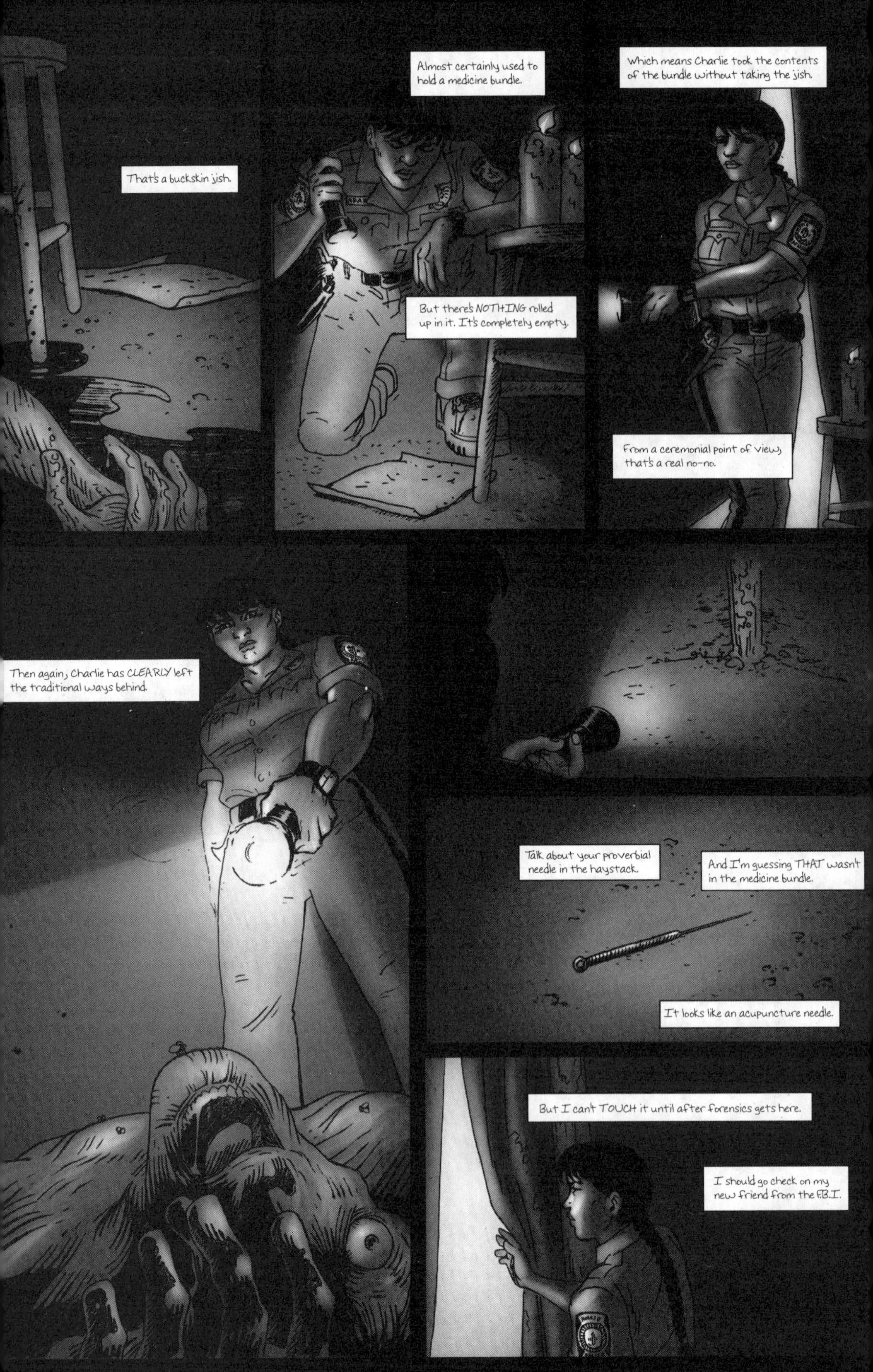
That's a buckskin jish.
Almost certainly used to hold a medicine bundle.
But there's NOTHING rolled up in it. It's completely empty.
Which means Charlie took the contents of the bundle without taking the jish.
From a ceremonial point of view, that's a real no-no.
Then again, Charlie has CLEARLY left the traditional ways behind.
Talk about your proverbial needle in the haystack.
And I'm guessing THAT wasn't in the medicine bundle.
It looks like an acupuncture needle.
But I can't TOUCH it until after forensics gets here.
I should go check on my new friend from the F.B.I.

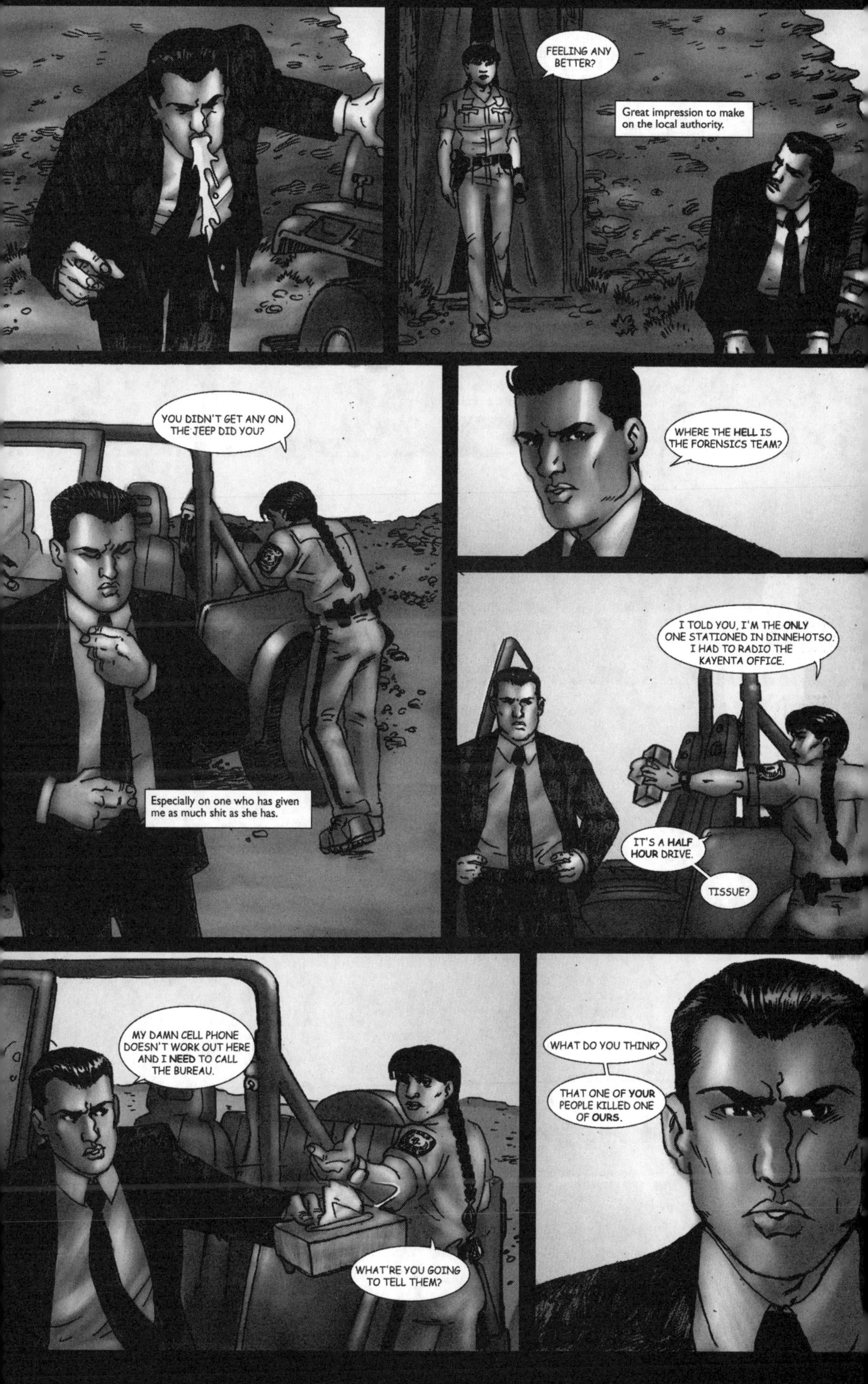
FEELING ANY BETTER?
Great impression to make on the local authority.
YOU DIDN'T GET ANY ON THE JEEP DID YOU?
Especially on one who has given me as much shit as she has.
WHERE THE HELL IS THE FORENSICS TEAM?
I TOLD YOU, I'M THE ONLY ONE STATIONED IN DINNEHOTSO. I HAD TO RADIO THE KAYENTA OFFICE.
IT'S A HALF HOUR DRIVE.
TISSUE?
MY DAMN CELL PHONE DOESN'T WORK OUT HERE AND I NEED TO CALL THE BUREAU.
WHAT'RE YOU GOING TO TELL THEM?
WHAT DO YOU THINK?
THAT ONE OF YOUR PEOPLE KILLED ONE OF OURS.

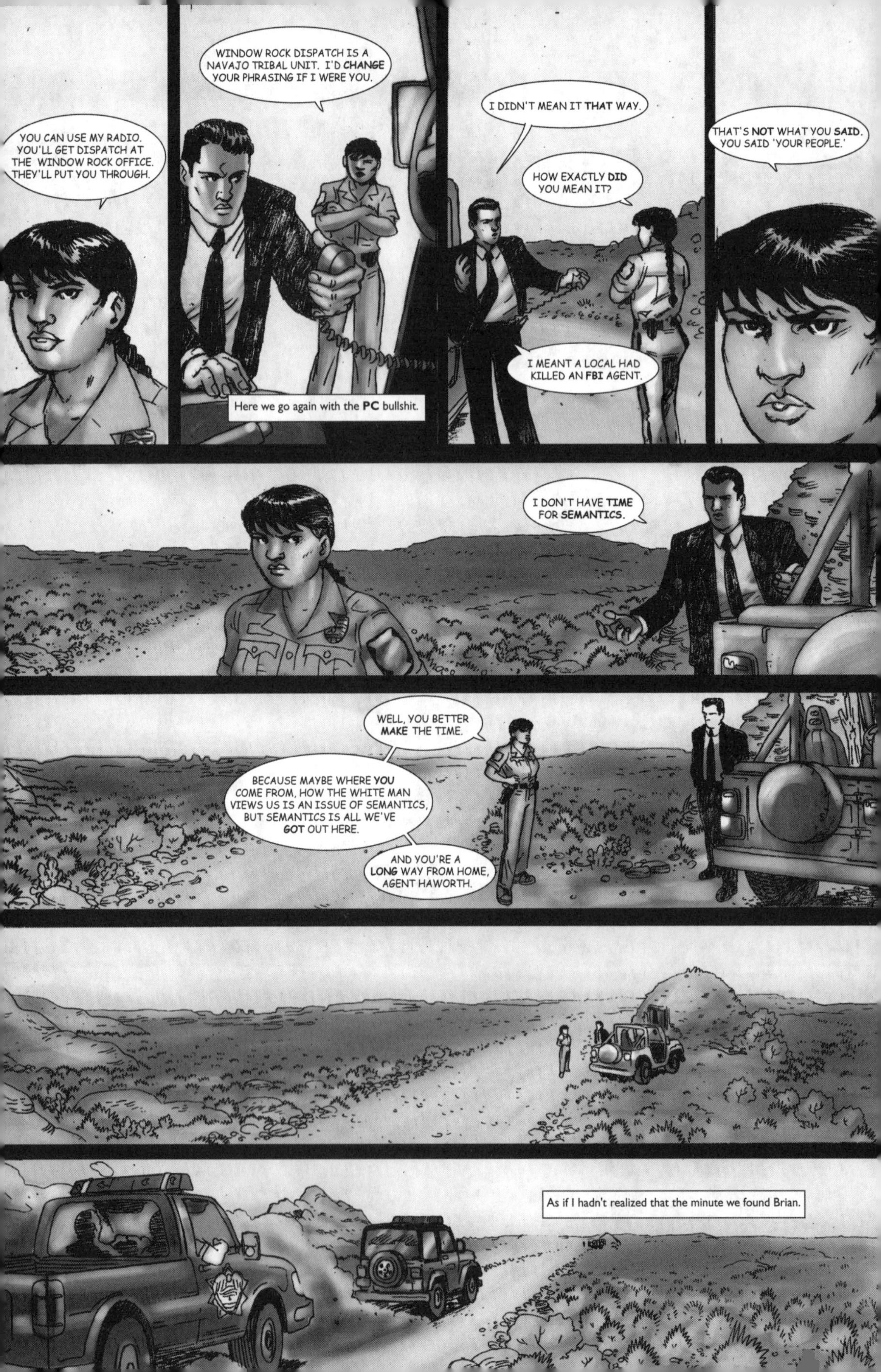

YOU CAN USE MY RADIO. YOU'LL GET DISPATCH AT THE WINDOW ROCK OFFICE. THEY'LL PUT YOU THROUGH.
WINDOW ROCK DISPATCH IS A NAVAJO TRIBAL UNIT. I'D **CHANGE** YOUR PHRASING IF I WERE YOU.
Here we go again with the **PC** bullshit.
I DIDN'T MEAN IT **THAT** WAY.
HOW EXACTLY **DID** YOU MEAN IT?
I MEANT A LOCAL HAD KILLED AN **FBI** AGENT.
THAT'S **NOT** WHAT YOU **SAID.** YOU SAID 'YOUR PEOPLE.'
I DON'T HAVE **TIME** FOR **SEMANTICS.**
WELL, YOU BETTER **MAKE** THE TIME.
BECAUSE MAYBE WHERE **YOU** COME FROM, HOW THE WHITE MAN VIEWS US IS AN ISSUE OF SEMANTICS, BUT SEMANTICS IS ALL WE'VE **GOT** OUT HERE.
AND YOU'RE A **LONG** WAY FROM HOME, AGENT HAWORTH.
As if I hadn't realized that the minute we found Brian.

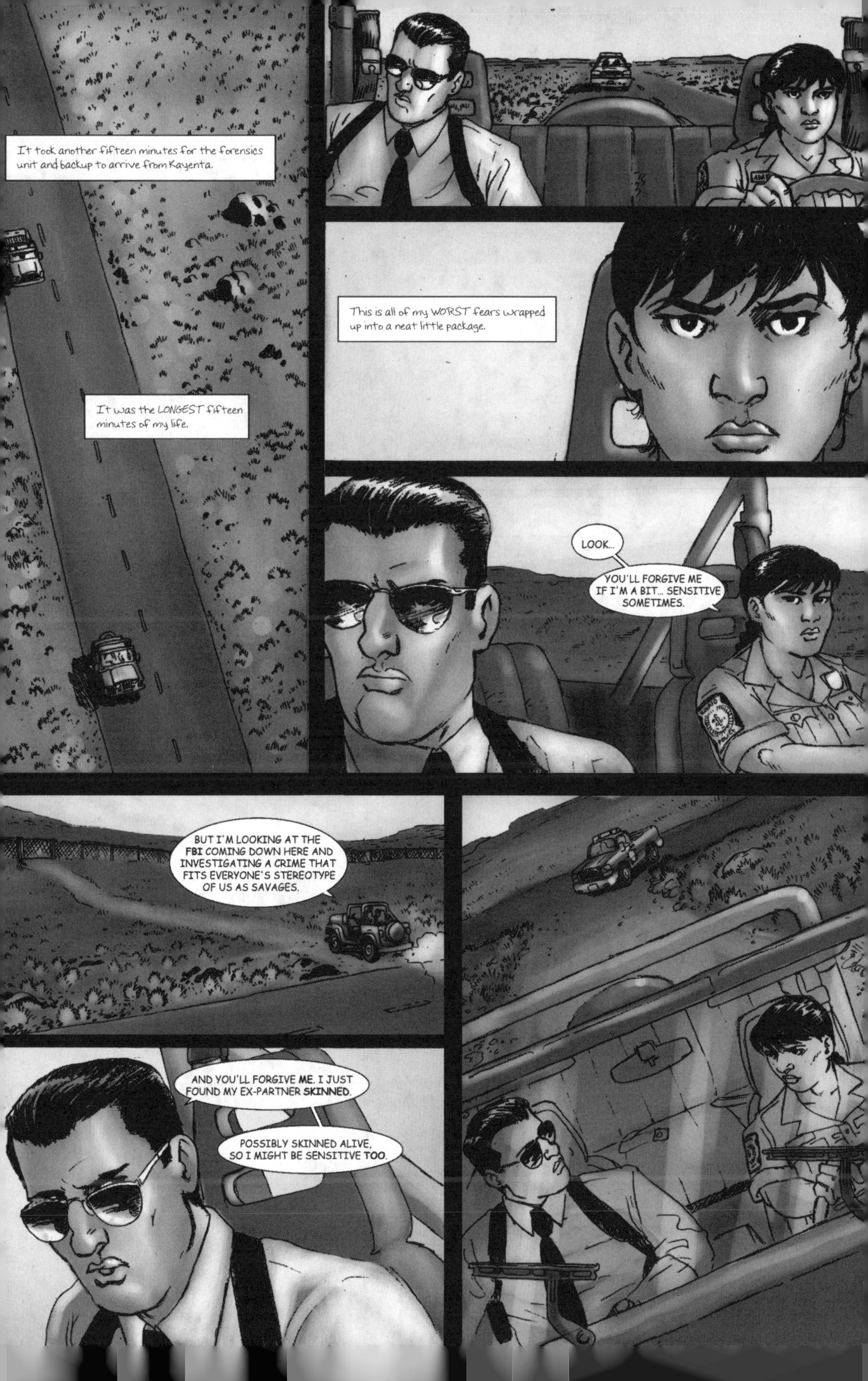

It took another fifteen minutes for the forensics unit and backup to arrive from Kayenta.
It was the LONGEST fifteen minutes of my life.
This is all of my WORST fears wrapped up into a neat little package.
LOOK...
YOU'LL FORGIVE ME IF I'M A BIT... SENSITIVE SOMETIMES.
BUT I'M LOOKING AT THE FBI COMING DOWN HERE AND INVESTIGATING A CRIME THAT FITS EVERYONE'S STEREOTYPE OF US AS SAVAGES.
AND YOU'LL FORGIVE ME. I JUST FOUND MY EX-PARTNER SKINNED.
POSSIBLY SKINNED ALIVE, SO I MIGHT BE SENSITIVE TOO.

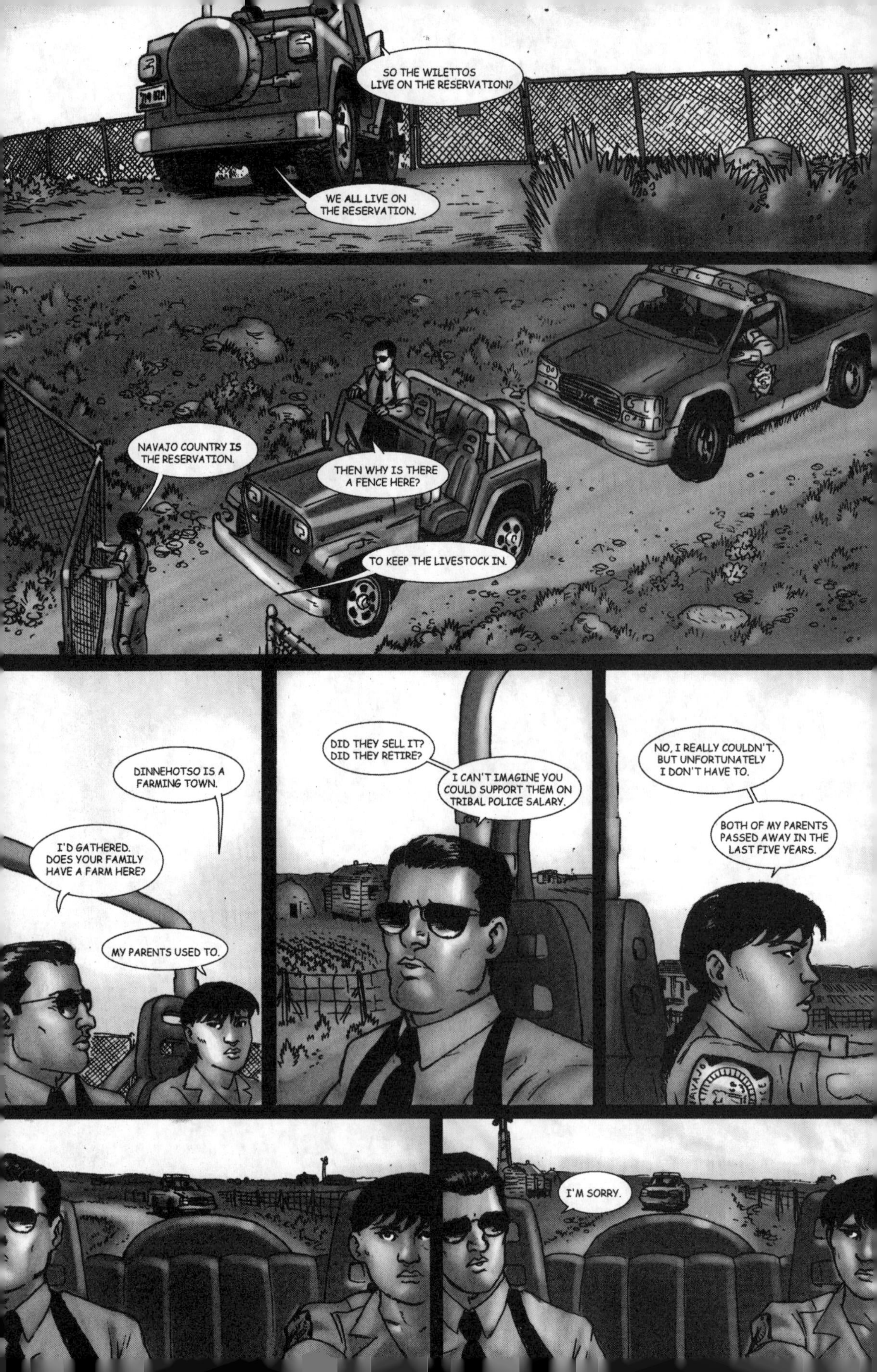

SO THE WILETTOS LIVE ON THE RESERVATION?
WE ALL LIVE ON THE RESERVATION.
NAVAJO COUNTRY IS THE RESERVATION.
THEN WHY IS THERE A FENCE HERE?
TO KEEP THE LIVESTOCK IN.
DINNEHOTSO IS A FARMING TOWN.
I'D GATHERED. DOES YOUR FAMILY HAVE A FARM HERE?
MY PARENTS USED TO.
DID THEY SELL IT? DID THEY RETIRE?
I CAN'T IMAGINE YOU COULD SUPPORT THEM ON TRIBAL POLICE SALARY.
NO, I REALLY COULDN'T. BUT UNFORTUNATELY I DON'T HAVE TO.
BOTH OF MY PARENTS PASSED AWAY IN THE LAST FIVE YEARS.
I'M SORRY.

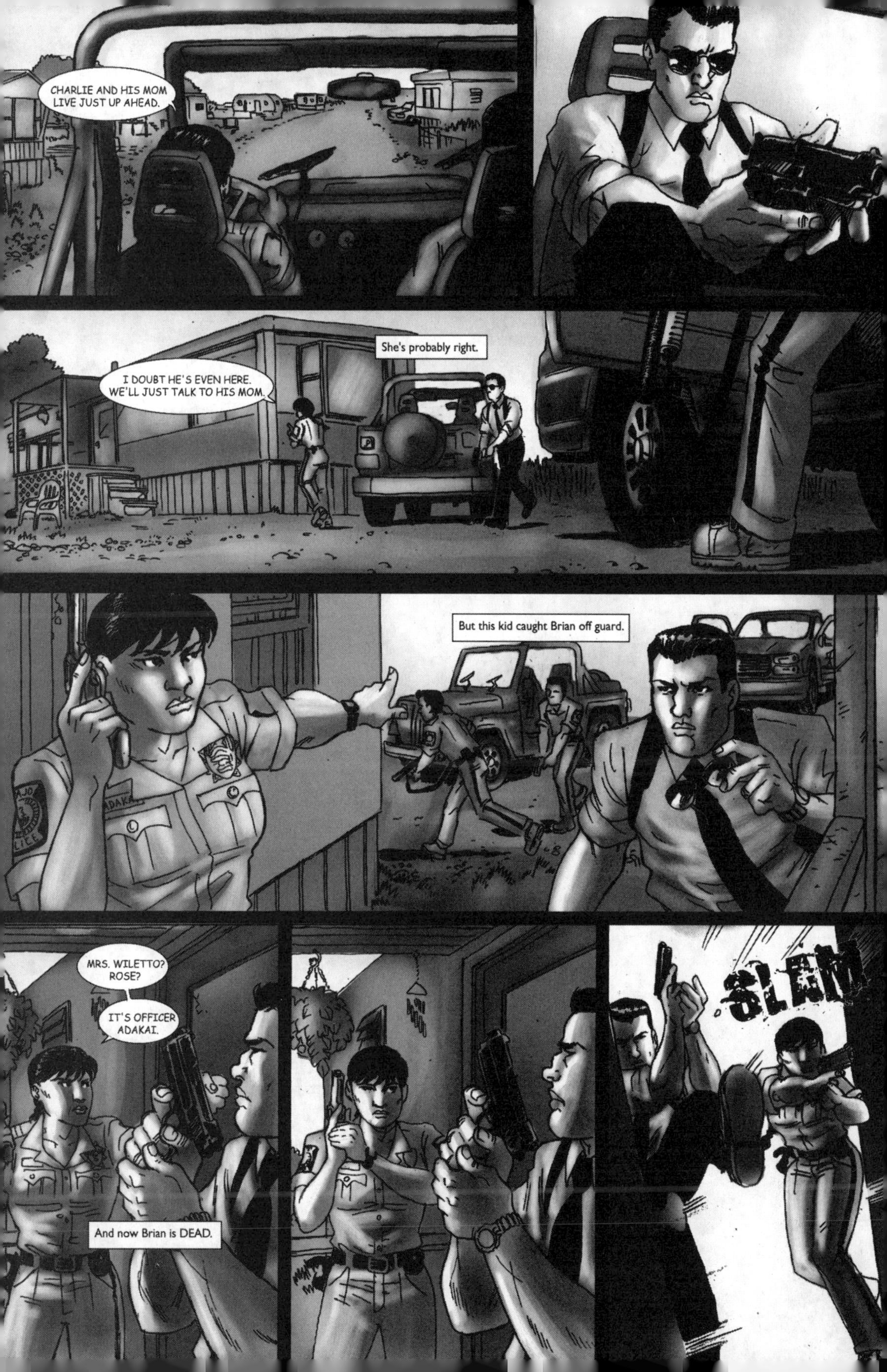

CHARLIE AND HIS MOM LIVE JUST UP AHEAD.
I DOUBT HE'S EVEN HERE. WE'LL JUST TALK TO HIS MOM.
She's probably right.
But this kid caught Brian off guard.
MRS. WILETTO? ROSE?
IT'S OFFICER ADAKAI.
And now Brian is DEAD.
SLAM

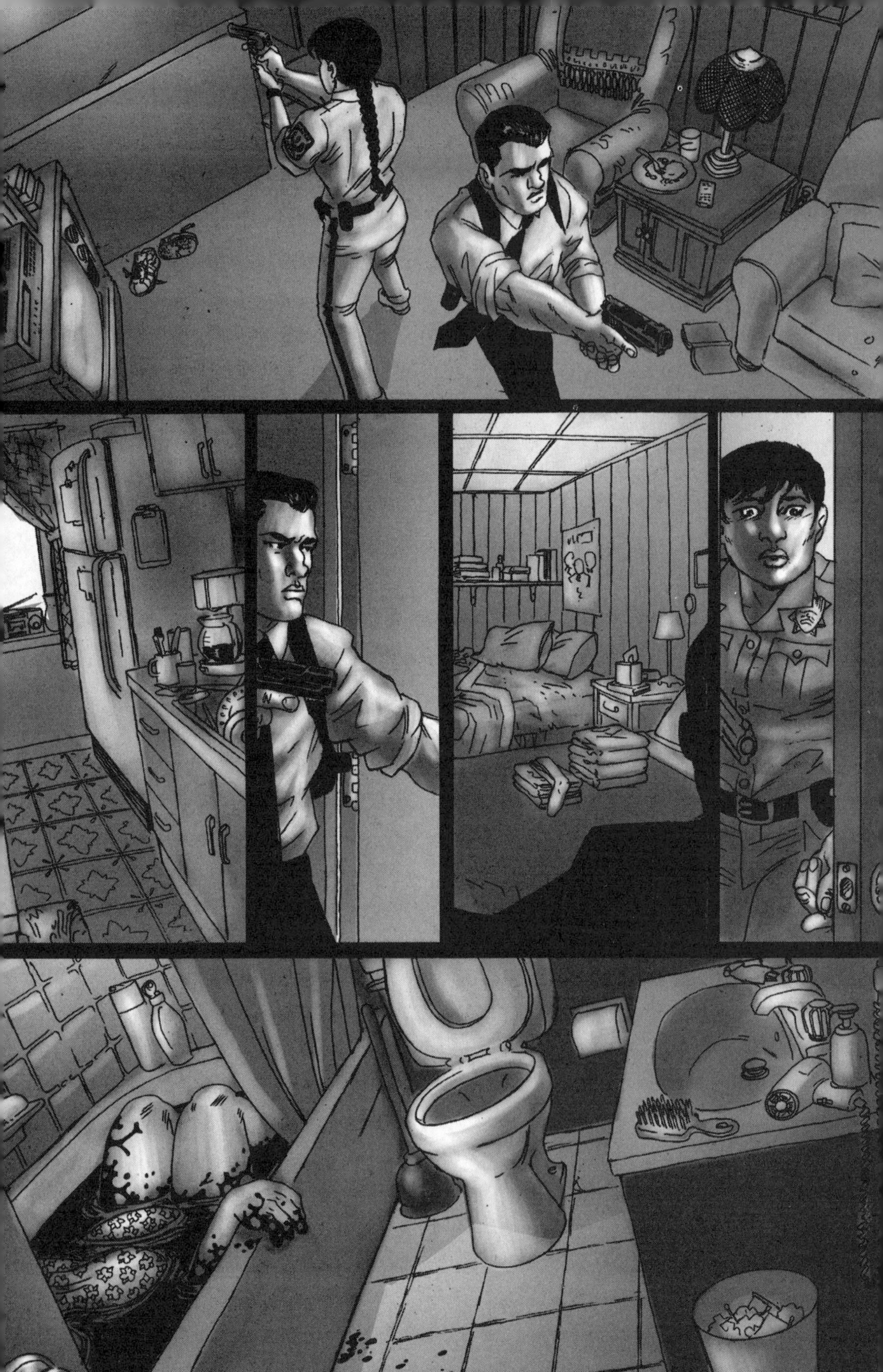

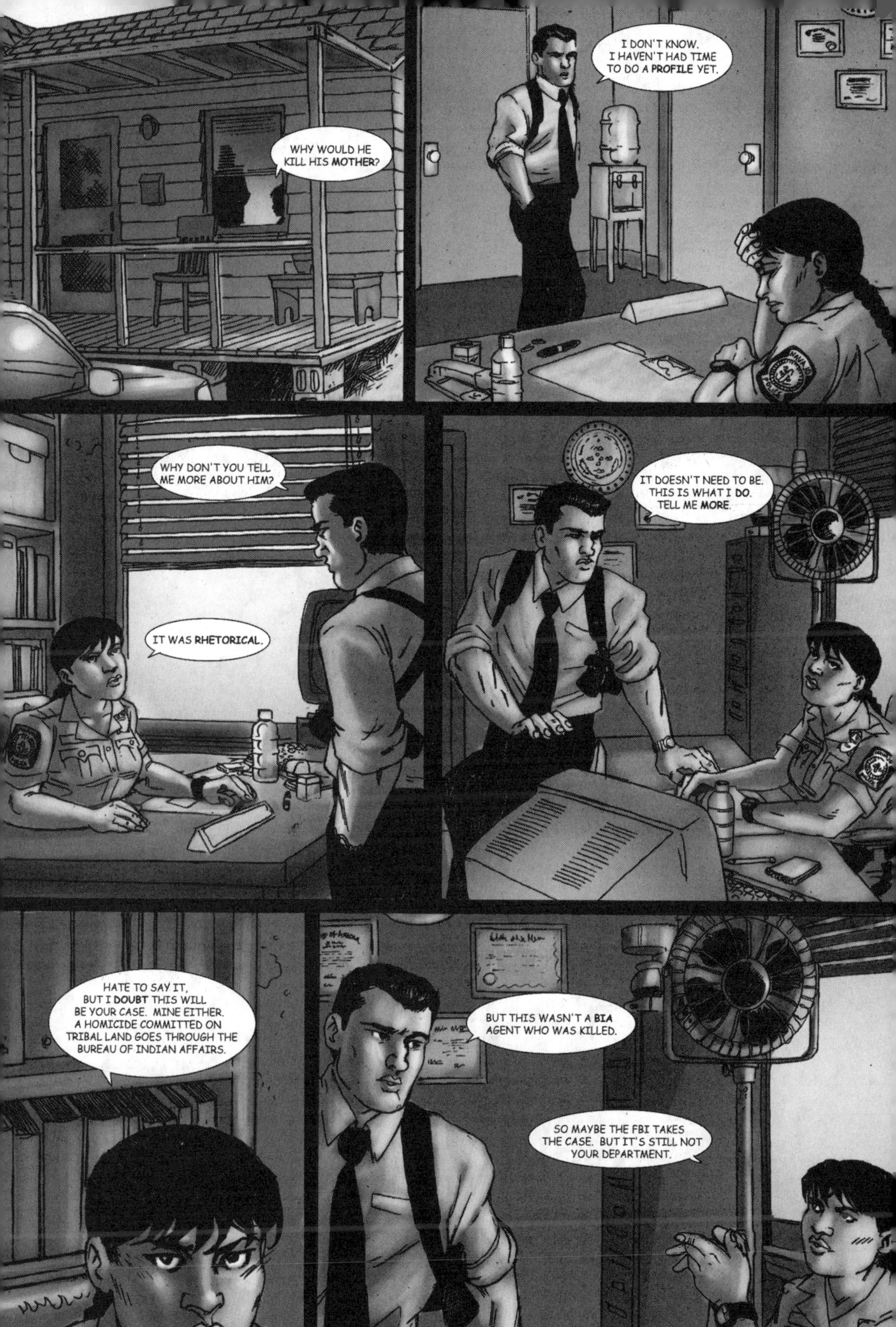
WHY WOULD HE KILL HIS MOTHER?
I DON'T KNOW. I HAVEN'T HAD TIME TO DO A PROFILE YET.
WHY DON'T YOU TELL ME MORE ABOUT HIM?
IT WAS RHETORICAL.
IT DOESN'T NEED TO BE. THIS IS WHAT I DO. TELL ME MORE.
HATE TO SAY IT, BUT I DOUBT THIS WILL BE YOUR CASE. MINE EITHER. A HOMICIDE COMMITTED ON TRIBAL LAND GOES THROUGH THE BUREAU OF INDIAN AFFAIRS.
BUT THIS WASN'T A BIA AGENT WHO WAS KILLED.
SO MAYBE THE FBI TAKES THE CASE. BUT IT'S STILL NOT YOUR DEPARTMENT.

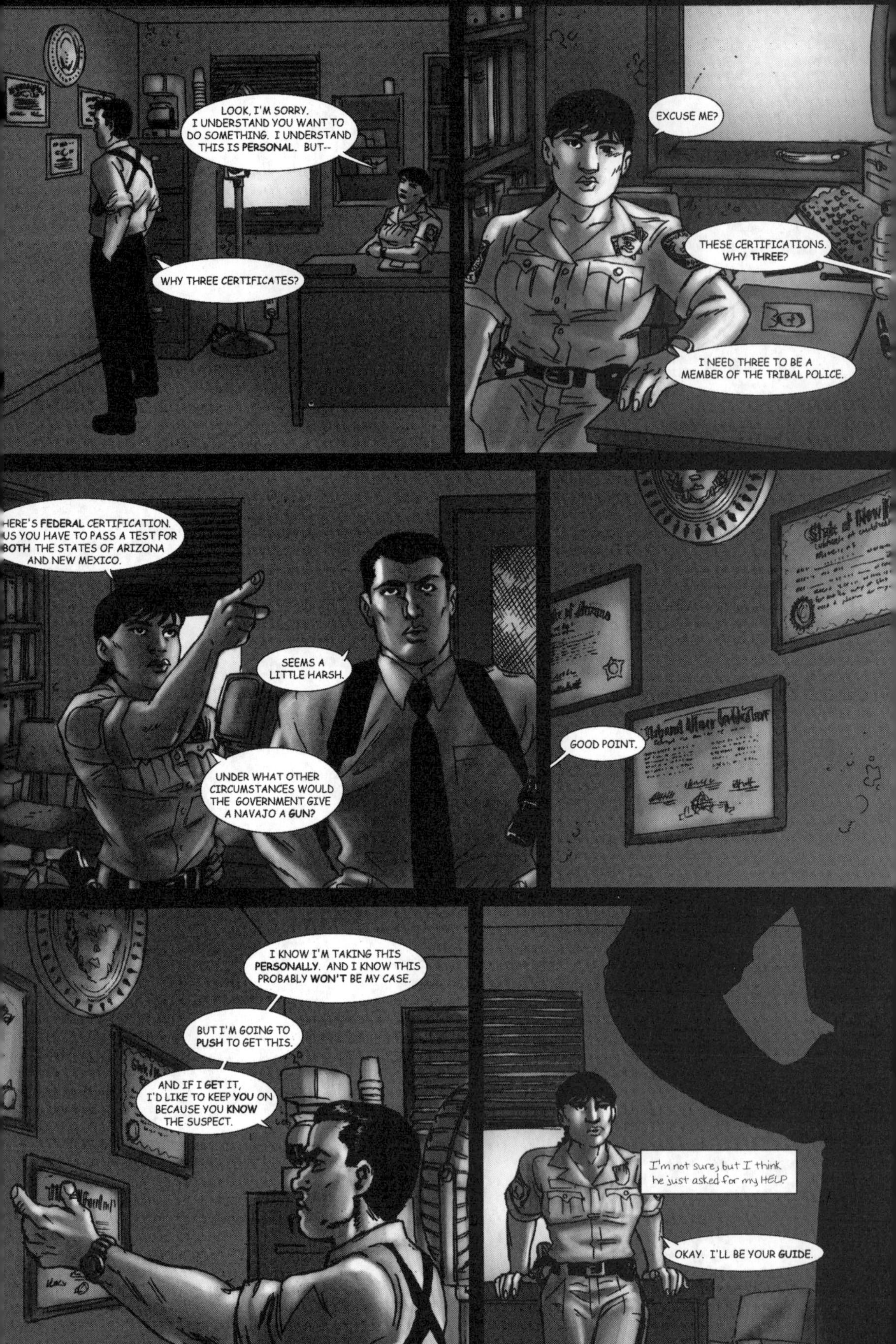
LOOK, I'M SORRY. I UNDERSTAND YOU WANT TO DO SOMETHING. I UNDERSTAND THIS IS PERSONAL. BUT--
WHY THREE CERTIFICATES?
EXCUSE ME?
THESE CERTIFICATIONS. WHY THREE?
I NEED THREE TO BE A MEMBER OF THE TRIBAL POLICE.
HERE'S FEDERAL CERTIFICATION. US YOU HAVE TO PASS A TEST FOR BOTH THE STATES OF ARIZONA AND NEW MEXICO.
SEEMS A LITTLE HARSH.
UNDER WHAT OTHER CIRCUMSTANCES WOULD THE GOVERNMENT GIVE A NAVAJO A GUN?
GOOD POINT.
I KNOW I'M TAKING THIS PERSONALLY. AND I KNOW THIS PROBABLY WON'T BE MY CASE.
BUT I'M GOING TO PUSH TO GET THIS.
AND IF I GET IT, I'D LIKE TO KEEP YOU ON BECAUSE YOU KNOW THE SUSPECT.
I'm not sure, but I think he just asked for my HELP.
OKAY. I'LL BE YOUR GUIDE.

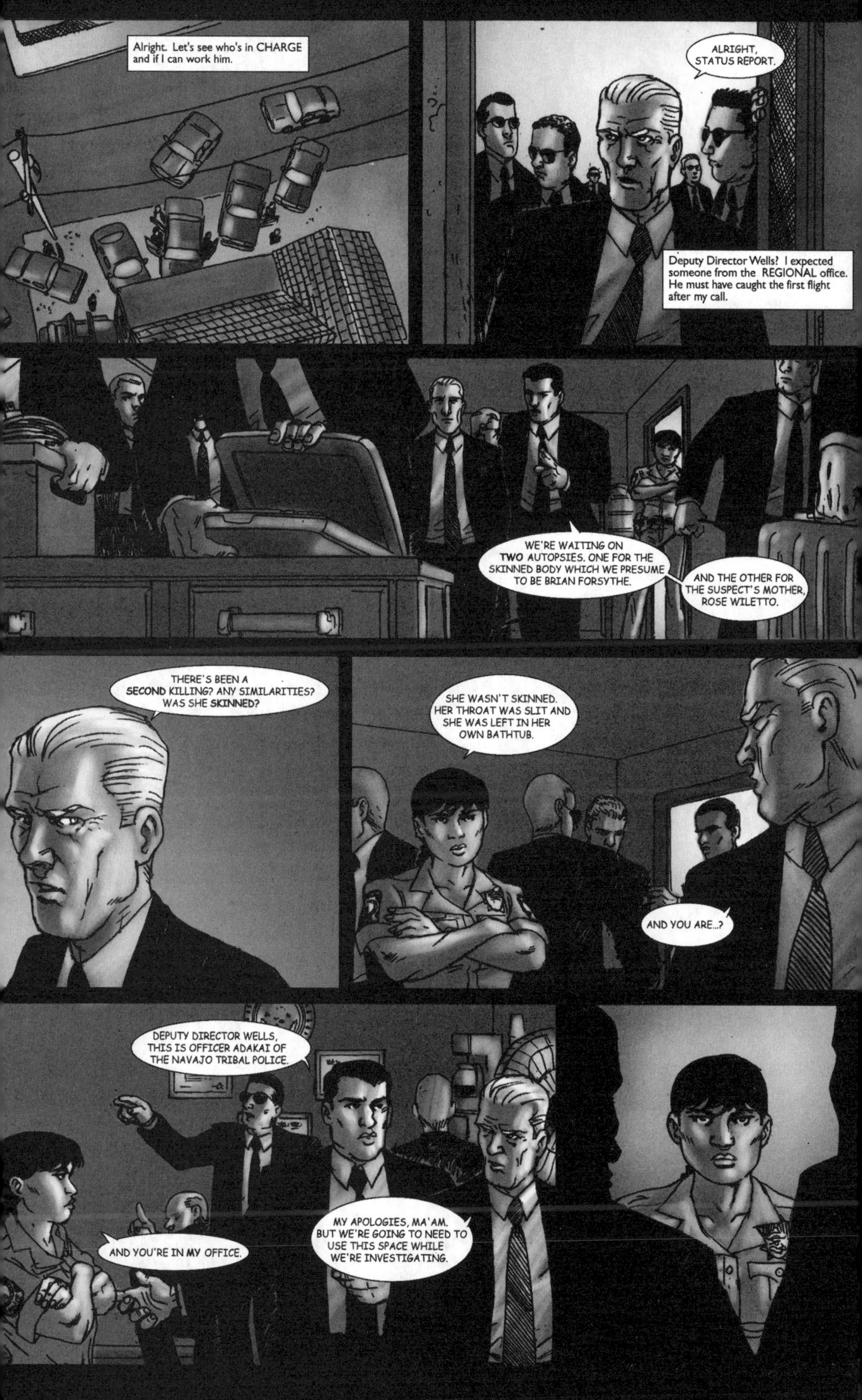
Alright. Let's see who's in CHARGE and if I can work him.
ALRIGHT, STATUS REPORT.
Deputy Director Wells? I expected someone from the REGIONAL office. He must have caught the first flight after my call.
WE'RE WAITING ON TWO AUTOPSIES. ONE FOR THE SKINNED BODY WHICH WE PRESUME TO BE BRIAN FORSYTHE.
AND THE OTHER FOR THE SUSPECT'S MOTHER, ROSE WILETTO.
THERE'S BEEN A SECOND KILLING? ANY SIMILARITIES? WAS SHE SKINNED?
SHE WASN'T SKINNED. HER THROAT WAS SLIT AND SHE WAS LEFT IN HER OWN BATHTUB.
AND YOU ARE...?
DEPUTY DIRECTOR WELLS, THIS IS OFFICER ADAKAI OF THE NAVAJO TRIBAL POLICE.
AND YOU'RE IN MY OFFICE.
MY APOLOGIES, MA'AM. BUT WE'RE GOING TO NEED TO USE THIS SPACE WHILE WE'RE INVESTIGATING.

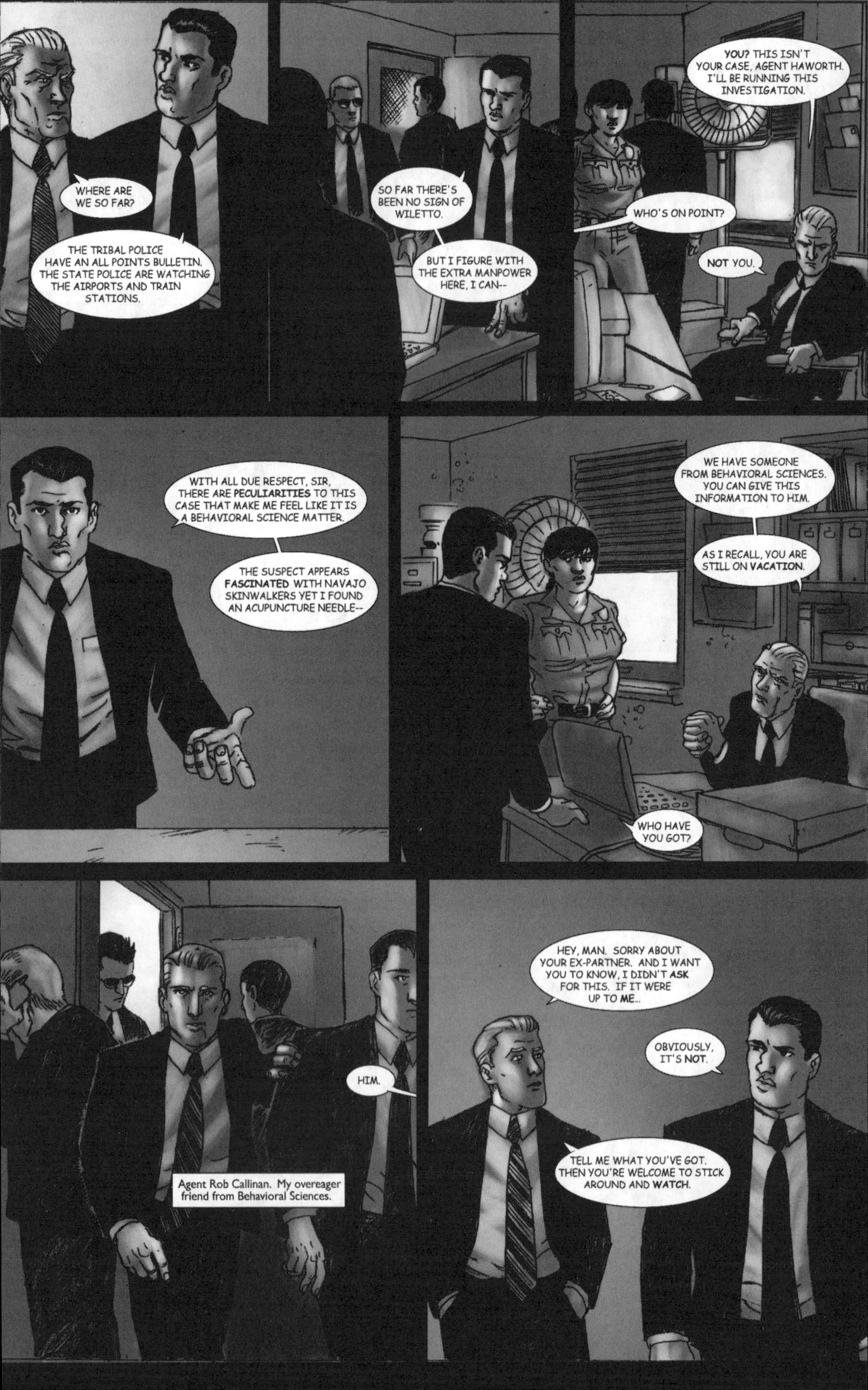
WHERE ARE WE SO FAR?
THE TRIBAL POLICE HAVE AN ALL POINTS BULLETIN. THE STATE POLICE ARE WATCHING THE AIRPORTS AND TRAIN STATIONS.
SO FAR THERE'S BEEN NO SIGN OF WILETTO.
BUT I FIGURE WITH THE EXTRA MANPOWER HERE, I CAN--
YOU? THIS ISN'T YOUR CASE, AGENT HAWORTH. I'LL BE RUNNING THIS INVESTIGATION.
WHO'S ON POINT?
NOT YOU.
WITH ALL DUE RESPECT, SIR, THERE ARE PECULIARITIES TO THIS CASE THAT MAKE ME FEEL LIKE IT IS A BEHAVIORAL SCIENCE MATTER.
THE SUSPECT APPEARS FASCINATED WITH NAVAJO SKINWALKERS YET I FOUND AN ACUPUNCTURE NEEDLE--
WE HAVE SOMEONE FROM BEHAVIORAL SCIENCES. YOU CAN GIVE THIS INFORMATION TO HIM.
AS I RECALL, YOU ARE STILL ON VACATION.
WHO HAVE YOU GOT?
HIM.
Agent Rob Callinan. My overeager friend from Behavioral Sciences.
HEY, MAN. SORRY ABOUT YOUR EX-PARTNER. AND I WANT YOU TO KNOW, I DIDN'T ASK FOR THIS. IF IT WERE UP TO ME...
OBVIOUSLY, IT'S NOT.
TELL ME WHAT YOU'VE GOT. THEN YOU'RE WELCOME TO STICK AROUND AND WATCH.

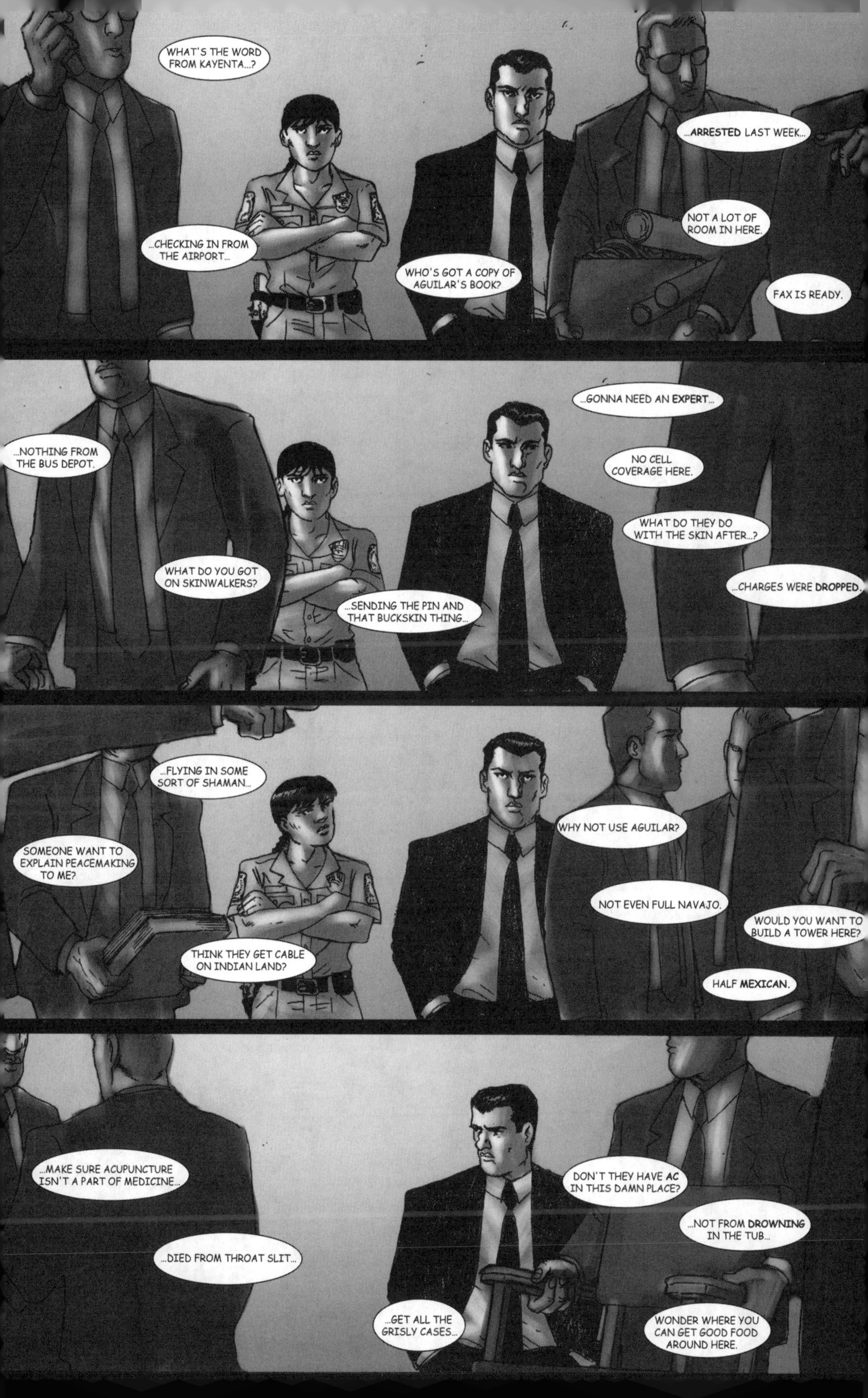
WHAT'S THE WORD FROM KAYENTA...?
...ARRESTED LAST WEEK...
NOT A LOT OF ROOM IN HERE.
...CHECKING IN FROM THE AIRPORT...
WHO'S GOT A COPY OF AGUILAR'S BOOK?
FAX IS READY.
...GONNA NEED AN EXPERT...
...NOTHING FROM THE BUS DEPOT.
NO CELL COVERAGE HERE.
WHAT DO THEY DO WITH THE SKIN AFTER...?
WHAT DO YOU GOT ON SKINWALKERS?
...CHARGES WERE DROPPED.
...SENDING THE PIN AND THAT BUCKSKIN THING...
...FLYING IN SOME SORT OF SHAMAN...
WHY NOT USE AGUILAR?
SOMEONE WANT TO EXPLAIN PEACEMAKING TO ME?
NOT EVEN FULL NAVAJO.
WOULD YOU WANT TO BUILD A TOWER HERE?
THINK THEY GET CABLE ON INDIAN LAND?
HALF MEXICAN.
...MAKE SURE ACUPUNCTURE ISN'T A PART OF MEDICINE...
DON'T THEY HAVE AC IN THIS DAMN PLACE?
...NOT FROM DROWNING IN THE TUB...
...DIED FROM THROAT SLIT...
...GET ALL THE GRISLY CASES...
WONDER WHERE YOU CAN GET GOOD FOOD AROUND HERE.

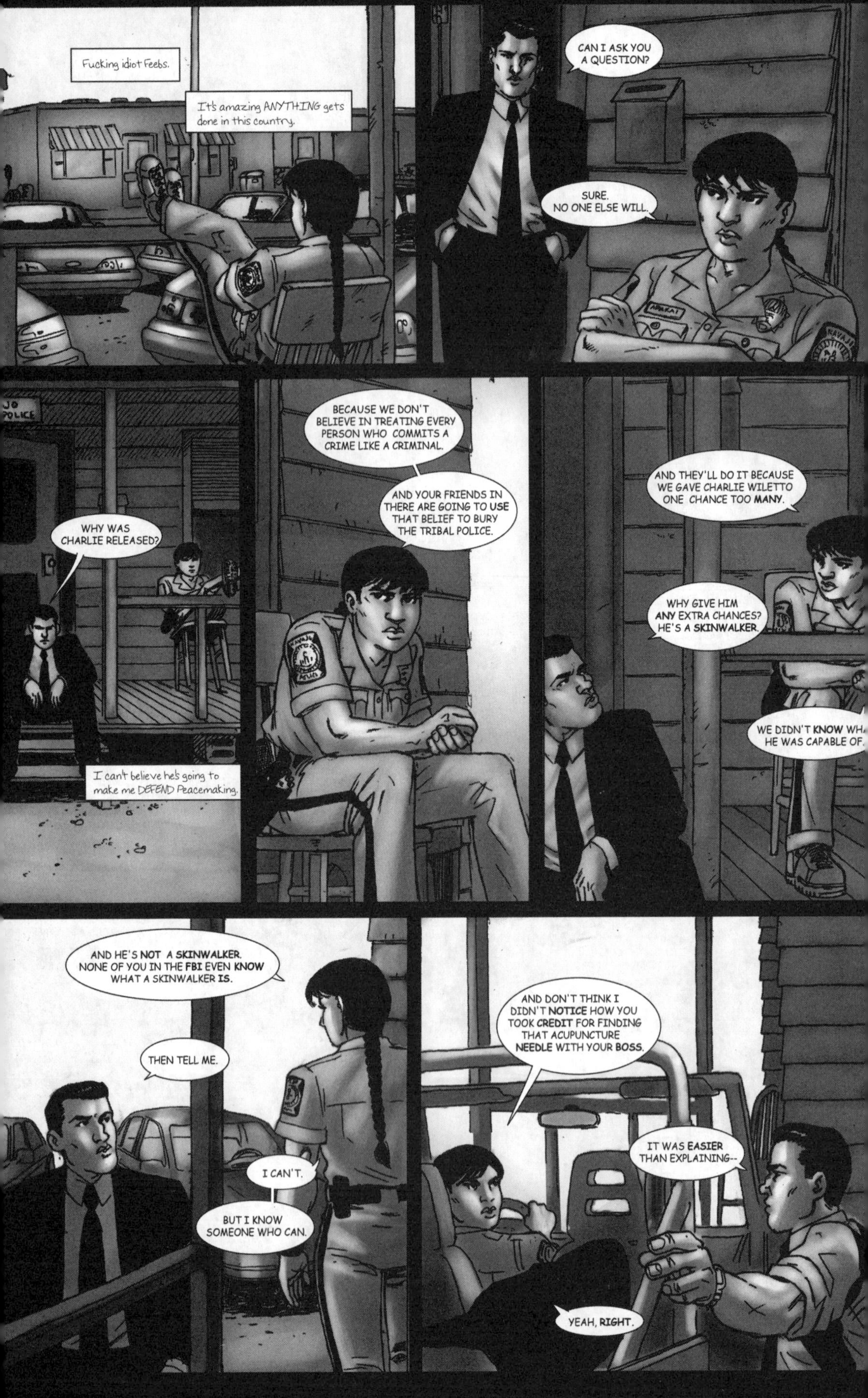
Fucking idiot Feebs.
It's amazing ANYTHING gets done in this country.
CAN I ASK YOU A QUESTION?
SURE. NO ONE ELSE WILL.
WHY WAS CHARLIE RELEASED?
I can't believe he's going to make me DEFEND Peacemaking.
BECAUSE WE DON'T BELIEVE IN TREATING EVERY PERSON WHO COMMITS A CRIME LIKE A CRIMINAL.
AND YOUR FRIENDS IN THERE ARE GOING TO USE THAT BELIEF TO BURY THE TRIBAL POLICE.
AND THEY'LL DO IT BECAUSE WE GAVE CHARLIE WILETTO ONE CHANCE TOO MANY.
WHY GIVE HIM ANY EXTRA CHANCES? HE'S A SKINWALKER.
WE DIDN'T KNOW WH HE WAS CAPABLE OF.
AND HE'S NOT A SKINWALKER. NONE OF YOU IN THE FBI EVEN KNOW WHAT A SKINWALKER IS.
THEN TELL ME.
I CAN'T.
BUT I KNOW SOMEONE WHO CAN.
AND DON'T THINK I DIDN'T NOTICE HOW YOU TOOK CREDIT FOR FINDING THAT ACUPUNCTURE NEEDLE WITH YOUR BOSS.
IT WAS EASIER THAN EXPLAINING--
YEAH, RIGHT.

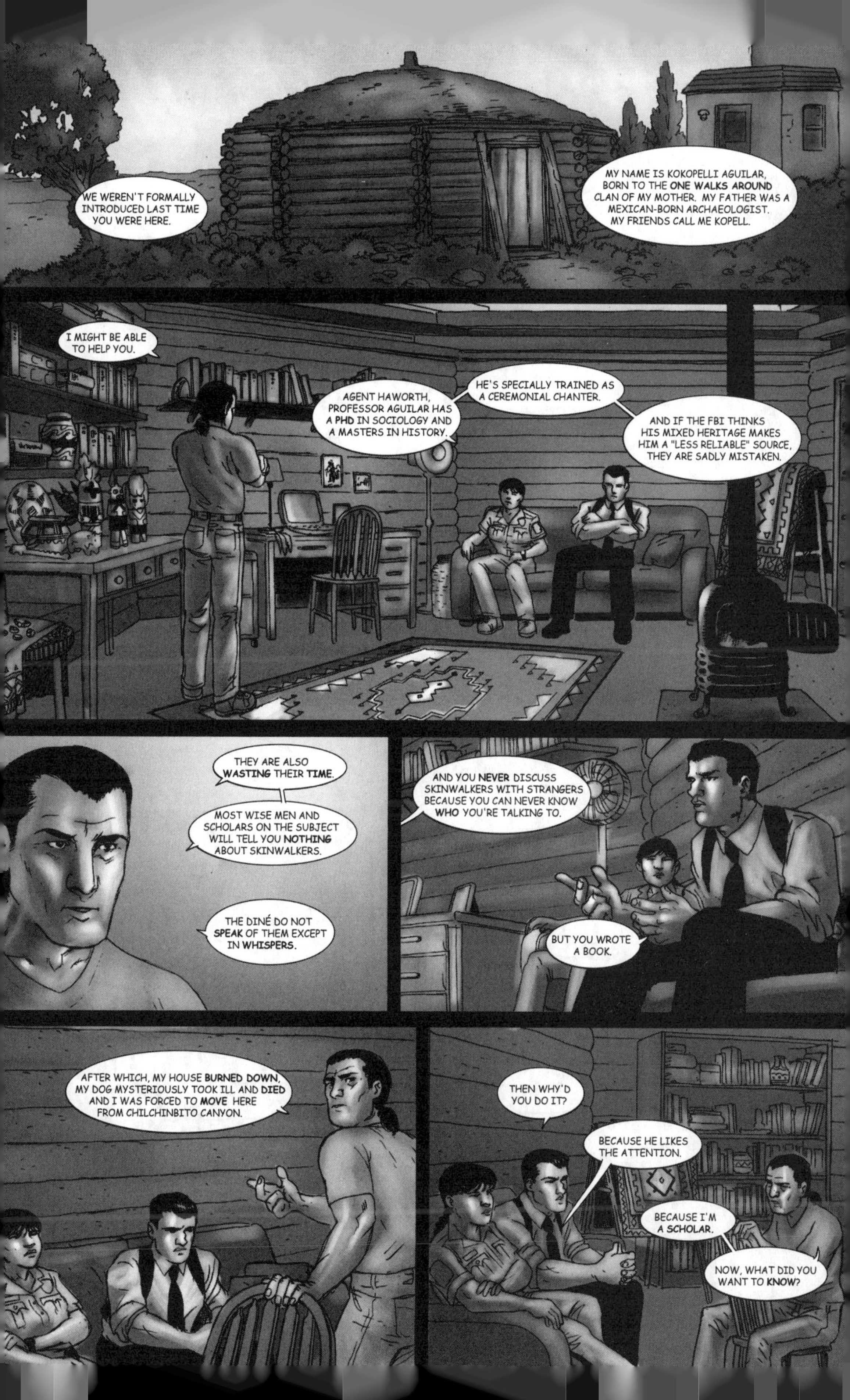
WE WEREN'T FORMALLY INTRODUCED LAST TIME YOU WERE HERE.
MY NAME IS KOKOPELLI AGUILAR, BORN TO THE ONE WALKS AROUND CLAN OF MY MOTHER. MY FATHER WAS A MEXICAN-BORN ARCHAEOLOGIST. MY FRIENDS CALL ME KOPELL.
I MIGHT BE ABLE TO HELP YOU.
AGENT HAWORTH, PROFESSOR AGUILAR HAS A PHD IN SOCIOLOGY AND A MASTERS IN HISTORY.
HE'S SPECIALLY TRAINED AS A CEREMONIAL CHANTER.
AND IF THE FBI THINKS HIS MIXED HERITAGE MAKES HIM A "LESS RELIABLE" SOURCE, THEY ARE SADLY MISTAKEN.
THEY ARE ALSO WASTING THEIR TIME.
MOST WISE MEN AND SCHOLARS ON THE SUBJECT WILL TELL YOU NOTHING ABOUT SKINWALKERS.
THE DINÉ DO NOT SPEAK OF THEM EXCEPT IN WHISPERS.
AND YOU NEVER DISCUSS SKINWALKERS WITH STRANGERS BECAUSE YOU CAN NEVER KNOW WHO YOU'RE TALKING TO.
BUT YOU WROTE A BOOK.
AFTER WHICH, MY HOUSE BURNED DOWN, MY DOG MYSTERIOUSLY TOOK ILL AND DIED AND I WAS FORCED TO MOVE HERE FROM CHILCHINBITO CANYON.
THEN WHY'D YOU DO IT?
BECAUSE HE LIKES THE ATTENTION.
BECAUSE I'M A SCHOLAR.
NOW, WHAT DID YOU WANT TO KNOW?

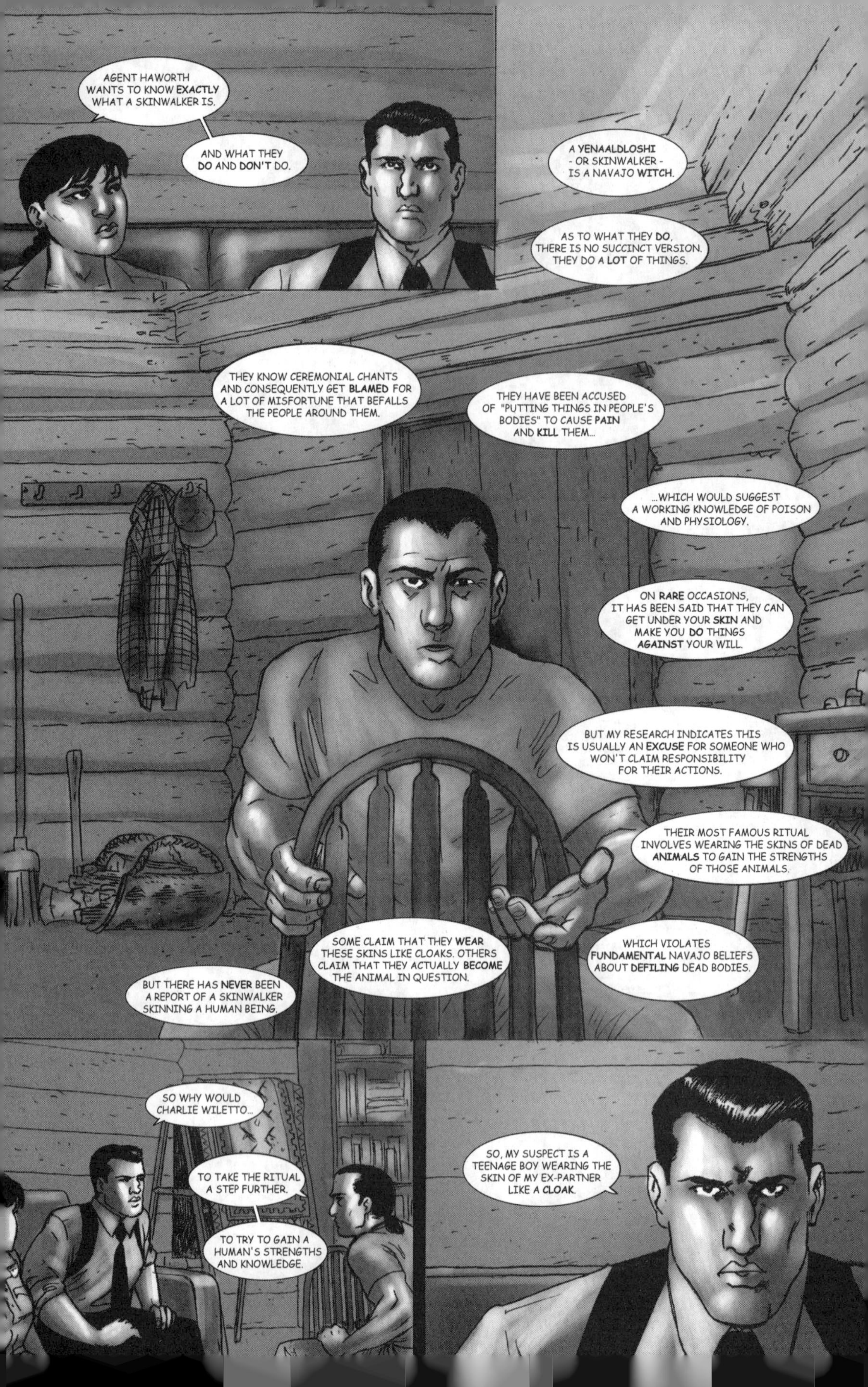
AGENT HAWORTH WANTS TO KNOW EXACTLY WHAT A SKINWALKER IS.
AND WHAT THEY DO AND DON'T DO.
A YENAALDLOSHI - OR SKINWALKER - IS A NAVAJO WITCH.
AS TO WHAT THEY DO, THERE IS NO SUCCINCT VERSION. THEY DO A LOT OF THINGS.
THEY KNOW CEREMONIAL CHANTS AND CONSEQUENTLY GET BLAMED FOR A LOT OF MISFORTUNE THAT BEFALLS THE PEOPLE AROUND THEM.
THEY HAVE BEEN ACCUSED OF "PUTTING THINGS IN PEOPLE'S BODIES" TO CAUSE PAIN AND KILL THEM...
...WHICH WOULD SUGGEST A WORKING KNOWLEDGE OF POISON AND PHYSIOLOGY.
ON RARE OCCASIONS, IT HAS BEEN SAID THAT THEY CAN GET UNDER YOUR SKIN AND MAKE YOU DO THINGS AGAINST YOUR WILL.
BUT MY RESEARCH INDICATES THIS IS USUALLY AN EXCUSE FOR SOMEONE WHO WON'T CLAIM RESPONSIBILITY FOR THEIR ACTIONS.
THEIR MOST FAMOUS RITUAL INVOLVES WEARING THE SKINS OF DEAD ANIMALS TO GAIN THE STRENGTHS OF THOSE ANIMALS.
WHICH VIOLATES FUNDAMENTAL NAVAJO BELIEFS ABOUT DEFILING DEAD BODIES.
SOME CLAIM THAT THEY WEAR THESE SKINS LIKE CLOAKS. OTHERS CLAIM THAT THEY ACTUALLY BECOME THE ANIMAL IN QUESTION.
BUT THERE HAS NEVER BEEN A REPORT OF A SKINWALKER SKINNING A HUMAN BEING.
SO WHY WOULD CHARLIE WILETTO...
TO TAKE THE RITUAL A STEP FURTHER.
TO TRY TO GAIN A HUMAN'S STRENGTHS AND KNOWLEDGE.
SO, MY SUSPECT IS A TEENAGE BOY WEARING THE SKIN OF MY EX-PARTNER LIKE A CLOAK.

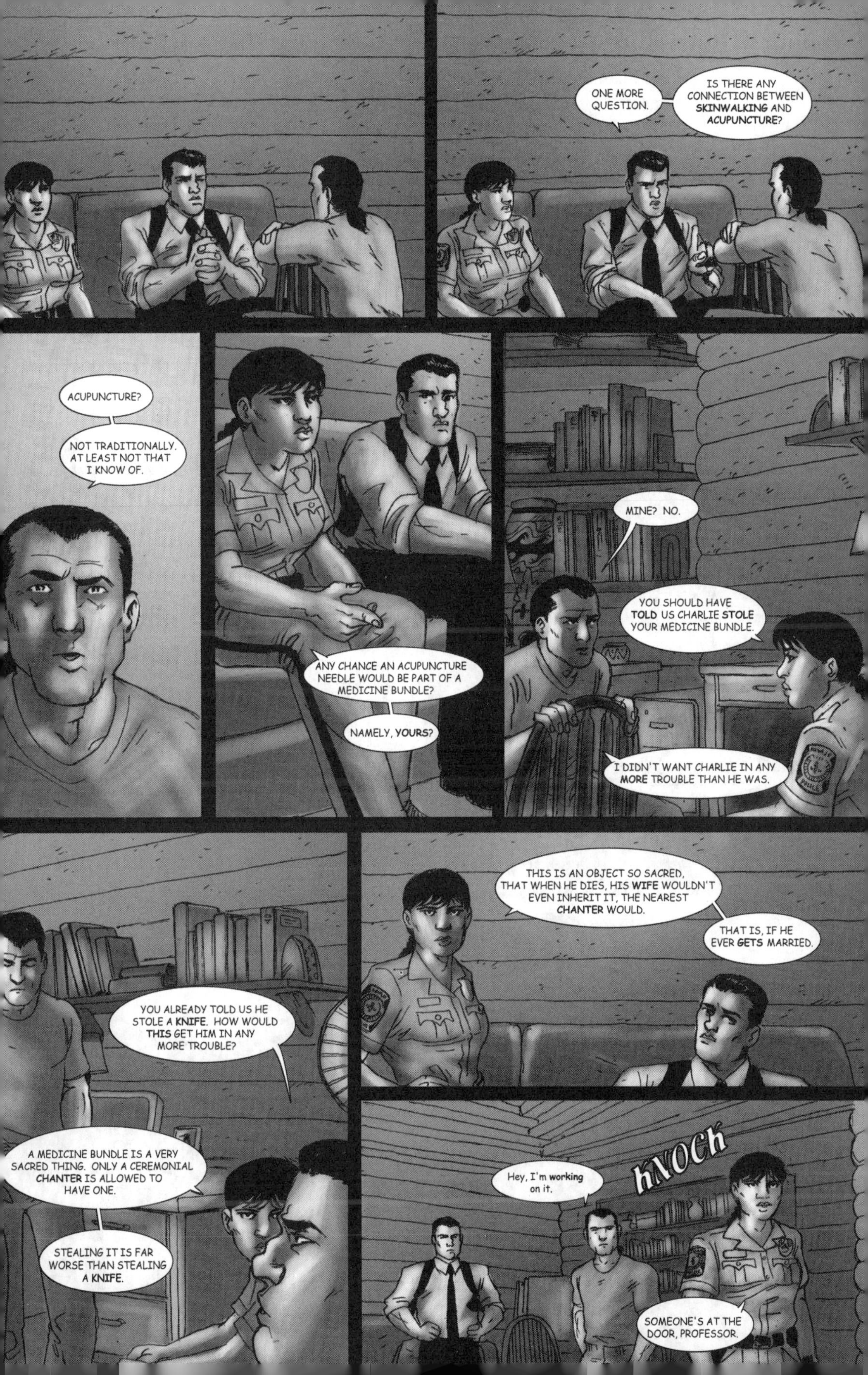
ONE MORE QUESTION.
IS THERE ANY CONNECTION BETWEEN SKINWALKING AND ACUPUNCTURE?
ACUPUNCTURE?
NOT TRADITIONALLY. AT LEAST NOT THAT I KNOW OF.
ANY CHANCE AN ACUPUNCTURE NEEDLE WOULD BE PART OF A MEDICINE BUNDLE?
NAMELY, YOURS?
MINE? NO.
YOU SHOULD HAVE TOLD US CHARLIE STOLE YOUR MEDICINE BUNDLE.
I DIDN'T WANT CHARLIE IN ANY MORE TROUBLE THAN HE WAS.
YOU ALREADY TOLD US HE STOLE A KNIFE. HOW WOULD THIS GET HIM IN ANY MORE TROUBLE?
A MEDICINE BUNDLE IS A VERY SACRED THING. ONLY A CEREMONIAL CHANTER IS ALLOWED TO HAVE ONE.
STEALING IT IS FAR WORSE THAN STEALING A KNIFE.
THIS IS AN OBJECT SO SACRED, THAT WHEN HE DIES, HIS WIFE WOULDN'T EVEN INHERIT IT, THE NEAREST CHANTER WOULD.
THAT IS, IF HE EVER GETS MARRIED.
KNOCK
Hey, I'm working on it.
SOMEONE'S AT THE DOOR, PROFESSOR.

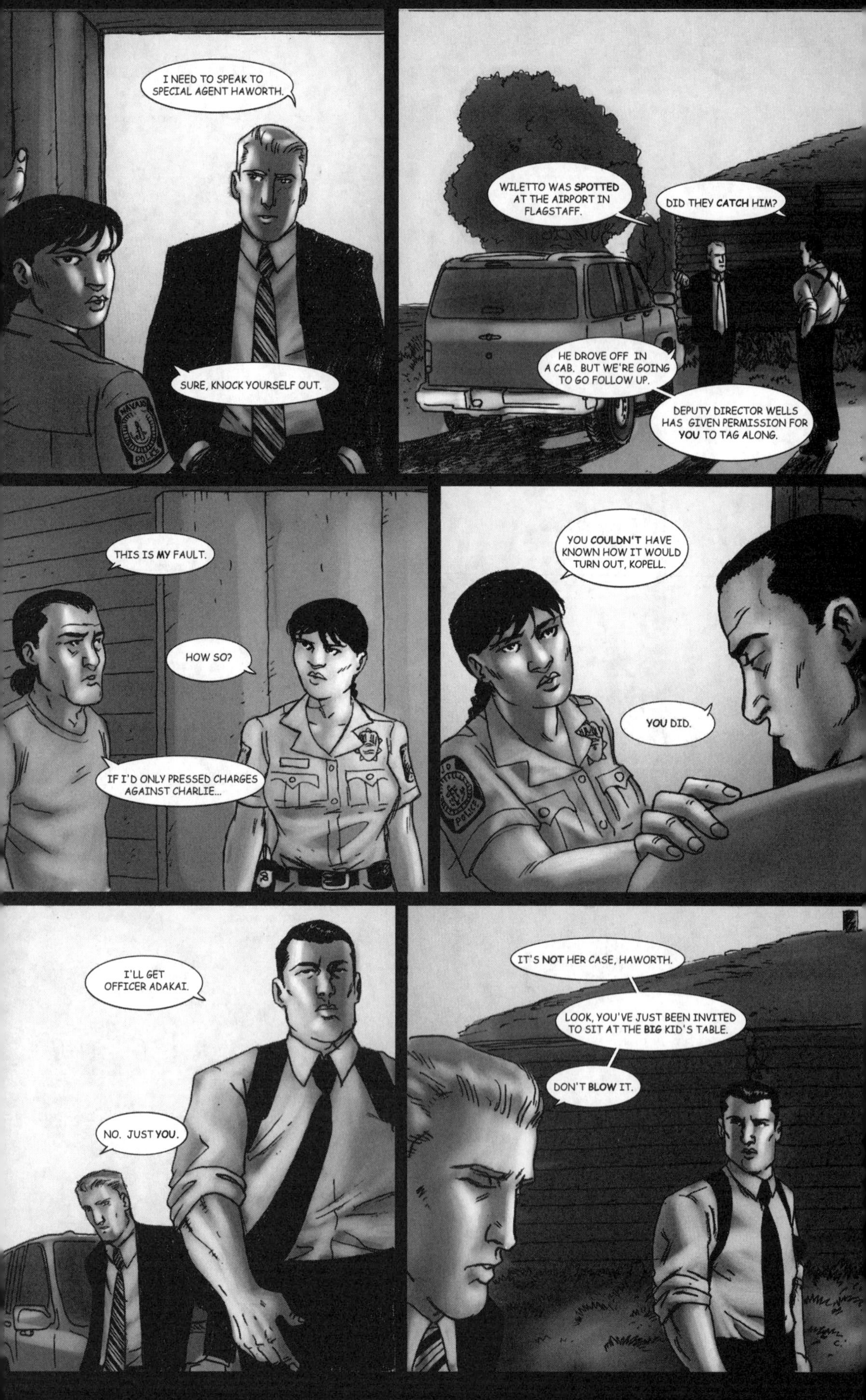
I NEED TO SPEAK TO SPECIAL AGENT HAWORTH.
SURE, KNOCK YOURSELF OUT.
WILETTO WAS SPOTTED AT THE AIRPORT IN FLAGSTAFF.
DID THEY CATCH HIM?
HE DROVE OFF IN A CAB. BUT WE'RE GOING TO GO FOLLOW UP.
DEPUTY DIRECTOR WELLS HAS GIVEN PERMISSION FOR YOU TO TAG ALONG.
THIS IS MY FAULT.
HOW SO?
IF I'D ONLY PRESSED CHARGES AGAINST CHARLIE...
YOU COULDN'T HAVE KNOWN HOW IT WOULD TURN OUT, KOPELL.
YOU DID.
I'LL GET OFFICER ADAKAI.
NO. JUST YOU.
IT'S NOT HER CASE, HAWORTH.
LOOK, YOU'VE JUST BEEN INVITED TO SIT AT THE BIG KID'S TABLE.
DON'T BLOW IT.

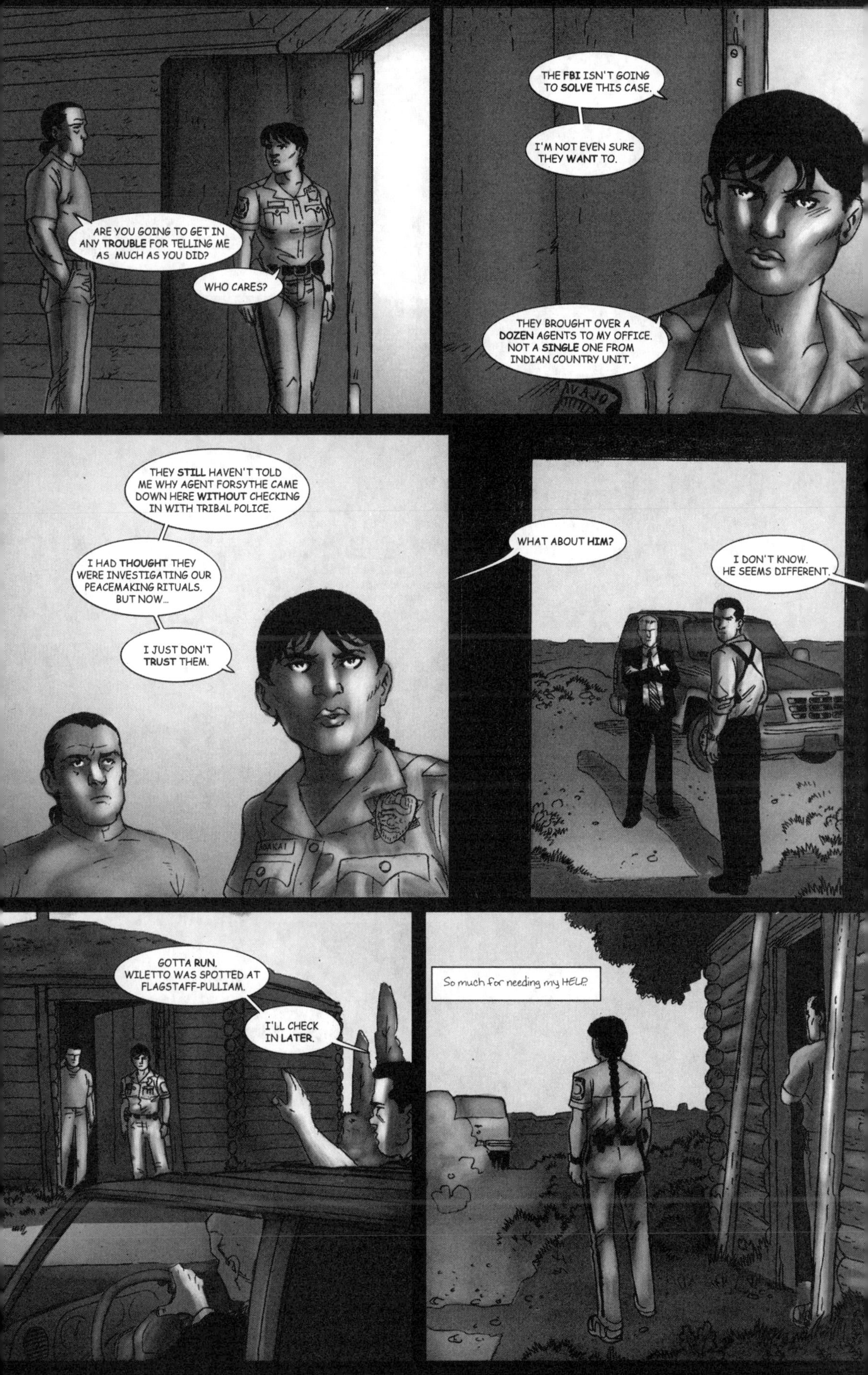

ARE YOU GOING TO GET IN ANY TROUBLE FOR TELLING ME AS MUCH AS YOU DID?
WHO CARES?
THE FBI ISN'T GOING TO SOLVE THIS CASE.
I'M NOT EVEN SURE THEY WANT TO.
THEY BROUGHT OVER A DOZEN AGENTS TO MY OFFICE. NOT A SINGLE ONE FROM INDIAN COUNTRY UNIT.
THEY STILL HAVEN'T TOLD ME WHY AGENT FORSYTHE CAME DOWN HERE WITHOUT CHECKING IN WITH TRIBAL POLICE.
I HAD THOUGHT THEY WERE INVESTIGATING OUR PEACEMAKING RITUALS. BUT NOW...
I JUST DON'T TRUST THEM.
WHAT ABOUT HIM?
I DON'T KNOW. HE SEEMS DIFFERENT.
GOTTA RUN. WILETTO WAS SPOTTED AT FLAGSTAFF-PULLIAM.
I'LL CHECK IN LATER.
So much for needing my HELP.

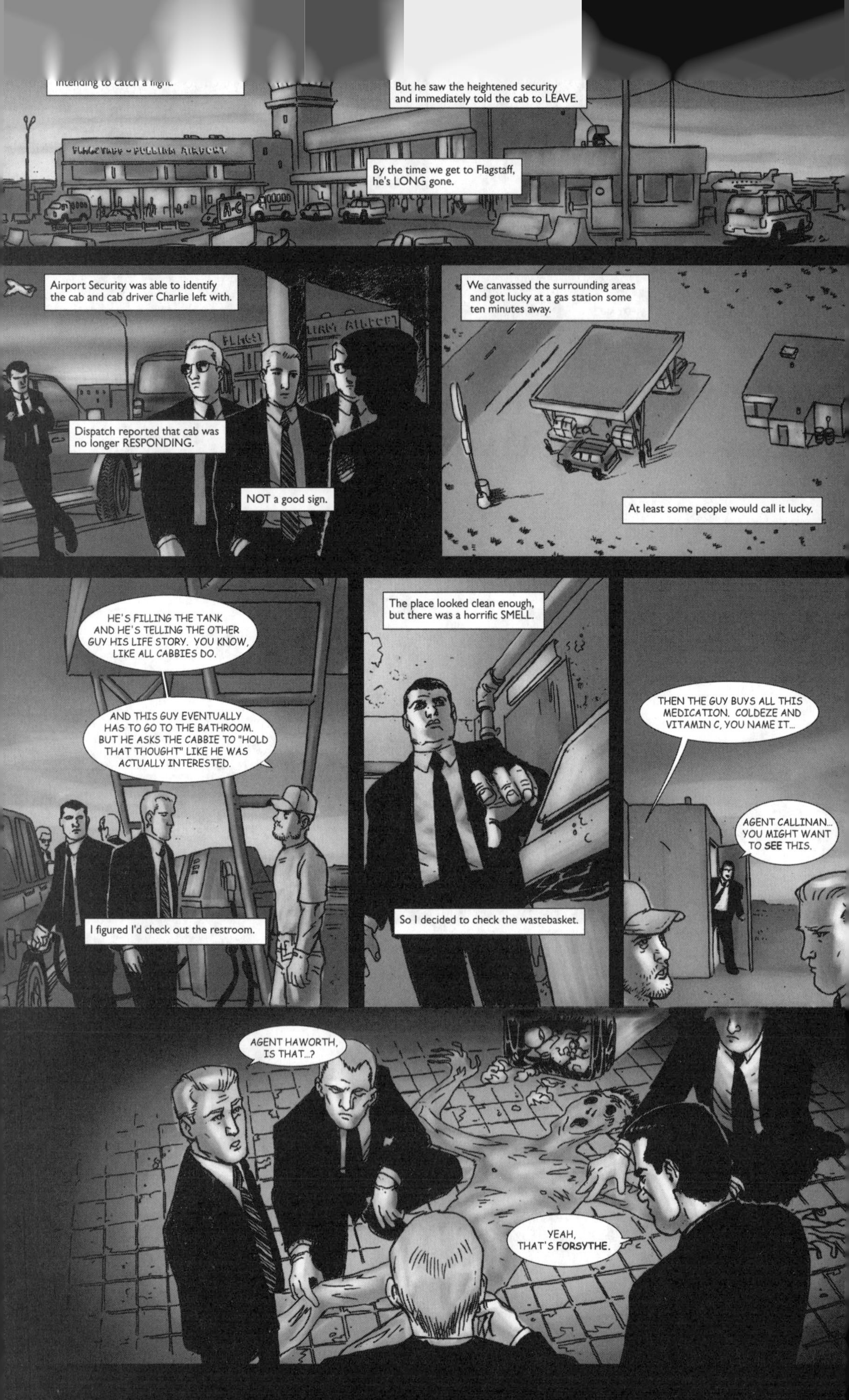
intending to catch a flight.
But he saw the heightened security and immediately told the cab to LEAVE.
By the time we get to Flagstaff, he's LONG gone.
Airport Security was able to identify the cab and cab driver Charlie left with.
Dispatch reported that cab was no longer RESPONDING.
NOT a good sign.
We canvassed the surrounding areas and got lucky at a gas station some ten minutes away.
At least some people would call it lucky.
HE'S FILLING THE TANK AND HE'S TELLING THE OTHER GUY HIS LIFE STORY. YOU KNOW, LIKE ALL CABBIES DO.
AND THIS GUY EVENTUALLY HAS TO GO TO THE BATHROOM. BUT HE ASKS THE CABBIE TO "HOLD THAT THOUGHT" LIKE HE WAS ACTUALLY INTERESTED.
I figured I'd check out the restroom.
The place looked clean enough, but there was a horrific SMELL.
So I decided to check the wastebasket.
THEN THE GUY BUYS ALL THIS MEDICATION. COLDEZE AND VITAMIN C, YOU NAME IT...
AGENT CALLINAN... YOU MIGHT WANT TO SEE THIS.
AGENT HAWORTH, IS THAT...?
YEAH, THAT'S FORSYTHE.

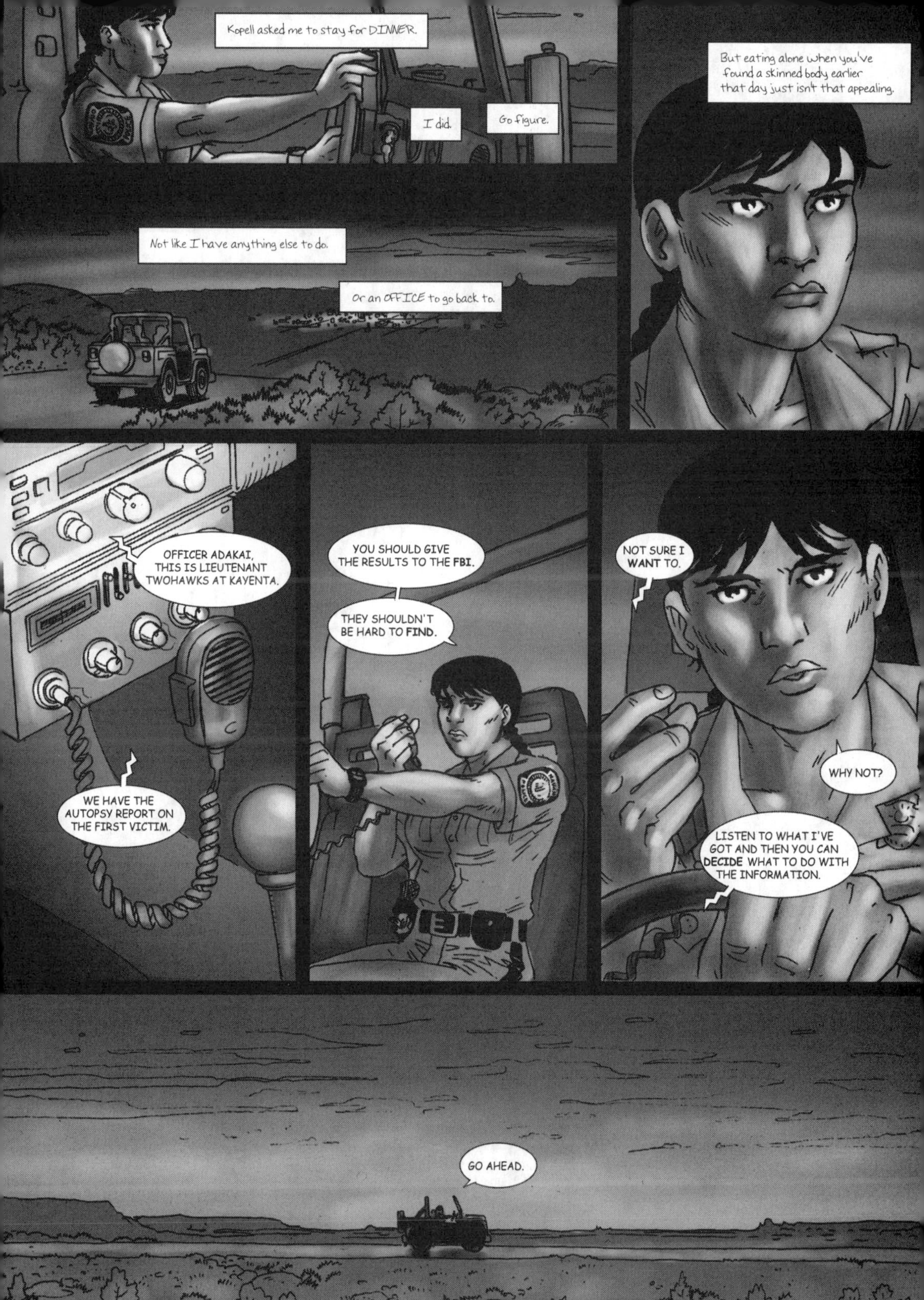

Kopell asked me to stay for DINNER.
I did.
Go figure.
But eating alone when you've found a skinned body earlier that day just isn't that appealing.
Not like I have anything else to do.
Or an OFFICE to go back to.
OFFICER ADAKAI, THIS IS LIEUTENANT TWOHAWKS AT KAYENTA.
WE HAVE THE AUTOPSY REPORT ON THE FIRST VICTIM.
YOU SHOULD GIVE THE RESULTS TO THE FBI.
THEY SHOULDN'T BE HARD TO FIND.
NOT SURE I WANT TO.
WHY NOT?
LISTEN TO WHAT I'VE GOT AND THEN YOU CAN DECIDE WHAT TO DO WITH THE INFORMATION.
GO AHEAD.

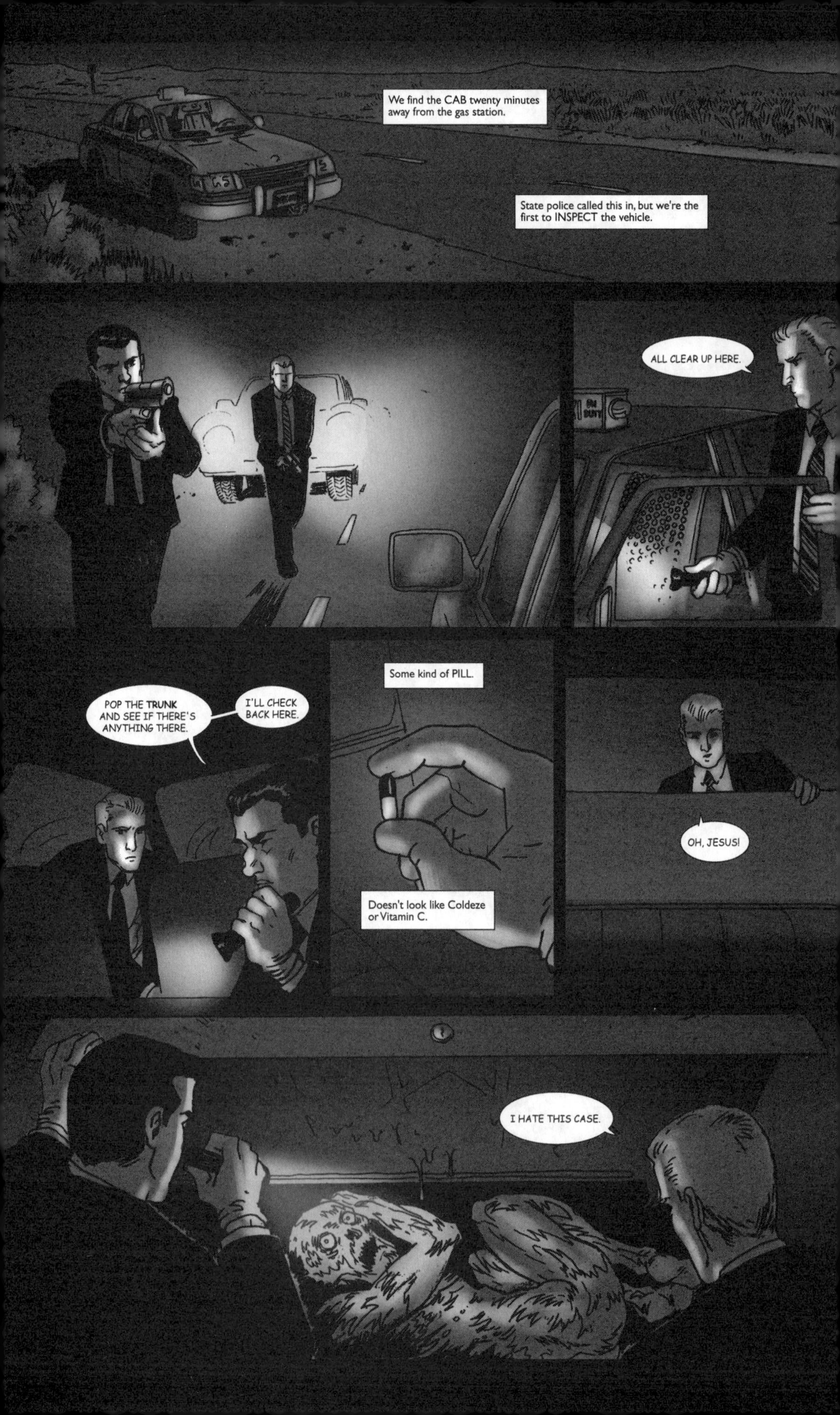

We find the CAB twenty minutes away from the gas station.
State police called this in, but we're the first to INSPECT the vehicle.
ALL CLEAR UP HERE.
POP THE TRUNK AND SEE IF THERE'S ANYTHING THERE.
I'LL CHECK BACK HERE.
Some kind of PILL.
Doesn't look like Coldeze or Vitamin C.
OH, JESUS!
I HATE THIS CASE.

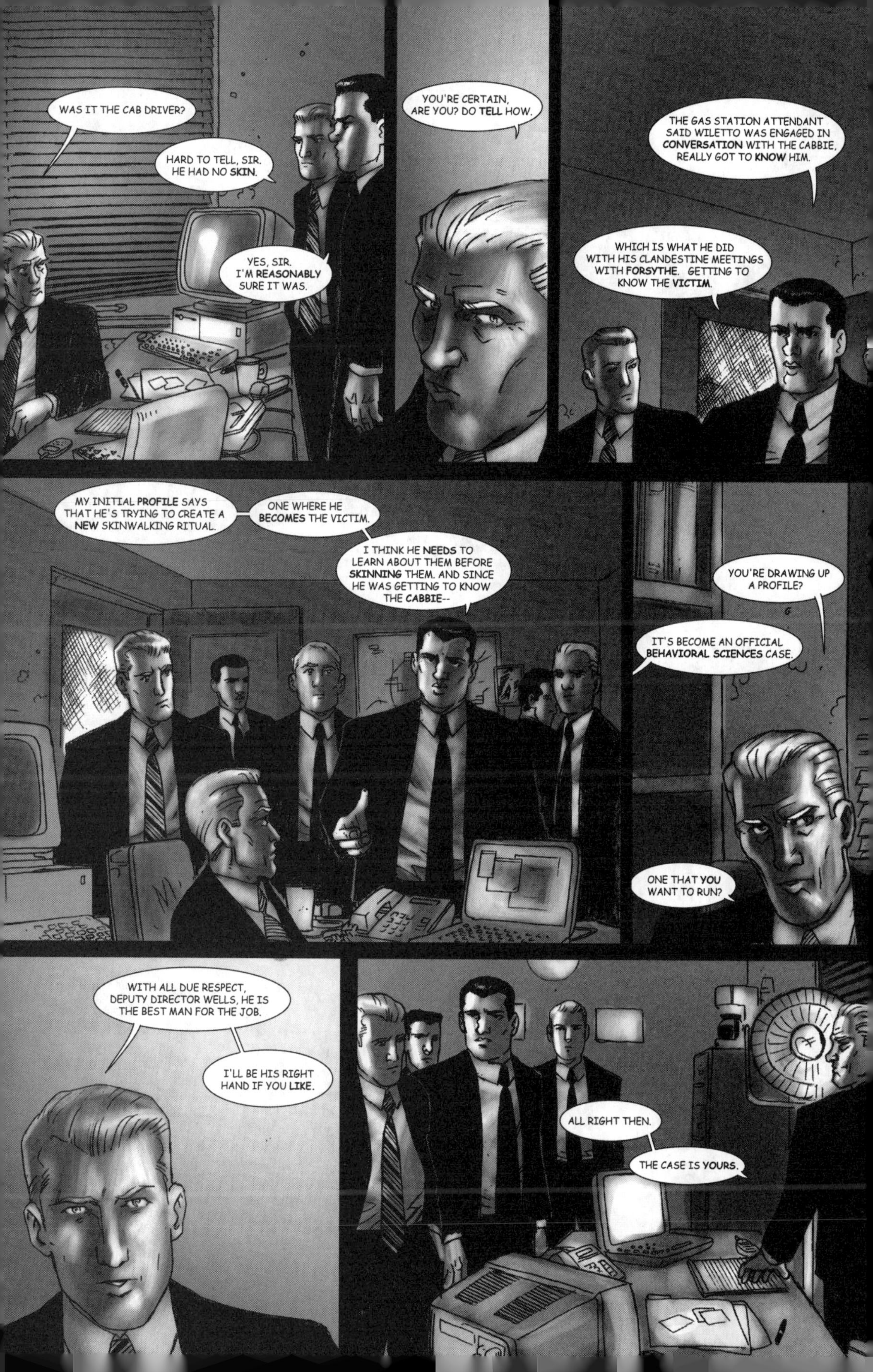
WAS IT THE CAB DRIVER?
HARD TO TELL, SIR. HE HAD NO SKIN.
YES, SIR. I'M REASONABLY SURE IT WAS.
YOU'RE CERTAIN, ARE YOU? DO TELL HOW.
THE GAS STATION ATTENDANT SAID WILETTO WAS ENGAGED IN CONVERSATION WITH THE CABBIE, REALLY GOT TO KNOW HIM.
WHICH IS WHAT HE DID WITH HIS CLANDESTINE MEETINGS WITH FORSYTHE. GETTING TO KNOW THE VICTIM.
MY INITIAL PROFILE SAYS THAT HE'S TRYING TO CREATE A NEW SKINWALKING RITUAL.
ONE WHERE HE BECOMES THE VICTIM.
I THINK HE NEEDS TO LEARN ABOUT THEM BEFORE SKINNING THEM. AND SINCE HE WAS GETTING TO KNOW THE CABBIE--
YOU'RE DRAWING UP A PROFILE?
IT'S BECOME AN OFFICIAL BEHAVIORAL SCIENCES CASE.
ONE THAT YOU WANT TO RUN?
WITH ALL DUE RESPECT, DEPUTY DIRECTOR WELLS, HE IS THE BEST MAN FOR THE JOB.
I'LL BE HIS RIGHT HAND IF YOU LIKE.
ALL RIGHT THEN.
THE CASE IS YOURS.

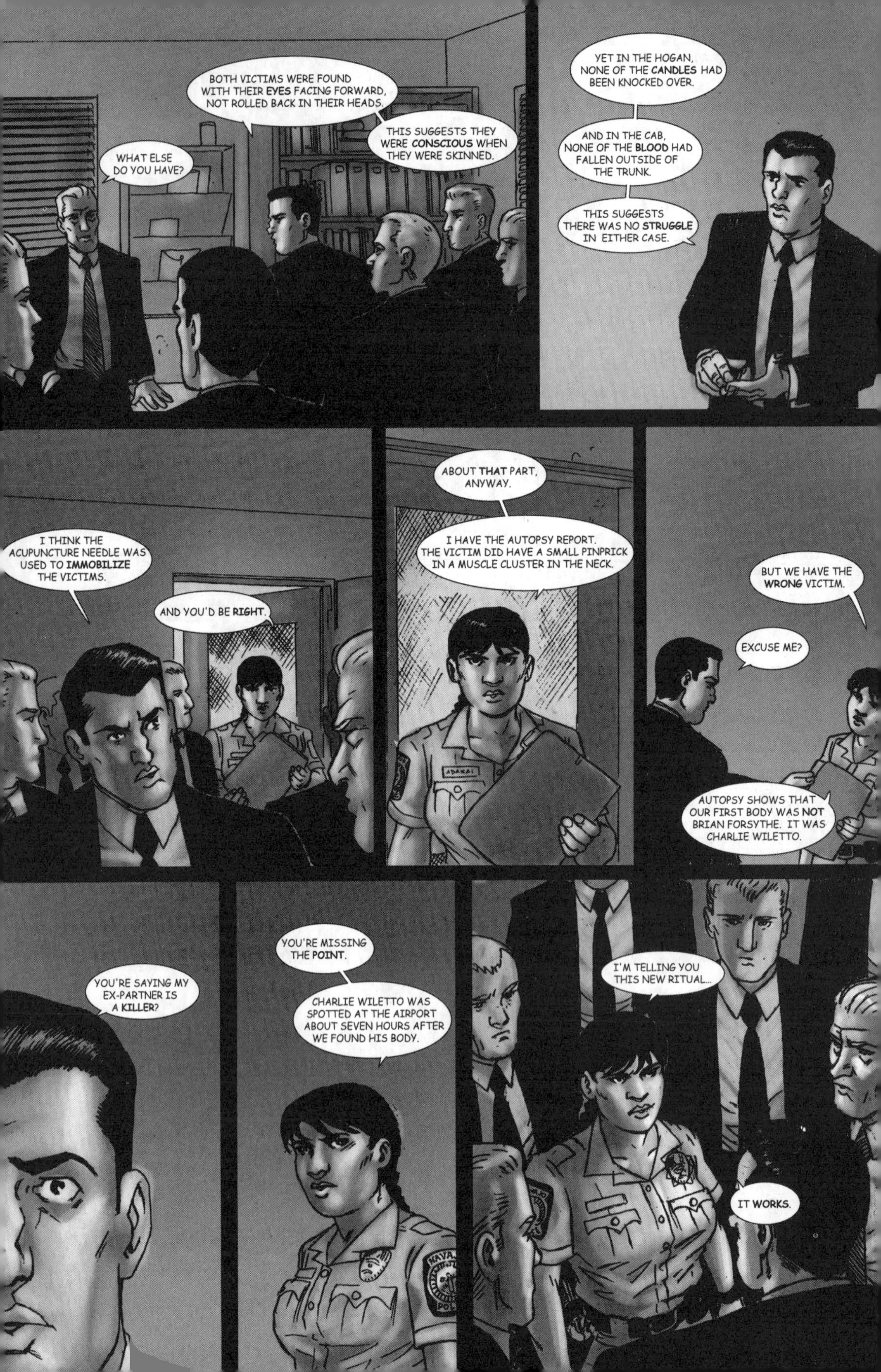

BOTH VICTIMS WERE FOUND WITH THEIR **EYES** FACING FORWARD, NOT ROLLED BACK IN THEIR HEADS.
THIS SUGGESTS THEY WERE **CONSCIOUS** WHEN THEY WERE SKINNED.
WHAT ELSE DO YOU HAVE?
YET IN THE HOGAN, NONE OF THE **CANDLES** HAD BEEN KNOCKED OVER.
AND IN THE CAB, NONE OF THE **BLOOD** HAD FALLEN OUTSIDE OF THE TRUNK.
THIS SUGGESTS THERE WAS NO **STRUGGLE** IN EITHER CASE.
I THINK THE ACUPUNCTURE NEEDLE WAS USED TO **IMMOBILIZE** THE VICTIMS.
AND YOU'D BE **RIGHT**.
ABOUT **THAT** PART, ANYWAY.
I HAVE THE AUTOPSY REPORT. THE VICTIM DID HAVE A SMALL PINPRICK IN A MUSCLE CLUSTER IN THE NECK.
BUT WE HAVE THE **WRONG** VICTIM.
EXCUSE ME?
AUTOPSY SHOWS THAT OUR FIRST BODY WAS **NOT** BRIAN FORSYTHE. IT WAS CHARLIE WILETTO.
YOU'RE SAYING MY EX-PARTNER IS A **KILLER**?
YOU'RE MISSING THE **POINT**.
CHARLIE WILETTO WAS SPOTTED AT THE AIRPORT ABOUT SEVEN HOURS AFTER WE FOUND HIS BODY.
I'M TELLING YOU THIS NEW RITUAL...
IT **WORKS**.

CHAPTER 3

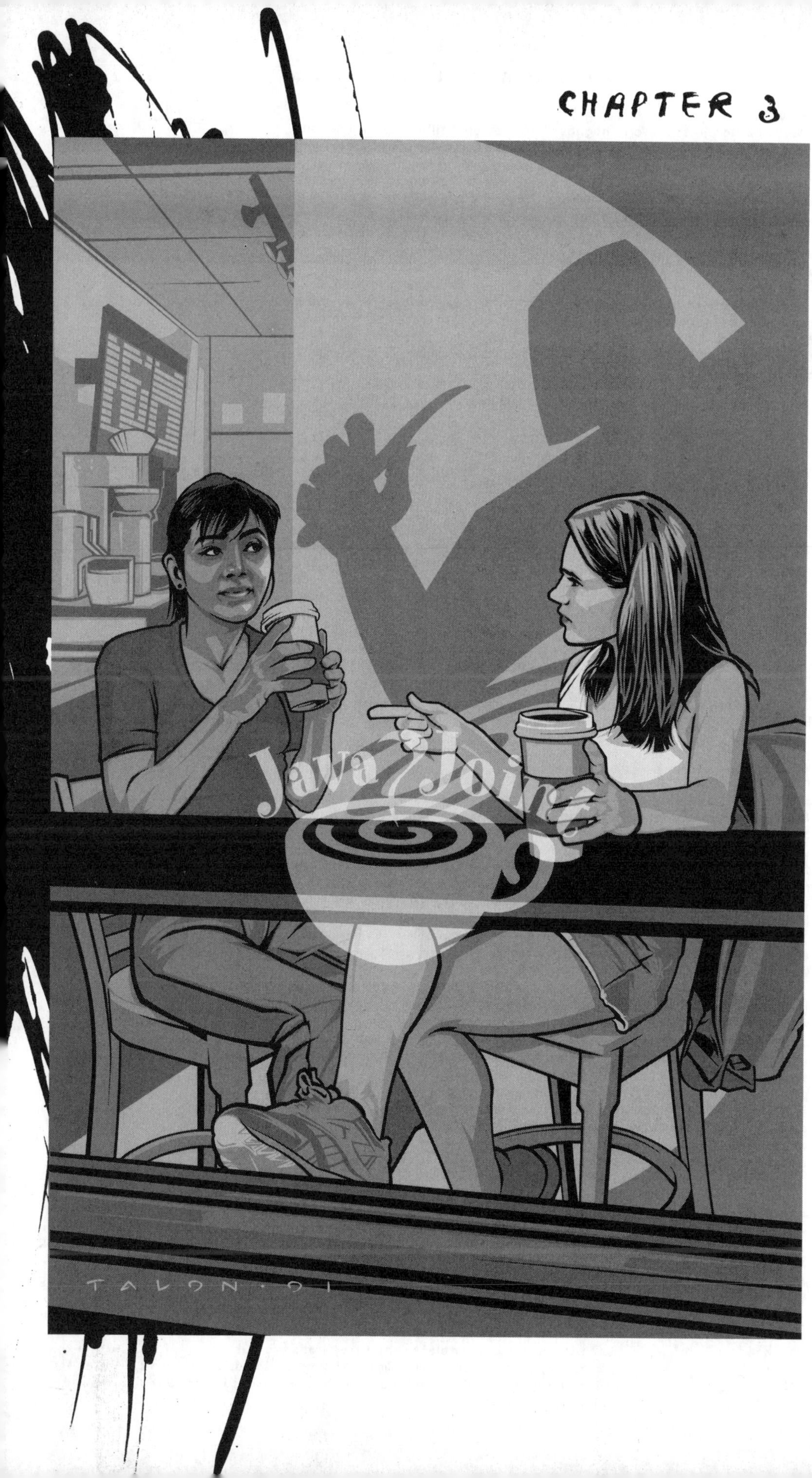

Java Joint
TALON·01

HOW TO BUILD A (FEMALE) HOGAN

female hogan

INTRODUCTION

Very few Navajo still live in hogans, but they are still in use throughout the reservation. There are two types of hogan, the male (with 5 sides) and the female (with 8). The male hogan is where one meets the enemy; it is also where the Navajo deal with illness. These things would contaminate the home. The female hogan is where the family lives and sleeps. It is a safe, warm environment. It is also much larger than the male hogan.

A female hogan is free standing, with a diameter on the inside of up to 23 feet. The design is very unique. It is such that it is warm during the winter and cool during the summer.

The door of the hogan must face to the east to meet the rising sun. It is made of wood with metal hinges (before metal hinges, rawhide hinges were used. And before wooden doors, a blanket hung to seal the opening). Behind the front door is a fire stick. The fire stick protects the family from those who would do them harm. It is about 3 feet long, and has been burned on one end.

male hogan

There are more modern construction techniques, but the hogans look similar to the hogans which Navajos have lived in for thousands of years.

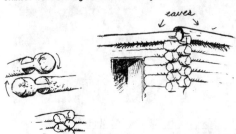

eaves

CONSTRUCTING THE WALLS

The female hogan has 8 sides and could be built without accurately measuring the length of a single pole or log. In some older hogans, the sides have different widths. Early hogans were built out of cedar, which allowed the hogan to last for generations.

The logs forming the walls are joined in the corners by notching them much like the log cabins of the pioneers. The cracks between the logs are sealed with a clay mud. After the walls are completed, a pole is added to the outer edges of the top logs of the wall. This forms a guard so the roof poles won't roll off.

diagram illustrates different stages of roof construction.

CONSTRUCTING THE ROOF

The roof is dome shaped, starting at shoulder height by the walls. At the center of the room the ceiling is about 10 feet high. The ceiling is built out of poles, carefully stacked in layers to form a strong, triangular structure. To give the roof its domed effect, fewer poles are used in the first layers and more poles are used towards the top, giving the hogan a relatively steep roof near the walls, but a shallow roof towards the top. The ceiling comes up at about a 45 degree angle until it reaches the fifth level. Then it quickly tapers off towards the center.

The first layer of poles are laid parallel to one another, beginning at each of the eight corners. Each pole forms an isometric triangle with the wall logs underneath it. The first pole is very short, enclosing just the corners. The next pole laying next to it is a little longer. The last pole on the first layer spans from the center of one wall to the center of the next wall. These last poles from each section touch each other.

The second layer of poles are laid parallel with the wall and form an isometric triangle with the first layer of roof poles underneath them. The second layer starts where the gap in the first layer of poles start. The poles forming the third layer lie parallel with the first layer of poles and form isometric triangles with the poles from the second layer directly below them and start where the gap in the second layer begins. And so this continues up to the fifth layer. At the fifth layer, the corners are reduced to 4 sides. This makes the roof doming effect begin to round. The total number of layers will be determined by the diameter of the poles used.

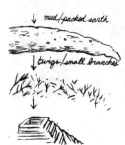

mud / packed earth

twigs / small branches

The top three levels are formed a bit differently, however. Two levels from the top, instead of forming isometric triangles like those levels below it, the poles run parallel across the top of the entire opening. The second to last layer is very small and reduces the size of this opening. The poles forming the top layer lie perpendicular to the poles of the 12th layer and reduce the size of this opening to about one foot square placing logs on both sides of the opening. This hole is used both as a chimney and a skylight. Aside from the front door, there won't be any other windows or openings besides this hole in the center of the ceiling.

Once the layers are complete, small tree limbs are put on top of this, with a thick layer of clay put on top of the limbs. After the clay dries, it forms a water tight barrier. This heavy earthen roof is one of the big reasons it was so cool in the summer and warm in the winter.

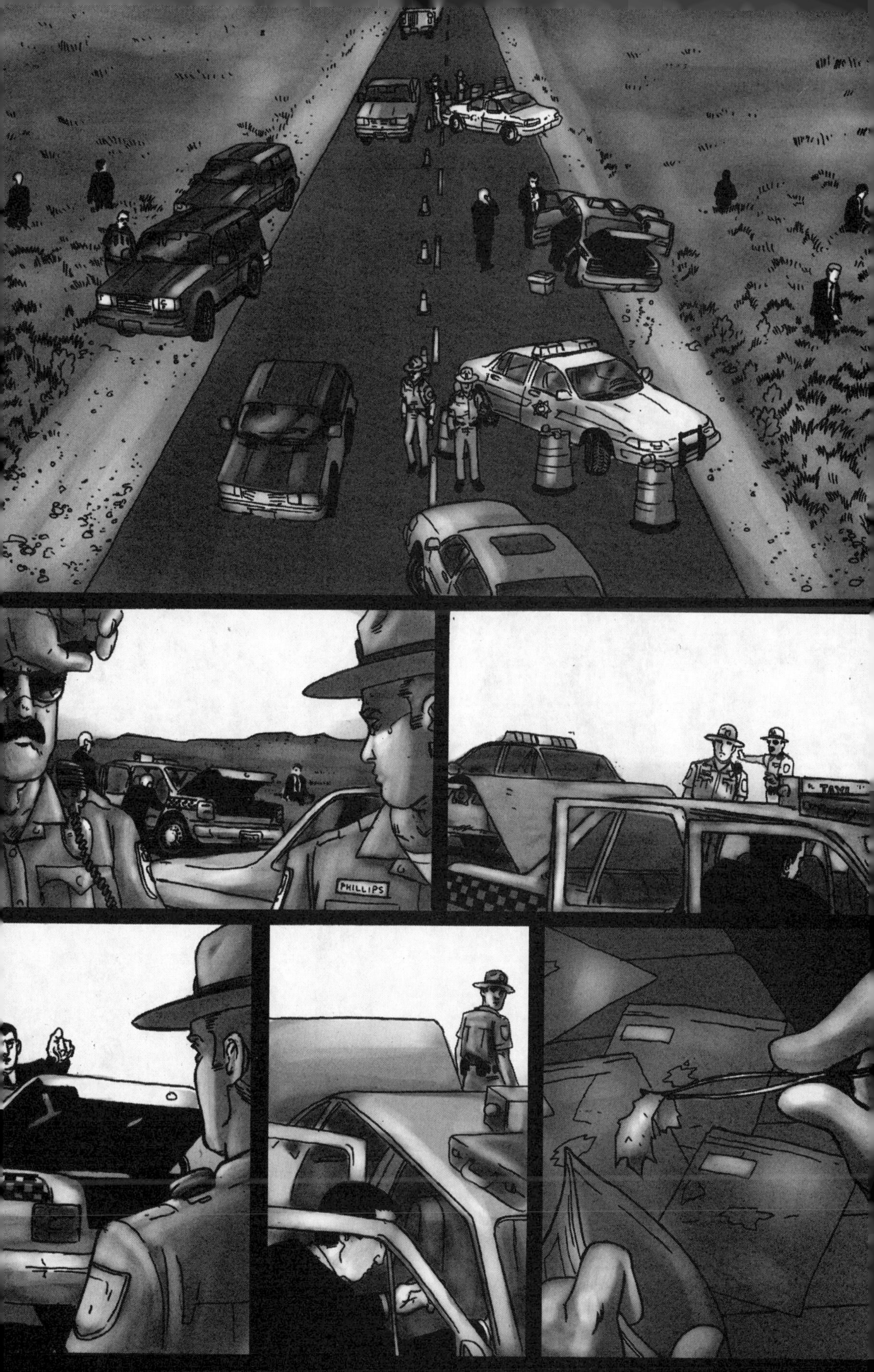
PHILLIPS
TAXI

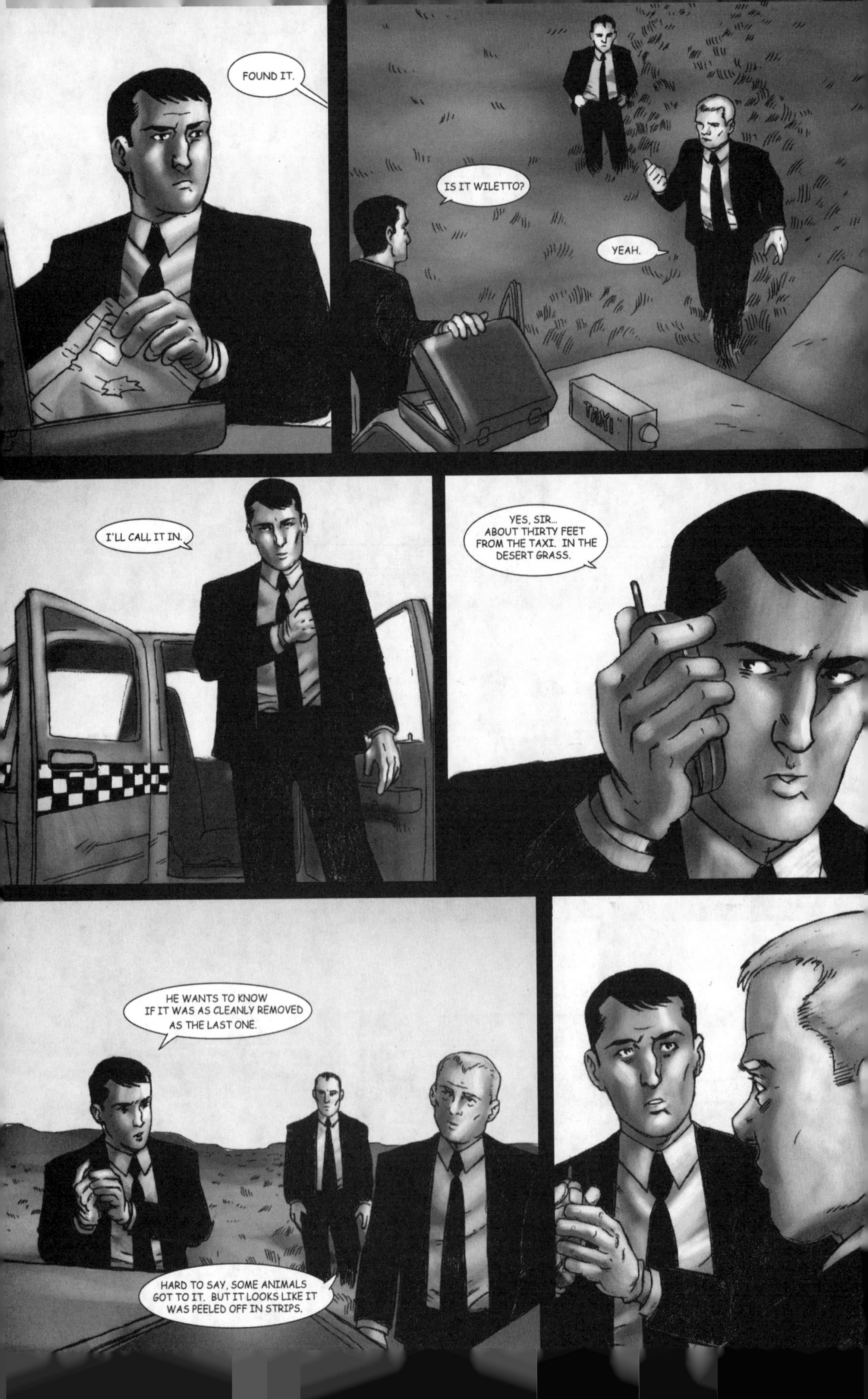
FOUND IT.
IS IT WILETTO?
YEAH.
TAXI
I'LL CALL IT IN.
YES, SIR... ABOUT THIRTY FEET FROM THE TAXI. IN THE DESERT GRASS.
HE WANTS TO KNOW IF IT WAS AS CLEANLY REMOVED AS THE LAST ONE.
HARD TO SAY, SOME ANIMALS GOT TO IT. BUT IT LOOKS LIKE IT WAS PEELED OFF IN STRIPS.

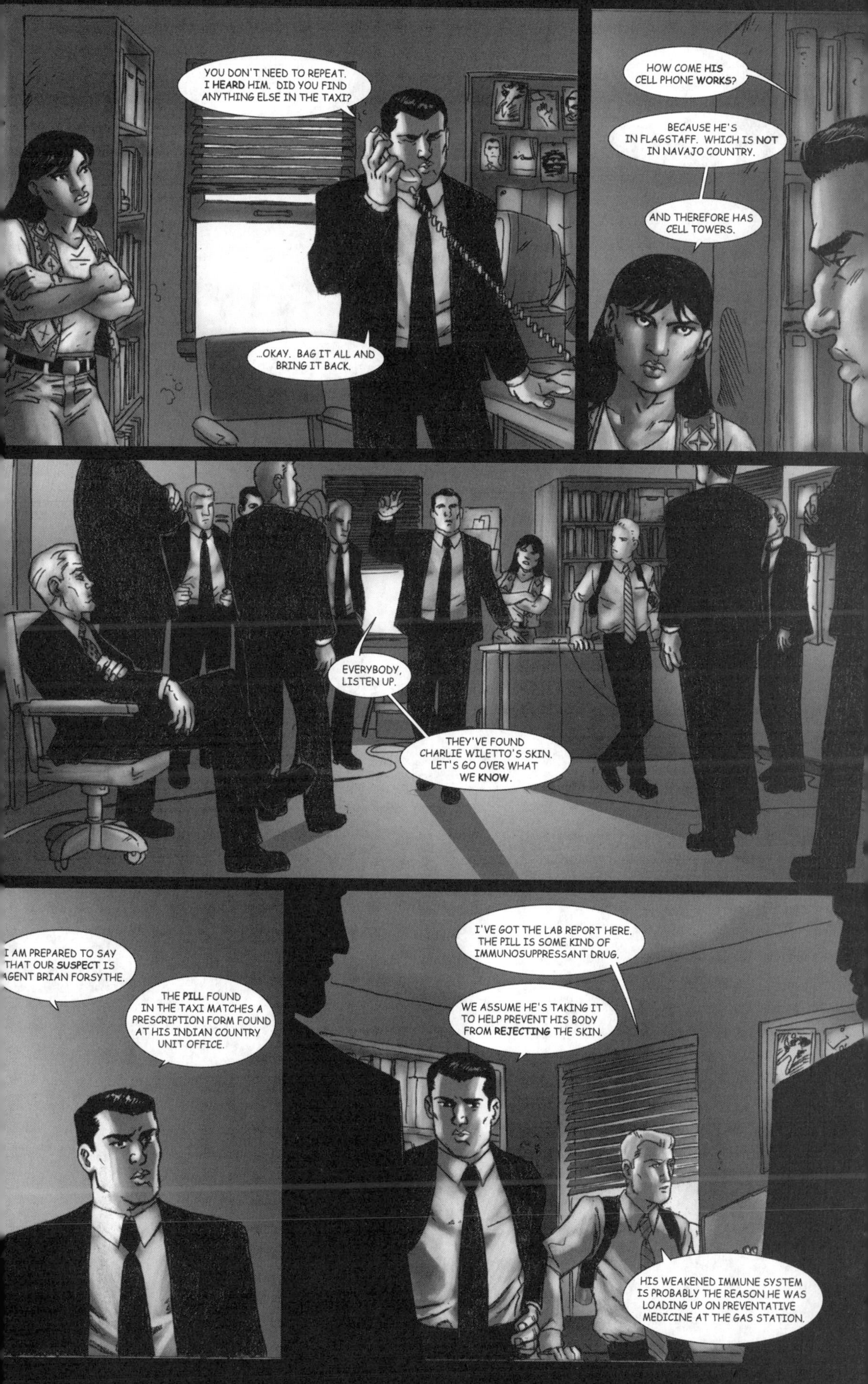

YOU DON'T NEED TO REPEAT. I HEARD HIM. DID YOU FIND ANYTHING ELSE IN THE TAXI?
...OKAY. BAG IT ALL AND BRING IT BACK.
HOW COME HIS CELL PHONE WORKS?
BECAUSE HE'S IN FLAGSTAFF. WHICH IS NOT IN NAVAJO COUNTRY.
AND THEREFORE HAS CELL TOWERS.
EVERYBODY, LISTEN UP.
THEY'VE FOUND CHARLIE WILETTO'S SKIN. LET'S GO OVER WHAT WE KNOW.
I AM PREPARED TO SAY THAT OUR SUSPECT IS AGENT BRIAN FORSYTHE.
THE PILL FOUND IN THE TAXI MATCHES A PRESCRIPTION FORM FOUND AT HIS INDIAN COUNTRY UNIT OFFICE.
I'VE GOT THE LAB REPORT HERE. THE PILL IS SOME KIND OF IMMUNOSUPPRESSANT DRUG.
WE ASSUME HE'S TAKING IT TO HELP PREVENT HIS BODY FROM REJECTING THE SKIN.
HIS WEAKENED IMMUNE SYSTEM IS PROBABLY THE REASON HE WAS LOADING UP ON PREVENTATIVE MEDICINE AT THE GAS STATION.

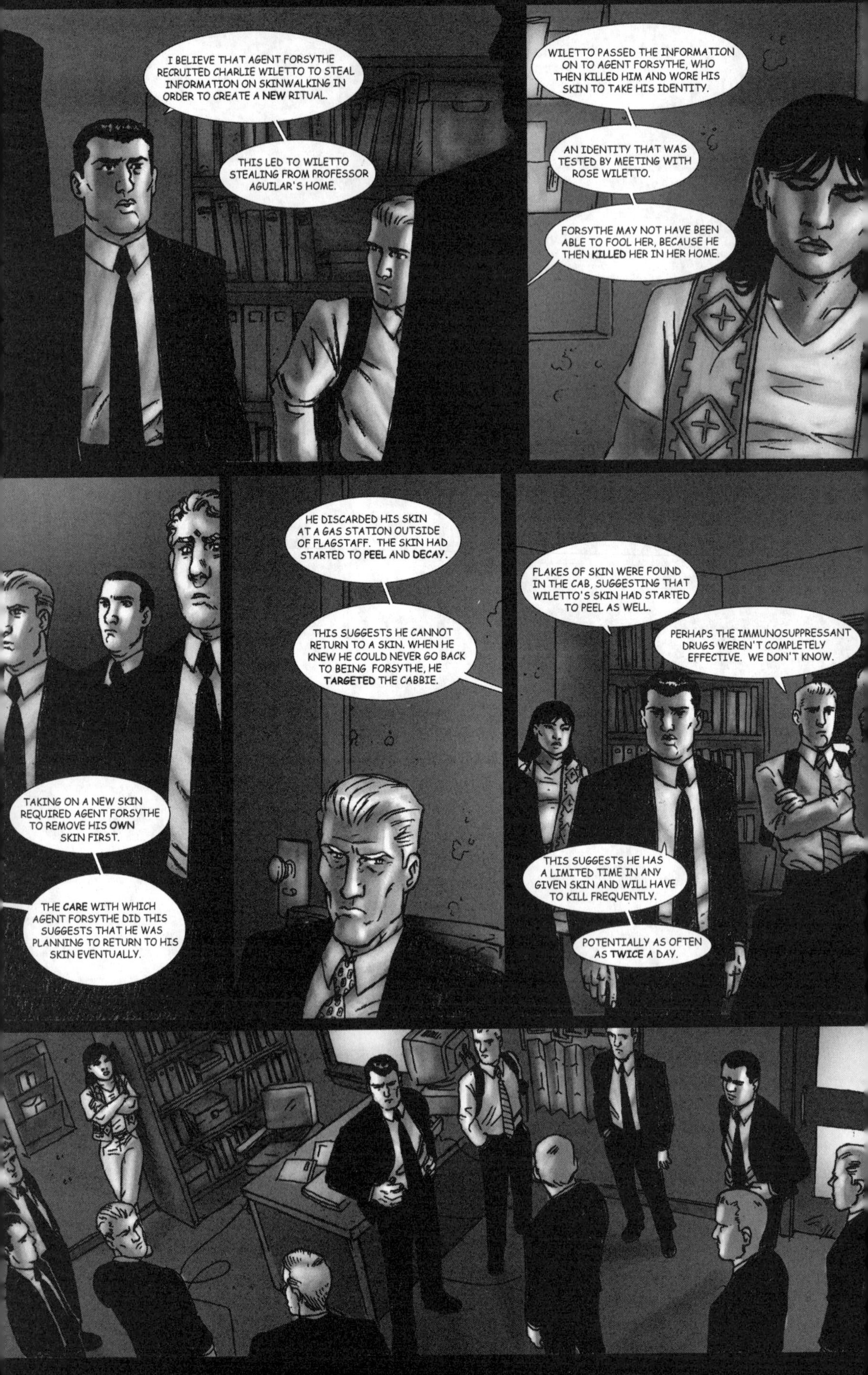

I BELIEVE THAT AGENT FORSYTHE RECRUITED CHARLIE WILETTO TO STEAL INFORMATION ON SKINWALKING IN ORDER TO CREATE A NEW RITUAL.
THIS LED TO WILETTO STEALING FROM PROFESSOR AGUILAR'S HOME.
WILETTO PASSED THE INFORMATION ON TO AGENT FORSYTHE, WHO THEN KILLED HIM AND WORE HIS SKIN TO TAKE HIS IDENTITY.
AN IDENTITY THAT WAS TESTED BY MEETING WITH ROSE WILETTO.
FORSYTHE MAY NOT HAVE BEEN ABLE TO FOOL HER, BECAUSE HE THEN KILLED HER IN HER HOME.
TAKING ON A NEW SKIN REQUIRED AGENT FORSYTHE TO REMOVE HIS OWN SKIN FIRST.
THE CARE WITH WHICH AGENT FORSYTHE DID THIS SUGGESTS THAT HE WAS PLANNING TO RETURN TO HIS SKIN EVENTUALLY.
HE DISCARDED HIS SKIN AT A GAS STATION OUTSIDE OF FLAGSTAFF. THE SKIN HAD STARTED TO PEEL AND DECAY.
THIS SUGGESTS HE CANNOT RETURN TO A SKIN. WHEN HE KNEW HE COULD NEVER GO BACK TO BEING FORSYTHE, HE TARGETED THE CABBIE.
FLAKES OF SKIN WERE FOUND IN THE CAB, SUGGESTING THAT WILETTO'S SKIN HAD STARTED TO PEEL AS WELL.
PERHAPS THE IMMUNOSUPPRESSANT DRUGS WEREN'T COMPLETELY EFFECTIVE. WE DON'T KNOW.
THIS SUGGESTS HE HAS A LIMITED TIME IN ANY GIVEN SKIN AND WILL HAVE TO KILL FREQUENTLY.
POTENTIALLY AS OFTEN AS TWICE A DAY.

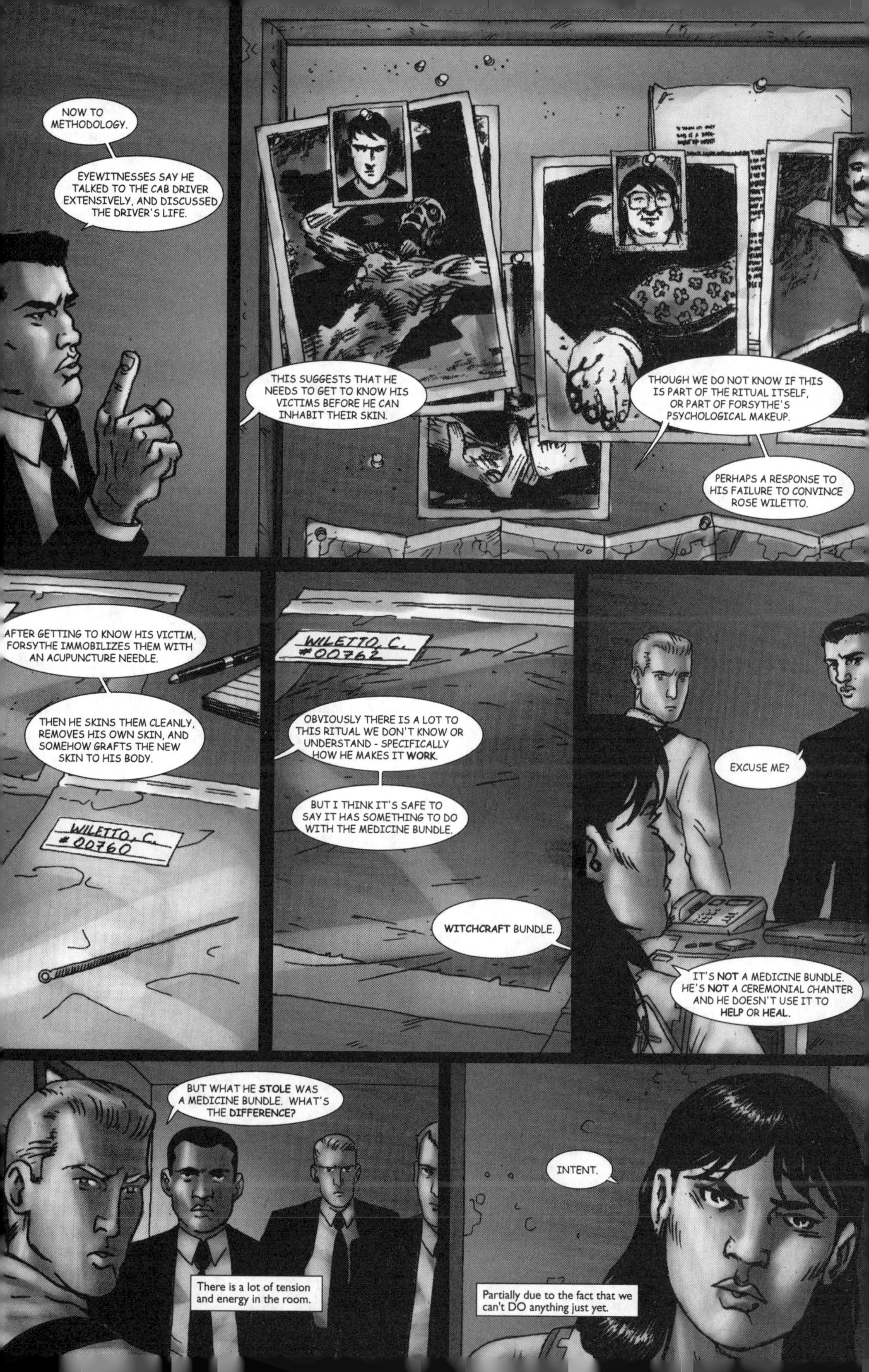

NOW TO METHODOLOGY.
EYEWITNESSES SAY HE TALKED TO THE CAB DRIVER EXTENSIVELY, AND DISCUSSED THE DRIVER'S LIFE.
THIS SUGGESTS THAT HE NEEDS TO GET TO KNOW HIS VICTIMS BEFORE HE CAN INHABIT THEIR SKIN.
THOUGH WE DO NOT KNOW IF THIS IS PART OF THE RITUAL ITSELF, OR PART OF FORSYTHE'S PSYCHOLOGICAL MAKEUP.
PERHAPS A RESPONSE TO HIS FAILURE TO CONVINCE ROSE WILETTO.
AFTER GETTING TO KNOW HIS VICTIM, FORSYTHE IMMOBILIZES THEM WITH AN ACUPUNCTURE NEEDLE.
THEN HE SKINS THEM CLEANLY, REMOVES HIS OWN SKIN, AND SOMEHOW GRAFTS THE NEW SKIN TO HIS BODY.
WILETTO, C. #00760
WILETTO, C. #00762
OBVIOUSLY THERE IS A LOT TO THIS RITUAL WE DON'T KNOW OR UNDERSTAND - SPECIFICALLY HOW HE MAKES IT WORK.
BUT I THINK IT'S SAFE TO SAY IT HAS SOMETHING TO DO WITH THE MEDICINE BUNDLE.
WITCHCRAFT BUNDLE.
EXCUSE ME?
IT'S NOT A MEDICINE BUNDLE. HE'S NOT A CEREMONIAL CHANTER AND HE DOESN'T USE IT TO HELP OR HEAL.
BUT WHAT HE STOLE WAS A MEDICINE BUNDLE. WHAT'S THE DIFFERENCE?
There is a lot of tension and energy in the room.
INTENT.
Partially due to the fact that we can't DO anything just yet.

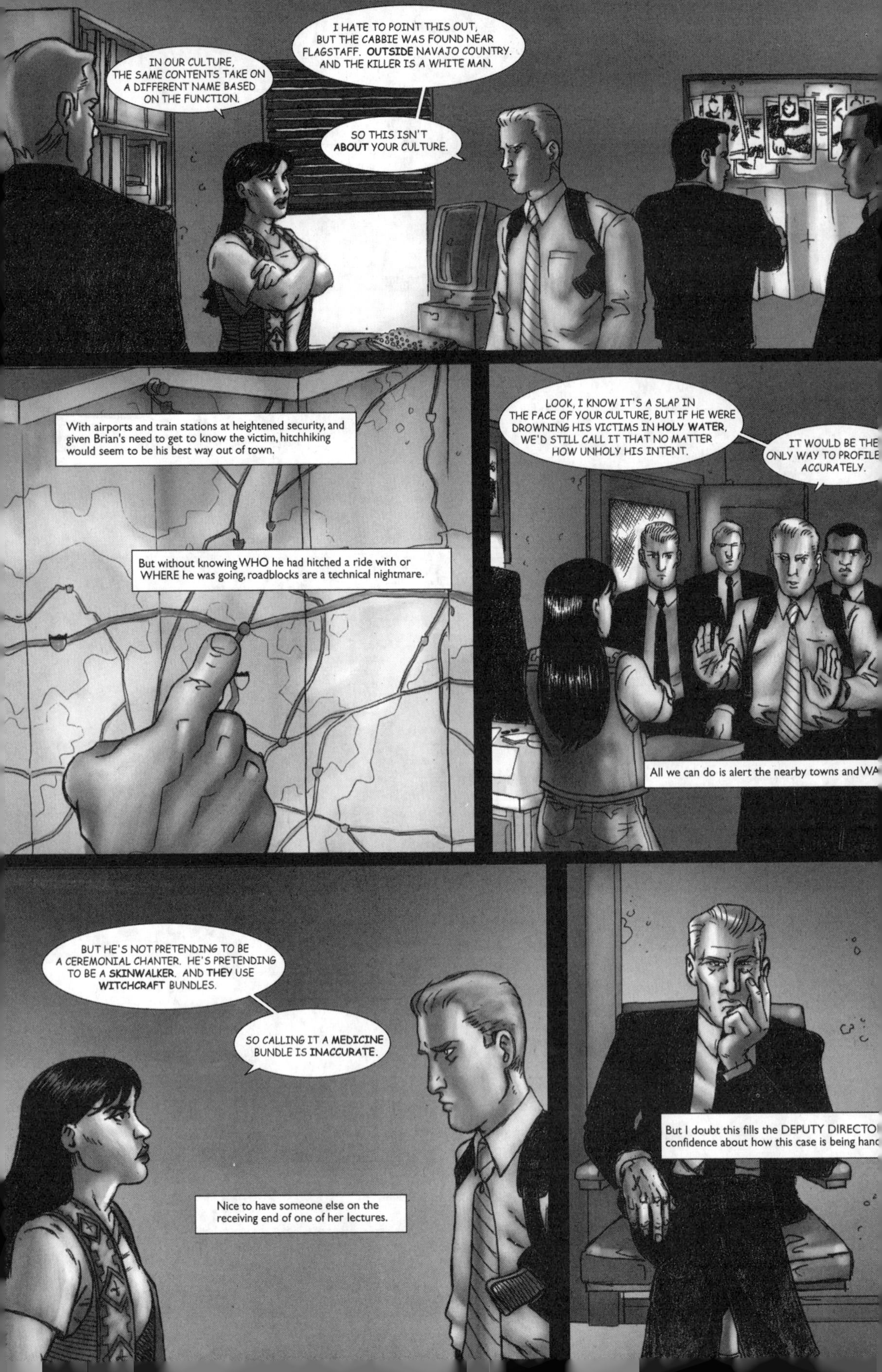
IN OUR CULTURE, THE SAME CONTENTS TAKE ON A DIFFERENT NAME BASED ON THE FUNCTION.
I HATE TO POINT THIS OUT, BUT THE CABBIE WAS FOUND NEAR FLAGSTAFF. **OUTSIDE** NAVAJO COUNTRY. AND THE KILLER IS A WHITE MAN.
SO THIS ISN'T **ABOUT** YOUR CULTURE.
With airports and train stations at heightened security, and given Brian's need to get to know the victim, hitchhiking would seem to be his best way out of town.
But without knowing WHO he had hitched a ride with or WHERE he was going, roadblocks are a technical nightmare.
LOOK, I KNOW IT'S A SLAP IN THE FACE OF YOUR CULTURE, BUT IF HE WERE DROWNING HIS VICTIMS IN **HOLY WATER**, WE'D STILL CALL IT THAT NO MATTER HOW UNHOLY HIS INTENT.
IT WOULD BE THE ONLY WAY TO PROFILE ACCURATELY.
All we can do is alert the nearby towns and WA
BUT HE'S NOT PRETENDING TO BE A CEREMONIAL CHANTER. HE'S PRETENDING TO BE A **SKINWALKER**. AND **THEY** USE **WITCHCRAFT** BUNDLES.
SO CALLING IT A **MEDICINE** BUNDLE IS **INACCURATE**.
Nice to have someone else on the receiving end of one of her lectures.
But I doubt this fills the DEPUTY DIRECTO
confidence about how this case is being hand

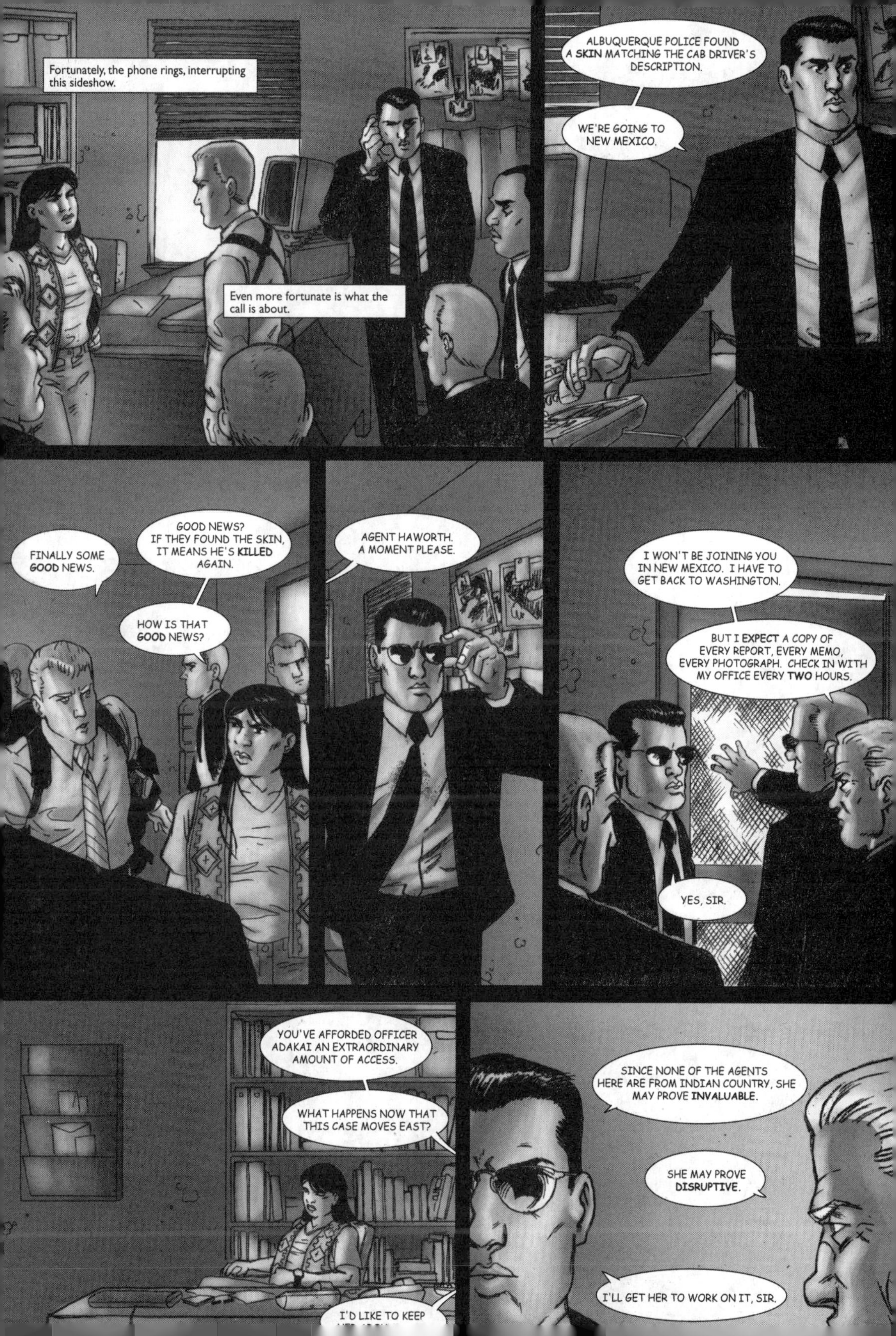
Fortunately, the phone rings, interrupting this sideshow.
Even more fortunate is what the call is about.
ALBUQUERQUE POLICE FOUND A SKIN MATCHING THE CAB DRIVER'S DESCRIPTION.
WE'RE GOING TO NEW MEXICO.
FINALLY SOME GOOD NEWS.
GOOD NEWS? IF THEY FOUND THE SKIN, IT MEANS HE'S KILLED AGAIN.
HOW IS THAT GOOD NEWS?
AGENT HAWORTH. A MOMENT PLEASE.
I WON'T BE JOINING YOU IN NEW MEXICO. I HAVE TO GET BACK TO WASHINGTON.
BUT I EXPECT A COPY OF EVERY REPORT, EVERY MEMO, EVERY PHOTOGRAPH. CHECK IN WITH MY OFFICE EVERY TWO HOURS.
YES, SIR.
YOU'VE AFFORDED OFFICER ADAKAI AN EXTRAORDINARY AMOUNT OF ACCESS.
WHAT HAPPENS NOW THAT THIS CASE MOVES EAST?
I'D LIKE TO KEEP
SINCE NONE OF THE AGENTS HERE ARE FROM INDIAN COUNTRY, SHE MAY PROVE INVALUABLE.
SHE MAY PROVE DISRUPTIVE.
I'LL GET HER TO WORK ON IT, SIR.

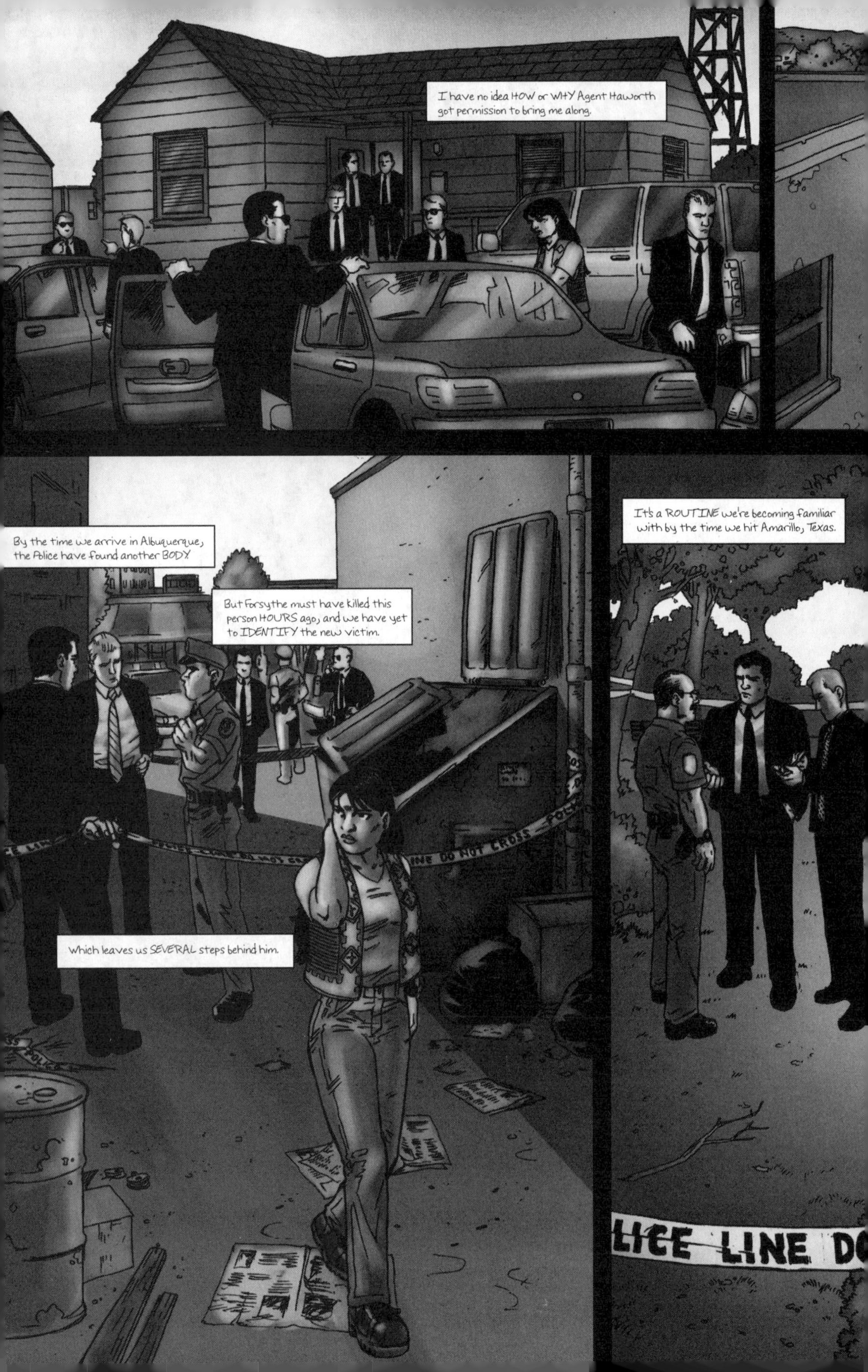
I have no idea HOW or WHY Agent Haworth got permission to bring me along.
By the time we arrive in Albuquerque, the Police have found another BODY.
But Forsythe must have killed this person HOURS ago, and we have yet to IDENTIFY the new victim.
Which leaves us SEVERAL steps behind him.
It's a ROUTINE we're becoming familiar with by the time we hit Amarillo, Texas.
LINE DO NOT CROSS
LICE LINE DO

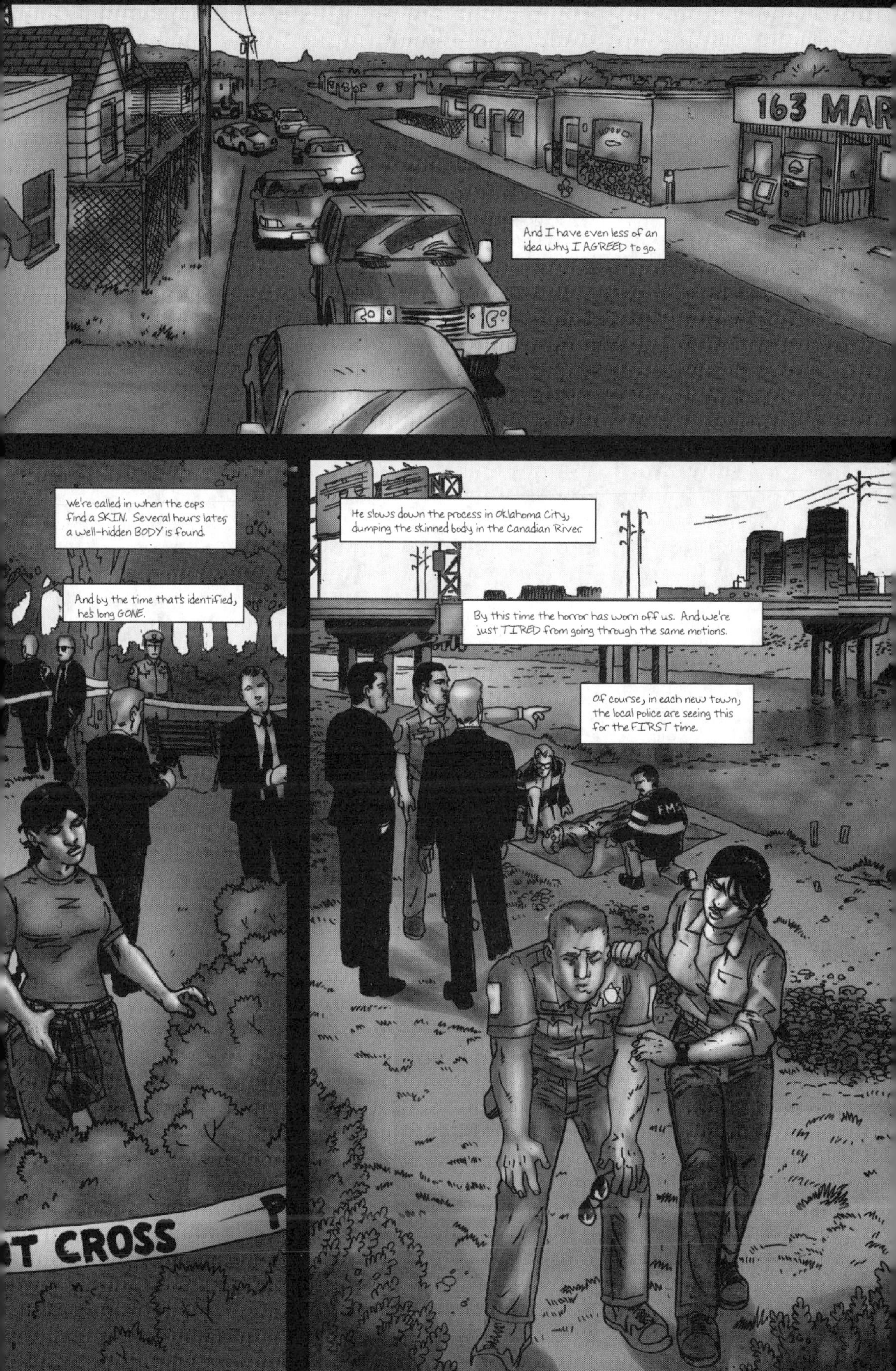
163 MAR
And I have even less of an idea why I AGREED to go.
We're called in when the cops find a SKIN. Several hours later a well-hidden BODY is found.
And by the time that's identified, he's long GONE.
T CROSS
He slows down the process in Oklahoma City, dumping the skinned body in the Canadian River.
By this time the horror has worn off us. And we're just TIRED from going through the same motions.
Of course, in each new town, the local police are seeing this for the FIRST time.
EMS

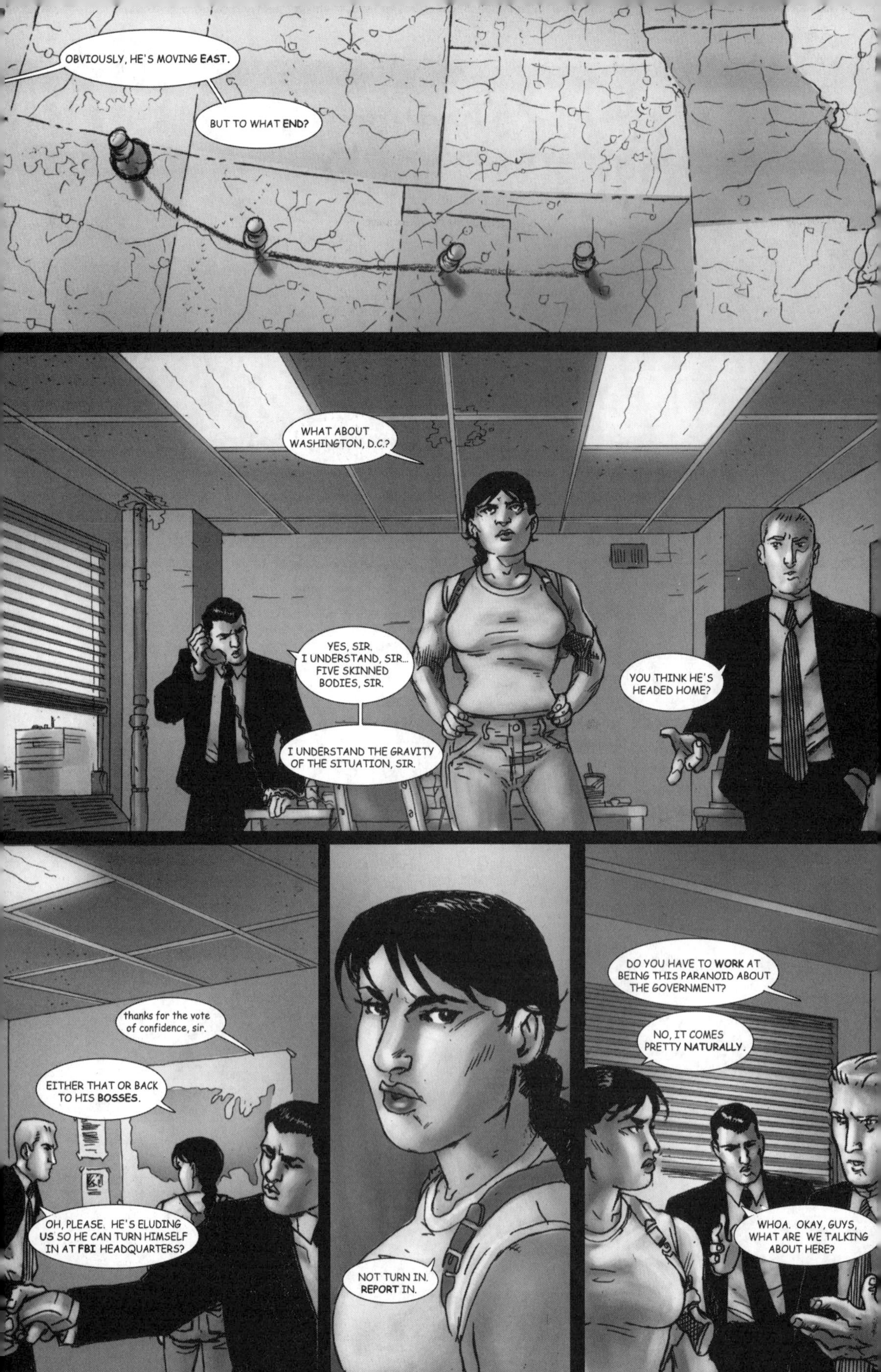
OBVIOUSLY, HE'S MOVING **EAST**.
BUT TO WHAT **END**?
WHAT ABOUT WASHINGTON, D.C.?
YES, SIR. I UNDERSTAND, SIR... FIVE SKINNED BODIES, SIR.
I UNDERSTAND THE GRAVITY OF THE SITUATION, SIR.
YOU THINK HE'S HEADED HOME?
thanks for the vote of confidence, sir.
EITHER THAT OR BACK TO HIS **BOSSES**.
OH, PLEASE. HE'S ELUDING **US** SO HE CAN TURN HIMSELF IN AT **FBI** HEADQUARTERS?
NOT TURN IN. **REPORT** IN.
DO YOU HAVE TO **WORK** AT BEING THIS PARANOID ABOUT THE GOVERNMENT?
NO, IT COMES PRETTY **NATURALLY**.
WHOA. OKAY, GUYS, WHAT ARE WE TALKING ABOUT HERE?

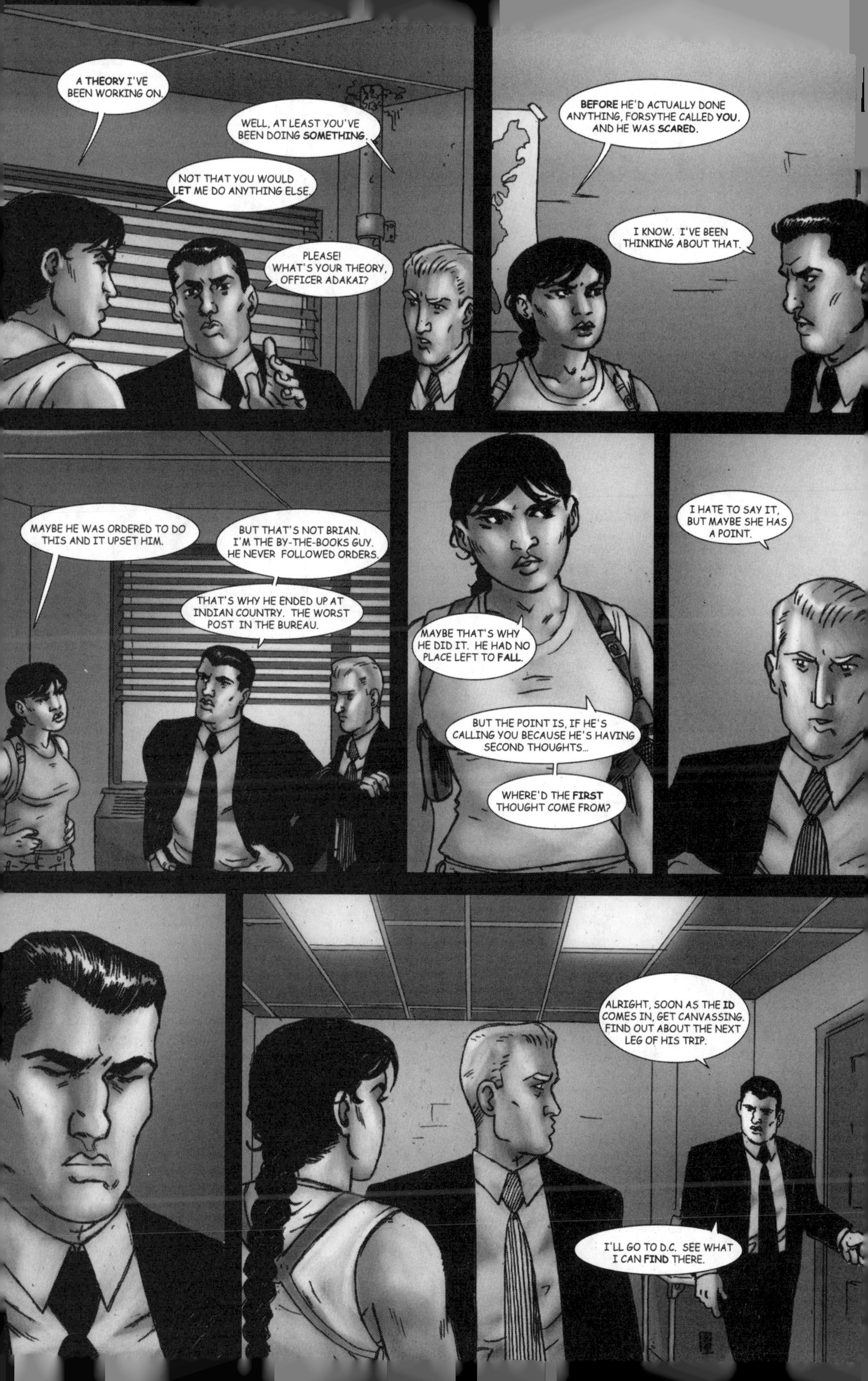
A THEORY I'VE BEEN WORKING ON.
WELL, AT LEAST YOU'VE BEEN DOING SOMETHING.
NOT THAT YOU WOULD LET ME DO ANYTHING ELSE.
PLEASE! WHAT'S YOUR THEORY, OFFICER ADAKAI?
BEFORE HE'D ACTUALLY DONE ANYTHING, FORSYTHE CALLED YOU. AND HE WAS SCARED.
I KNOW. I'VE BEEN THINKING ABOUT THAT.
MAYBE HE WAS ORDERED TO DO THIS AND IT UPSET HIM.
BUT THAT'S NOT BRIAN. I'M THE BY-THE-BOOKS GUY. HE NEVER FOLLOWED ORDERS.
THAT'S WHY HE ENDED UP AT INDIAN COUNTRY. THE WORST POST IN THE BUREAU.
MAYBE THAT'S WHY HE DID IT. HE HAD NO PLACE LEFT TO FALL.
BUT THE POINT IS, IF HE'S CALLING YOU BECAUSE HE'S HAVING SECOND THOUGHTS...
WHERE'D THE FIRST THOUGHT COME FROM?
I HATE TO SAY IT, BUT MAYBE SHE HAS A POINT.
ALRIGHT, SOON AS THE ID COMES IN, GET CANVASSING. FIND OUT ABOUT THE NEXT LEG OF HIS TRIP.
I'LL GO TO D.C. SEE WHAT I CAN FIND THERE.

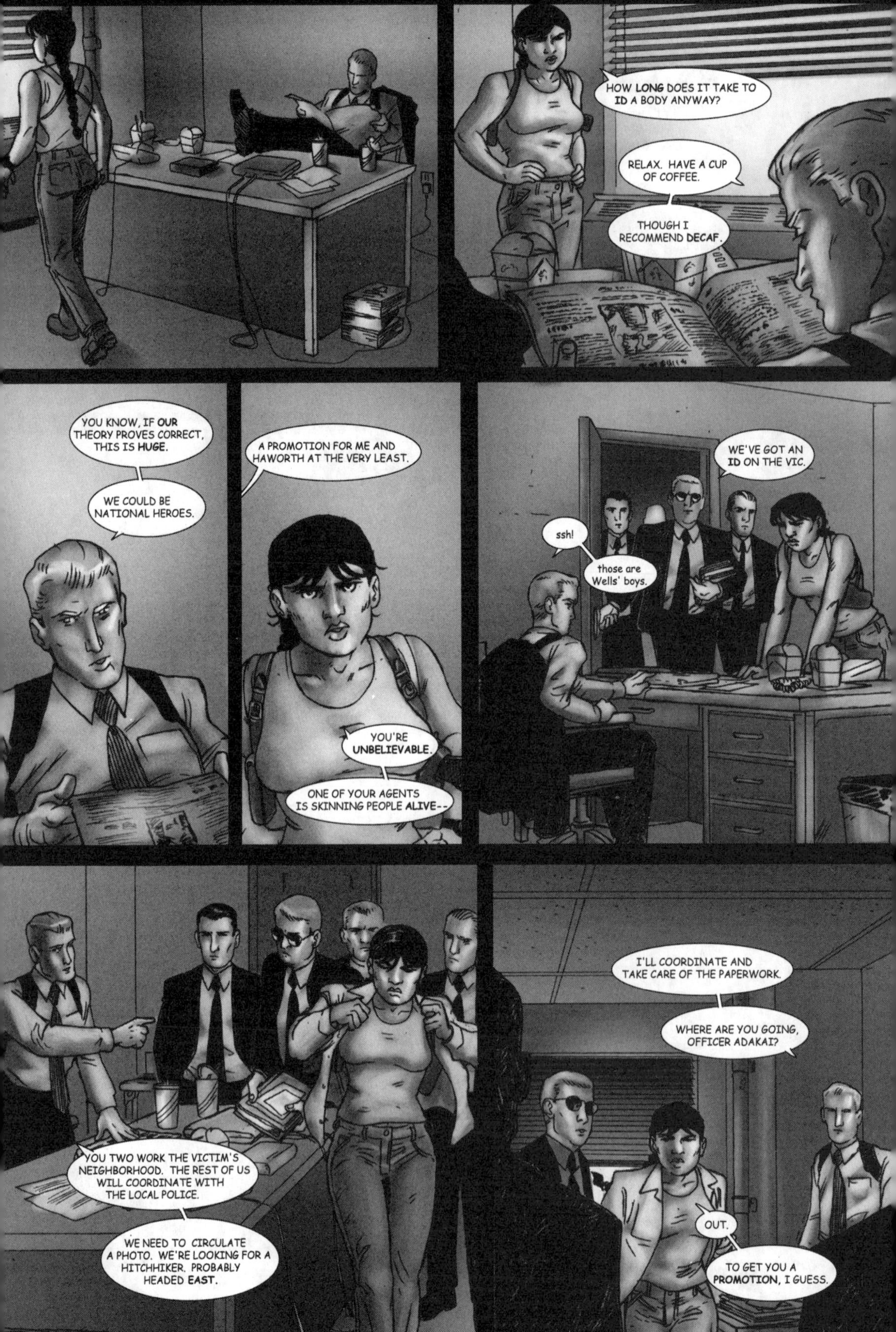
HOW LONG DOES IT TAKE TO ID A BODY ANYWAY?
RELAX. HAVE A CUP OF COFFEE.
THOUGH I RECOMMEND DECAF.
YOU KNOW, IF OUR THEORY PROVES CORRECT, THIS IS HUGE.
WE COULD BE NATIONAL HEROES.
A PROMOTION FOR ME AND HAWORTH AT THE VERY LEAST.
YOU'RE UNBELIEVABLE.
ONE OF YOUR AGENTS IS SKINNING PEOPLE ALIVE--
WE'VE GOT AN ID ON THE VIC.
ssh!
those are Wells' boys.
YOU TWO WORK THE VICTIM'S NEIGHBORHOOD. THE REST OF US WILL COORDINATE WITH THE LOCAL POLICE.
WE NEED TO CIRCULATE A PHOTO. WE'RE LOOKING FOR A HITCHHIKER. PROBABLY HEADED EAST.
I'LL COORDINATE AND TAKE CARE OF THE PAPERWORK.
WHERE ARE YOU GOING, OFFICER ADAKAI?
OUT.
TO GET YOU A PROMOTION, I GUESS.

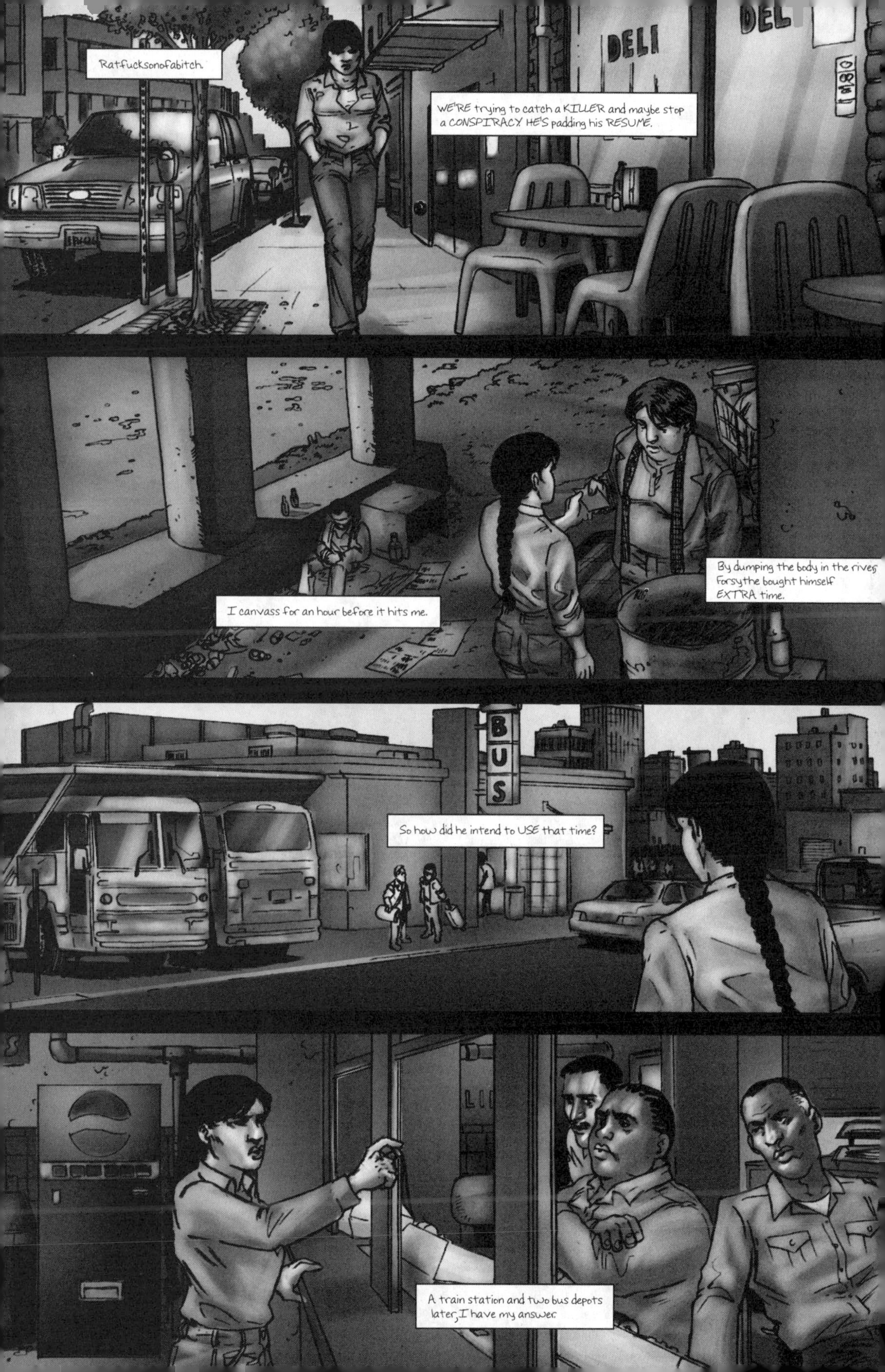

Ratfucksonofabitch.
WE'RE trying to catch a KILLER and maybe stop a CONSPIRACY. HE'S padding his RESUME.
I canvass for an hour before it hits me.
By dumping the body in the river, Forsythe bought himself EXTRA time.
So how did he intend to USE that time?
A train station and two bus depots later, I have my answer.

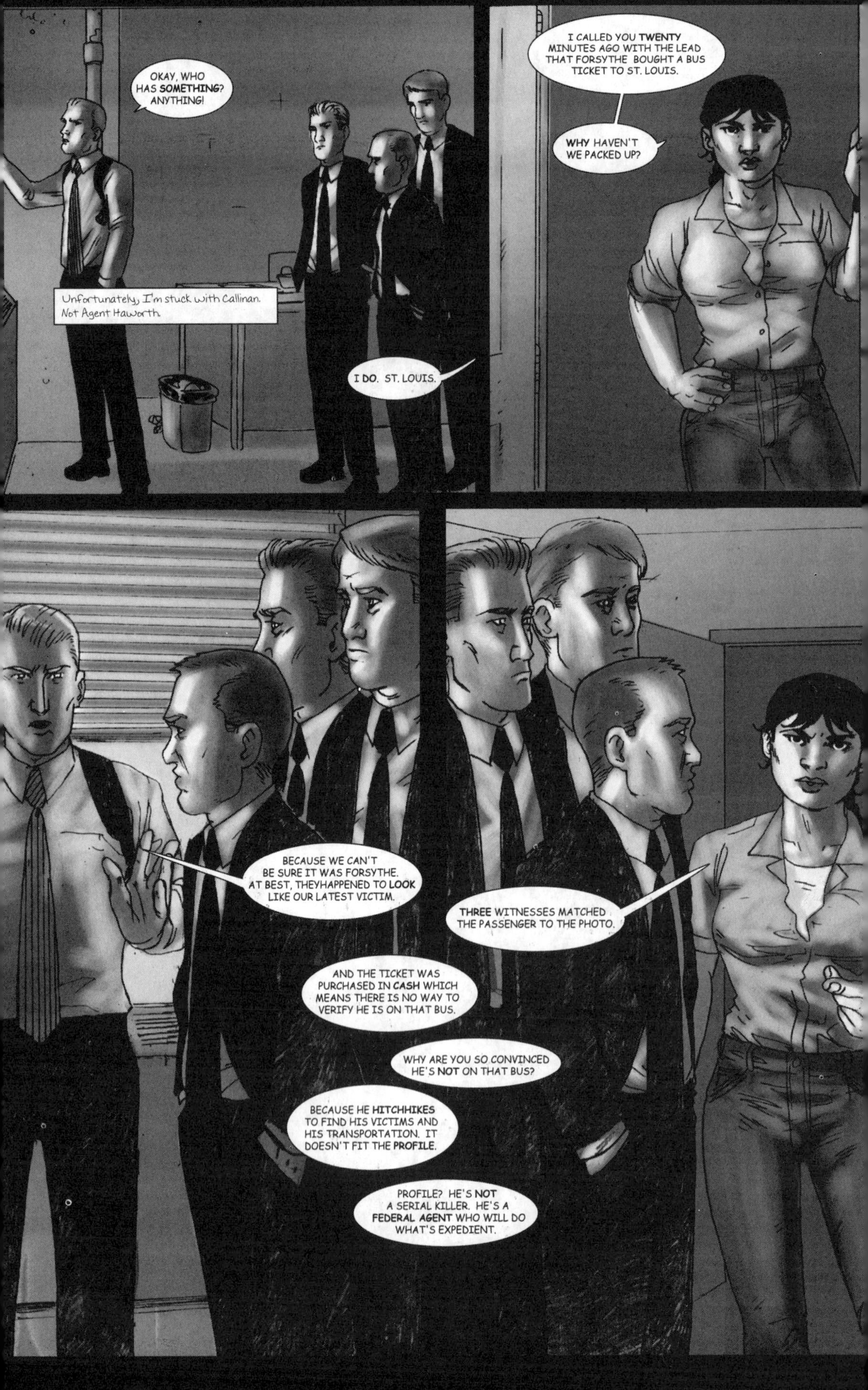

OKAY, WHO HAS SOMETHING? ANYTHING!
Unfortunately, I'm stuck with Callinan. Not Agent Haworth.
I DO. ST. LOUIS.
I CALLED YOU TWENTY MINUTES AGO WITH THE LEAD THAT FORSYTHE BOUGHT A BUS TICKET TO ST. LOUIS.
WHY HAVEN'T WE PACKED UP?
BECAUSE WE CAN'T BE SURE IT WAS FORSYTHE. AT BEST, THEYHAPPENED TO LOOK LIKE OUR LATEST VICTIM.
THREE WITNESSES MATCHED THE PASSENGER TO THE PHOTO.
AND THE TICKET WAS PURCHASED IN CASH WHICH MEANS THERE IS NO WAY TO VERIFY HE IS ON THAT BUS.
WHY ARE YOU SO CONVINCED HE'S NOT ON THAT BUS?
BECAUSE HE HITCHHIKES TO FIND HIS VICTIMS AND HIS TRANSPORTATION. IT DOESN'T FIT THE PROFILE.
PROFILE? HE'S NOT A SERIAL KILLER. HE'S A FEDERAL AGENT WHO WILL DO WHAT'S EXPEDIENT.

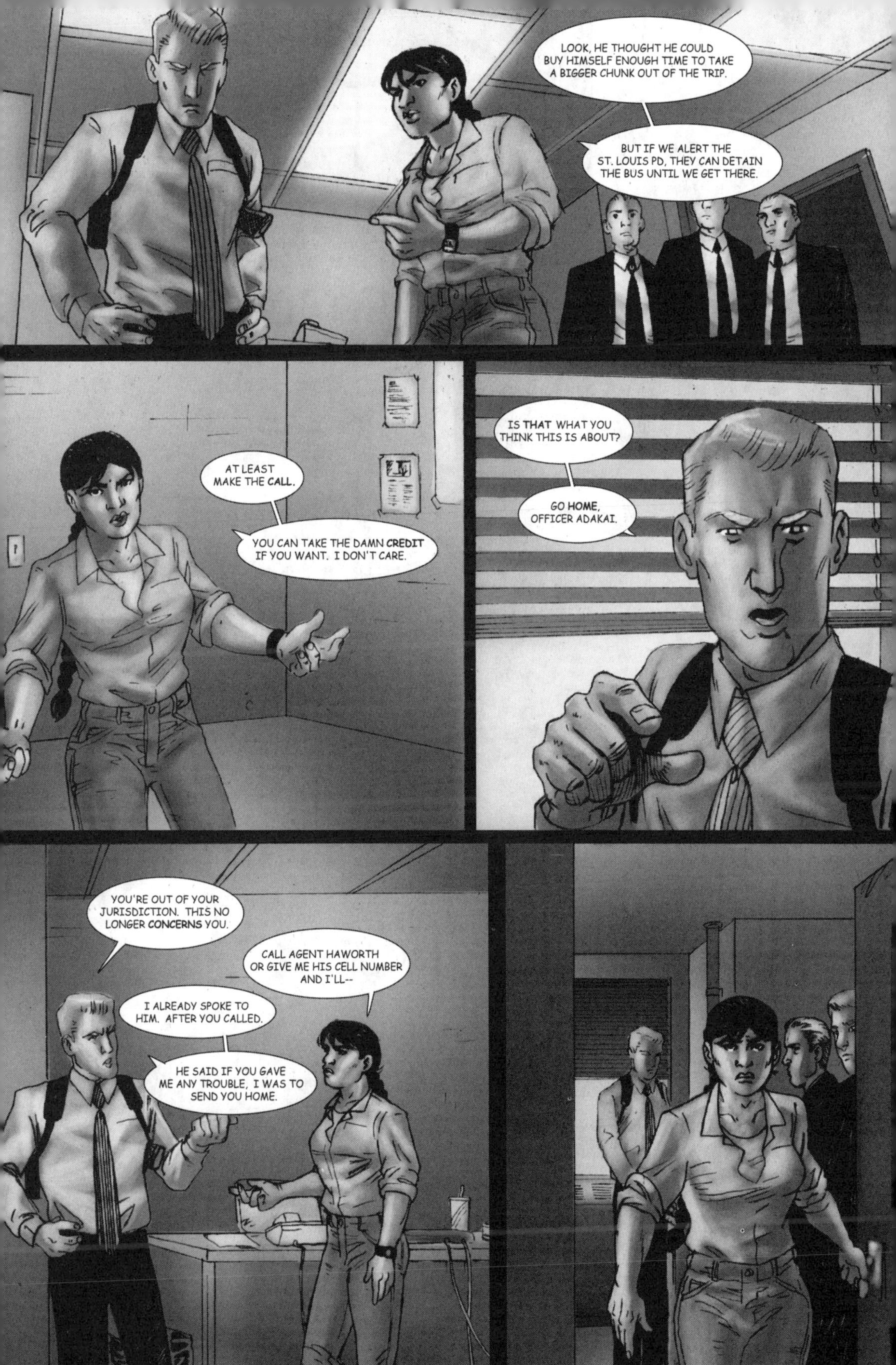
LOOK, HE THOUGHT HE COULD BUY HIMSELF ENOUGH TIME TO TAKE A BIGGER CHUNK OUT OF THE TRIP.
BUT IF WE ALERT THE ST. LOUIS PD, THEY CAN DETAIN THE BUS UNTIL WE GET THERE.
AT LEAST MAKE THE CALL.
YOU CAN TAKE THE DAMN CREDIT IF YOU WANT. I DON'T CARE.
IS THAT WHAT YOU THINK THIS IS ABOUT?
GO HOME, OFFICER ADAKAI.
YOU'RE OUT OF YOUR JURISDICTION. THIS NO LONGER CONCERNS YOU.
CALL AGENT HAWORTH OR GIVE ME HIS CELL NUMBER AND I'LL--
I ALREADY SPOKE TO HIM. AFTER YOU CALLED.
HE SAID IF YOU GAVE ME ANY TROUBLE, I WAS TO SEND YOU HOME.

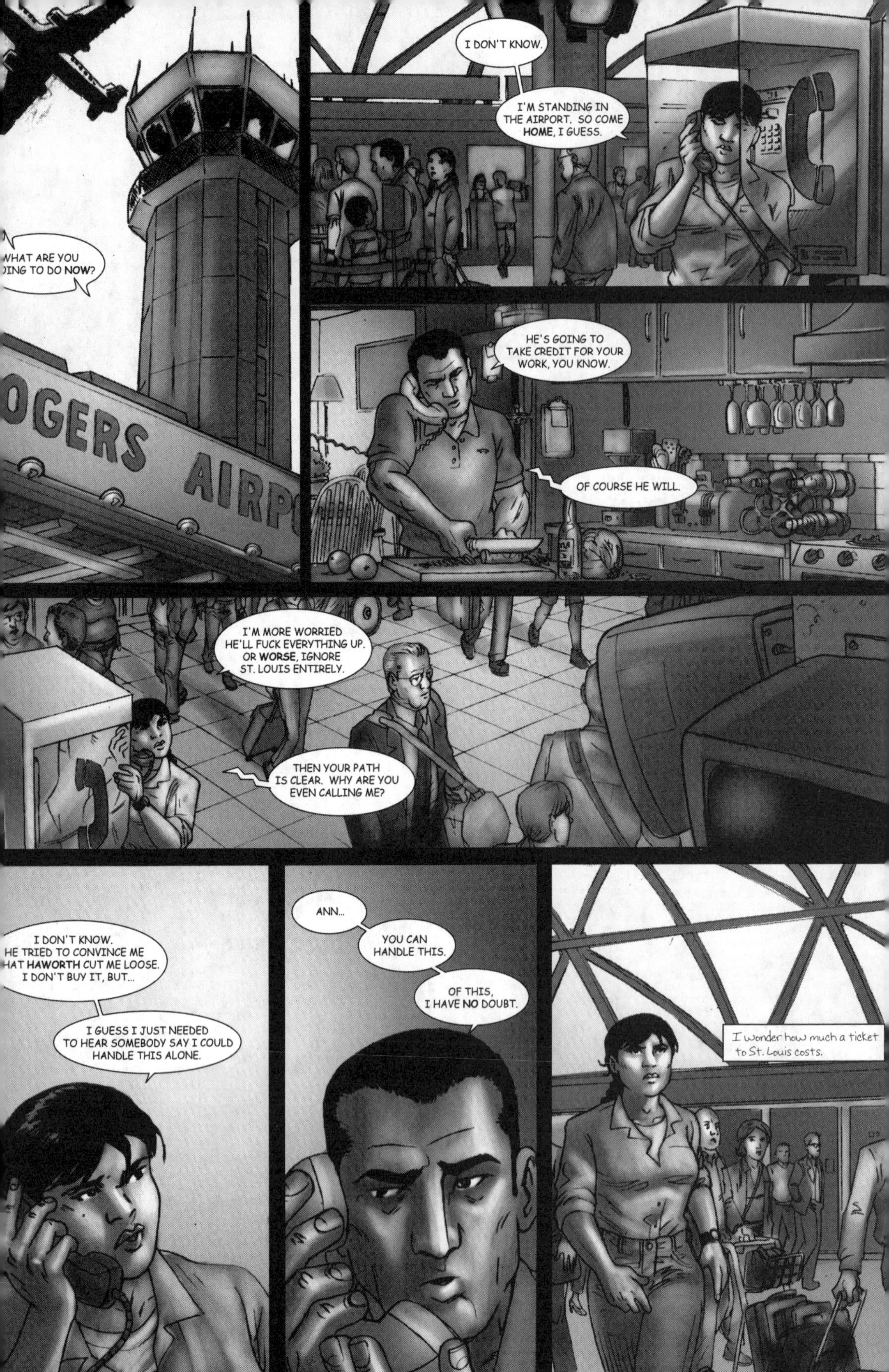
WHAT ARE YOU
OING TO DO NOW?
OGERS AIRP
I DON'T KNOW.
I'M STANDING IN THE AIRPORT. SO COME HOME, I GUESS.
HE'S GOING TO TAKE CREDIT FOR YOUR WORK, YOU KNOW.
OF COURSE HE WILL.
I'M MORE WORRIED HE'LL FUCK EVERYTHING UP. OR WORSE, IGNORE ST. LOUIS ENTIRELY.
THEN YOUR PATH IS CLEAR. WHY ARE YOU EVEN CALLING ME?
I DON'T KNOW. HE TRIED TO CONVINCE ME HAT HAWORTH CUT ME LOOSE. I DON'T BUY IT, BUT...
I GUESS I JUST NEEDED TO HEAR SOMEBODY SAY I COULD HANDLE THIS ALONE.
ANN...
YOU CAN HANDLE THIS.
OF THIS, I HAVE NO DOUBT.
I wonder how much a ticket to St. Louis costs.

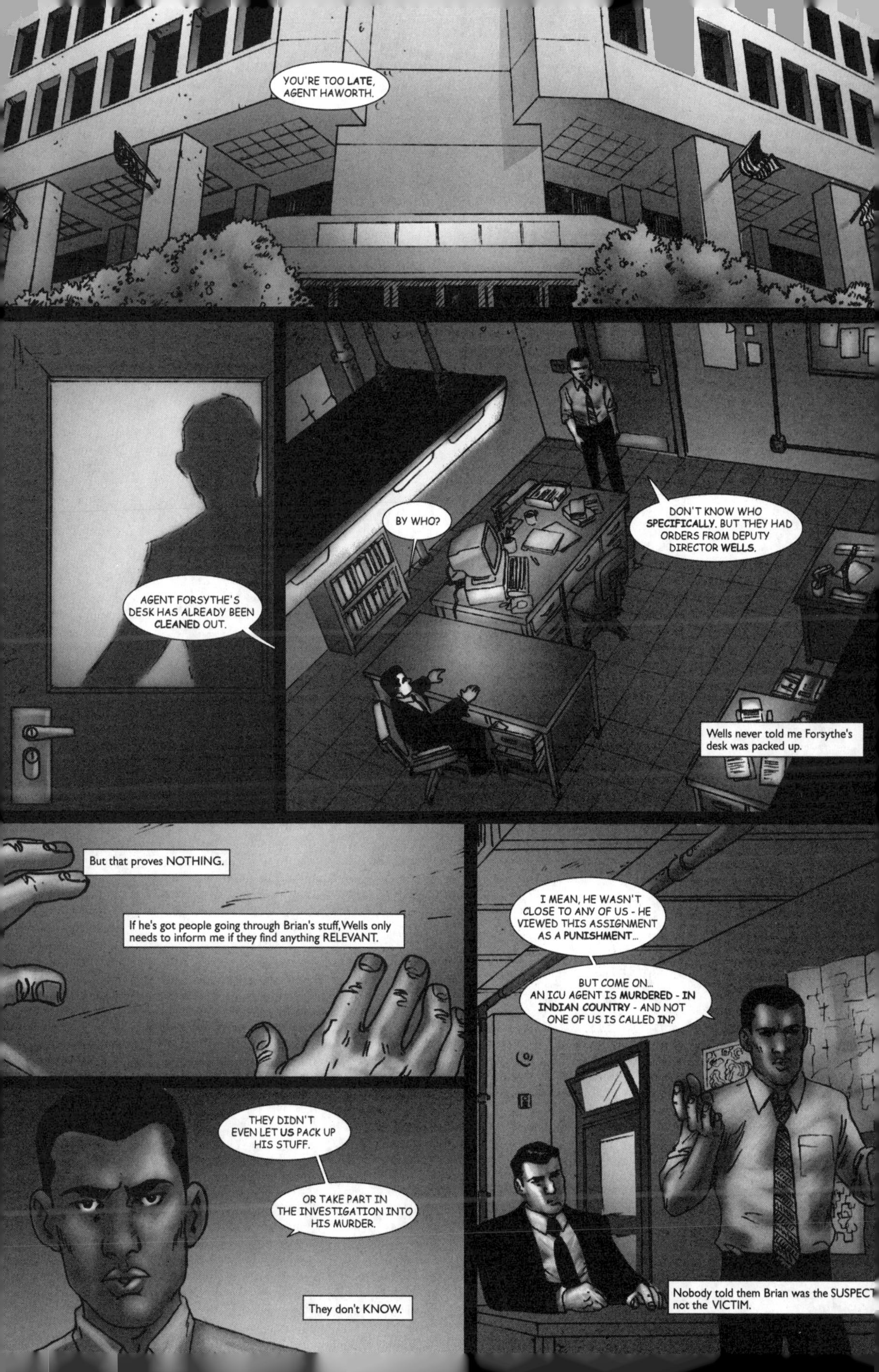
YOU'RE TOO LATE, AGENT HAWORTH.
AGENT FORSYTHE'S DESK HAS ALREADY BEEN CLEANED OUT.
BY WHO?
DON'T KNOW WHO SPECIFICALLY. BUT THEY HAD ORDERS FROM DEPUTY DIRECTOR WELLS.
Wells never told me Forsythe's desk was packed up.
But that proves NOTHING.
If he's got people going through Brian's stuff, Wells only needs to inform me if they find anything RELEVANT.
THEY DIDN'T EVEN LET US PACK UP HIS STUFF.
OR TAKE PART IN THE INVESTIGATION INTO HIS MURDER.
They don't KNOW.
I MEAN, HE WASN'T CLOSE TO ANY OF US - HE VIEWED THIS ASSIGNMENT AS A PUNISHMENT...
BUT COME ON... AN ICU AGENT IS MURDERED - IN INDIAN COUNTRY - AND NOT ONE OF US IS CALLED IN?
Nobody told them Brian was the SUSPECT not the VICTIM.

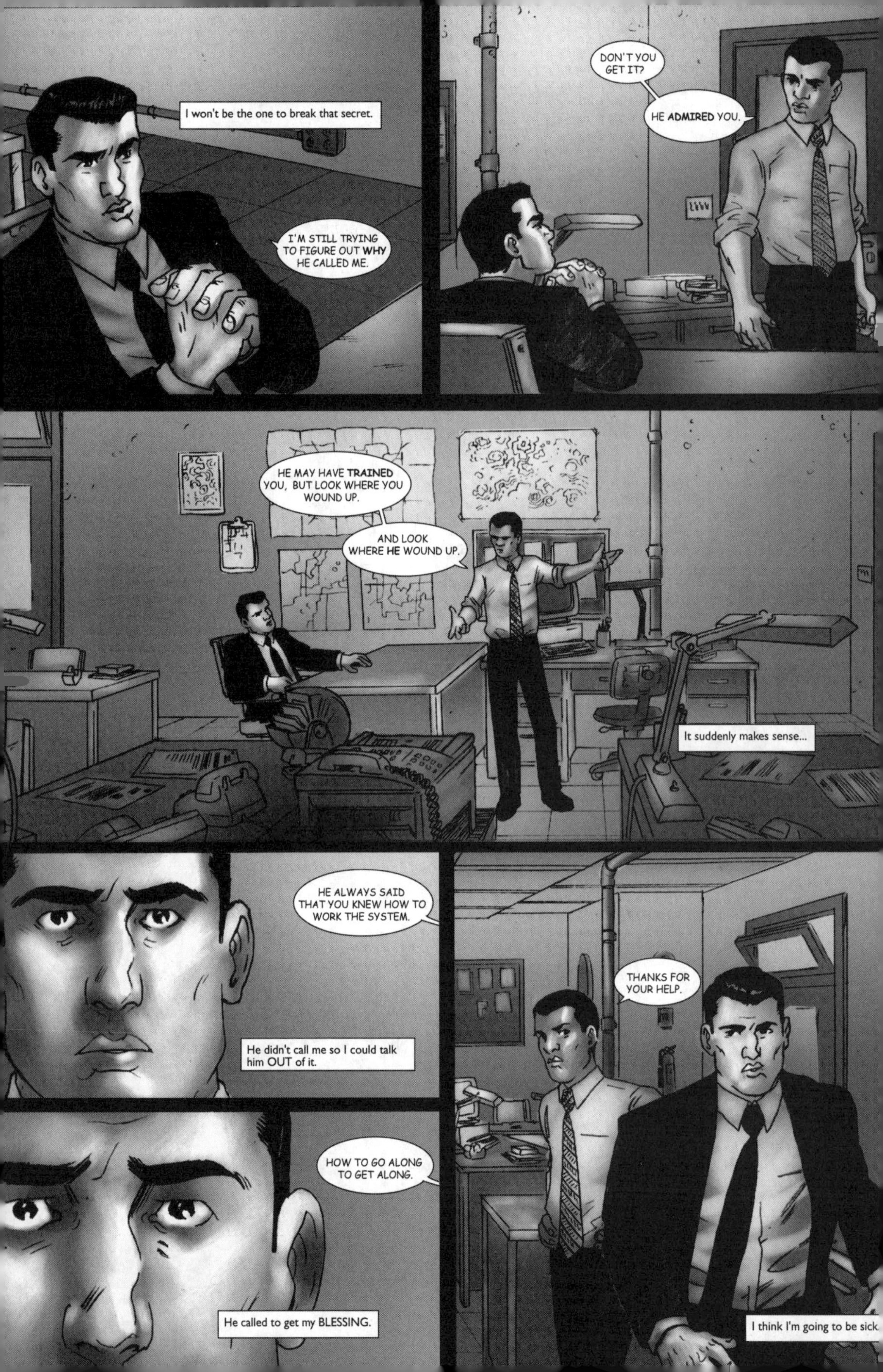
I won't be the one to break that secret.
I'M STILL TRYING TO FIGURE OUT WHY HE CALLED ME.
DON'T YOU GET IT?
HE ADMIRED YOU.
HE MAY HAVE TRAINED YOU, BUT LOOK WHERE YOU WOUND UP.
AND LOOK WHERE HE WOUND UP.
It suddenly makes sense...
HE ALWAYS SAID THAT YOU KNEW HOW TO WORK THE SYSTEM.
He didn't call me so I could talk him OUT of it.
HOW TO GO ALONG TO GET ALONG.
He called to get my BLESSING.
THANKS FOR YOUR HELP.
I think I'm going to be sick.

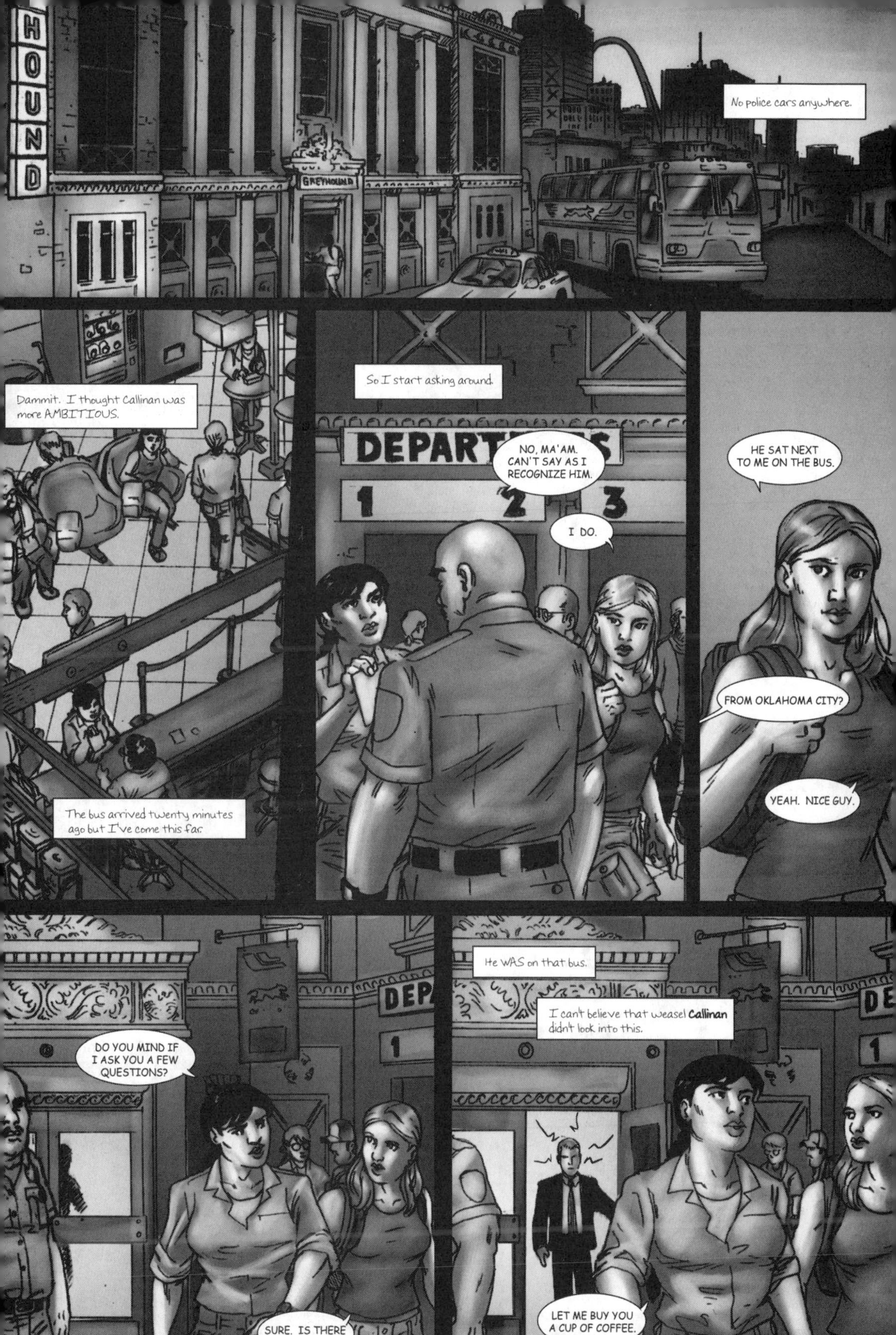
HOUND
GREYHOUND
No police cars anywhere.
Dammit. I thought Callinan was more AMBITIOUS.
The bus arrived twenty minutes ago but I've come this far.
So I start asking around.
DEPART
1
2
3
NO, MA'AM. CAN'T SAY AS I RECOGNIZE HIM.
I DO.
HE SAT NEXT TO ME ON THE BUS.
FROM OKLAHOMA CITY?
YEAH. NICE GUY.
DEPA
1
DO YOU MIND IF I ASK YOU A FEW QUESTIONS?
SURE. IS THERE A PROBLEM?
He WAS on that bus.
I can't believe that weasel **Callinan** didn't look into this.
DE
1
LET ME BUY YOU A CUP OF COFFEE.

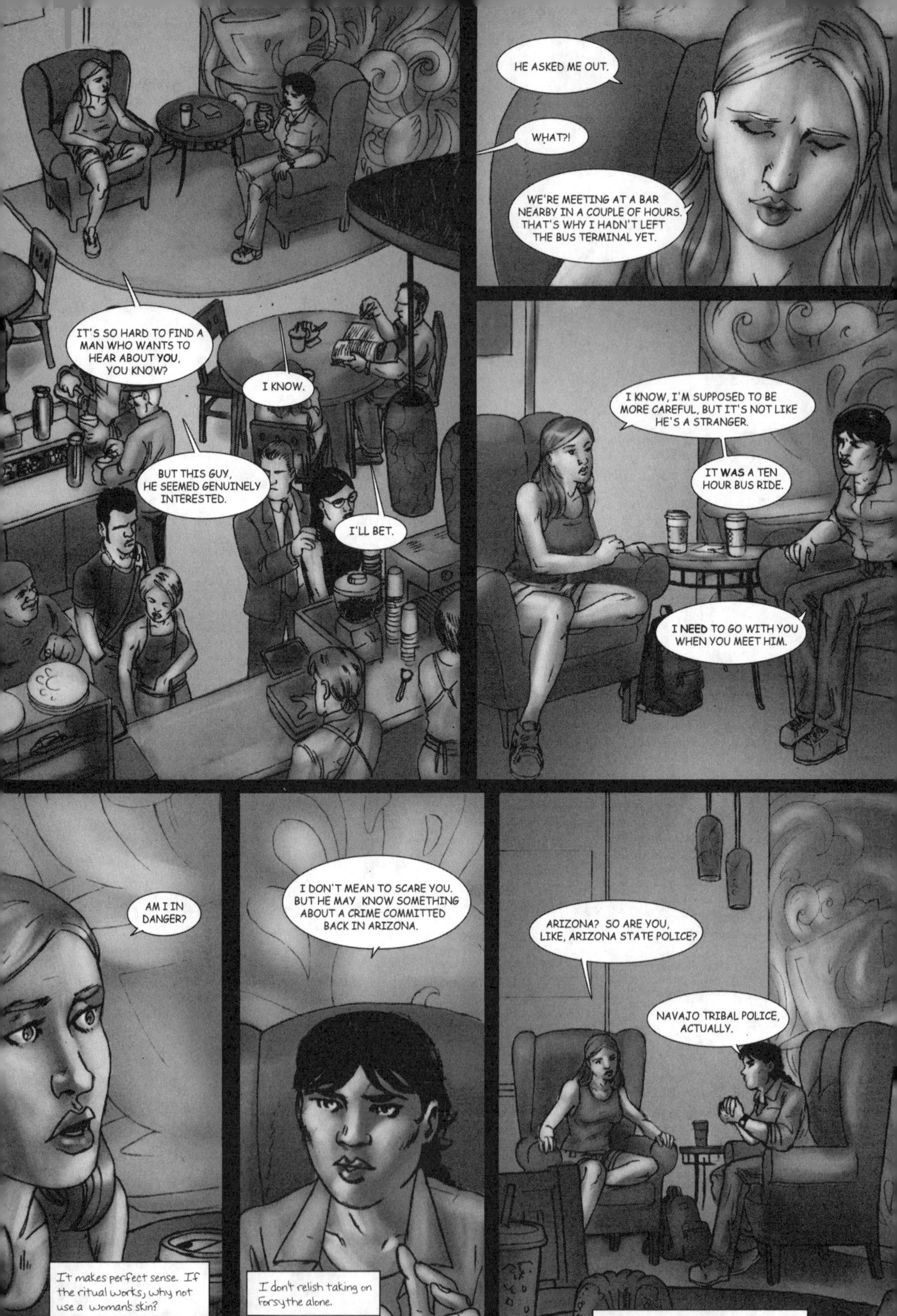
IT'S SO HARD TO FIND A MAN WHO WANTS TO HEAR ABOUT YOU, YOU KNOW?
I KNOW.
BUT THIS GUY, HE SEEMED GENUINELY INTERESTED.
I'LL BET.
HE ASKED ME OUT.
WHAT?!
WE'RE MEETING AT A BAR NEARBY IN A COUPLE OF HOURS. THAT'S WHY I HADN'T LEFT THE BUS TERMINAL YET.
I KNOW, I'M SUPPOSED TO BE MORE CAREFUL, BUT IT'S NOT LIKE HE'S A STRANGER.
IT WAS A TEN HOUR BUS RIDE.
I NEED TO GO WITH YOU WHEN YOU MEET HIM.
AM I IN DANGER?
It makes perfect sense. If the ritual works, why not use a woman's skin?
I DON'T MEAN TO SCARE YOU. BUT HE MAY KNOW SOMETHING ABOUT A CRIME COMMITTED BACK IN ARIZONA.
I don't relish taking on Forsythe alone.
ARIZONA? SO ARE YOU, LIKE, ARIZONA STATE POLICE?
NAVAJO TRIBAL POLICE, ACTUALLY.
One way or another, this ends tonight.

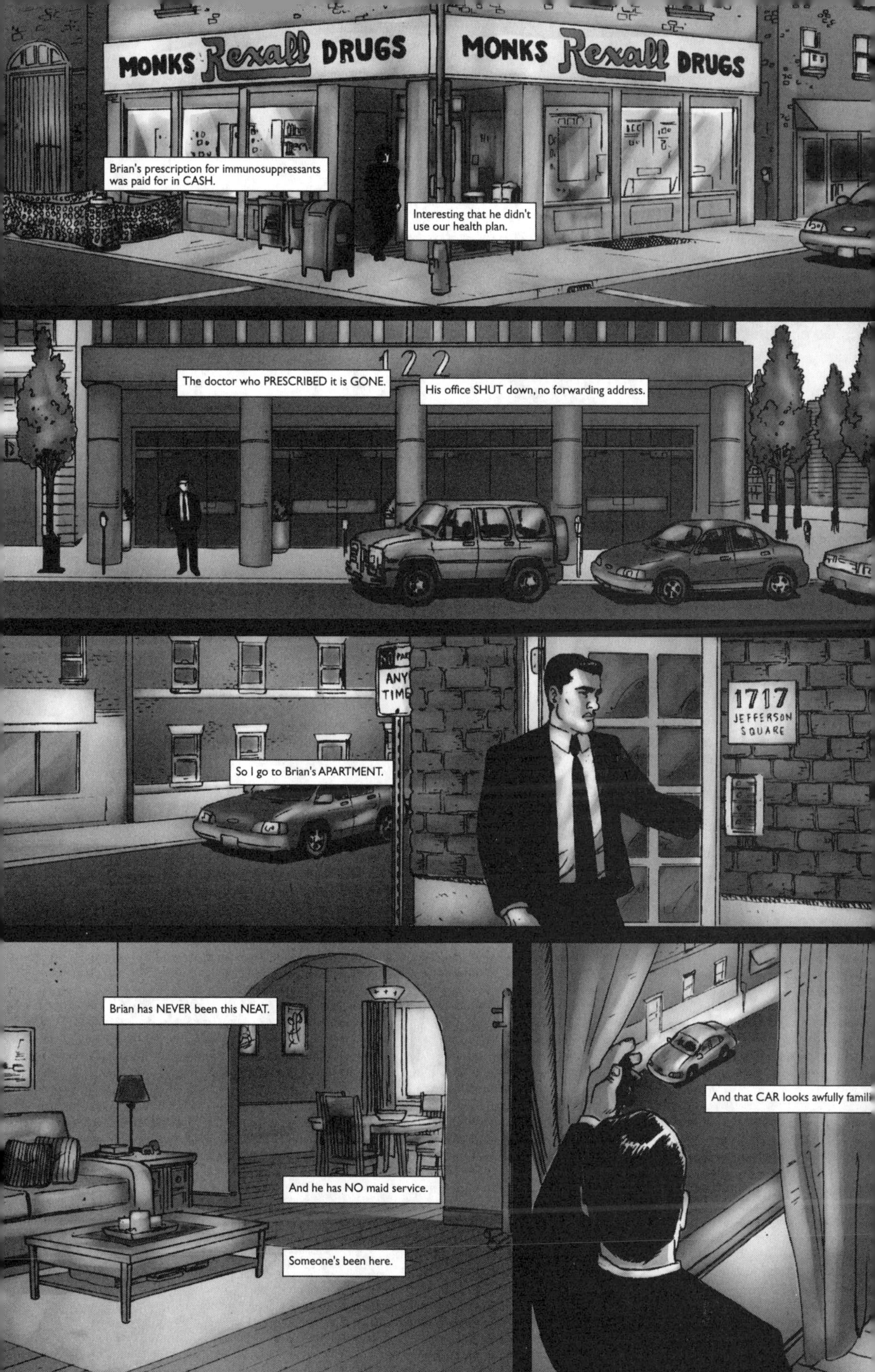
MONKS Rexall DRUGS
MONKS Rexall DRUGS
Brian's prescription for immunosuppressants was paid for in CASH.
Interesting that he didn't use our health plan.
122
The doctor who PRESCRIBED it is GONE.
His office SHUT down, no forwarding address.
ANY TIME
1717 JEFFERSON SQUARE
So I go to Brian's APARTMENT.
Brian has NEVER been this NEAT.
And he has NO maid service.
Someone's been here.
And that CAR looks awfully famili

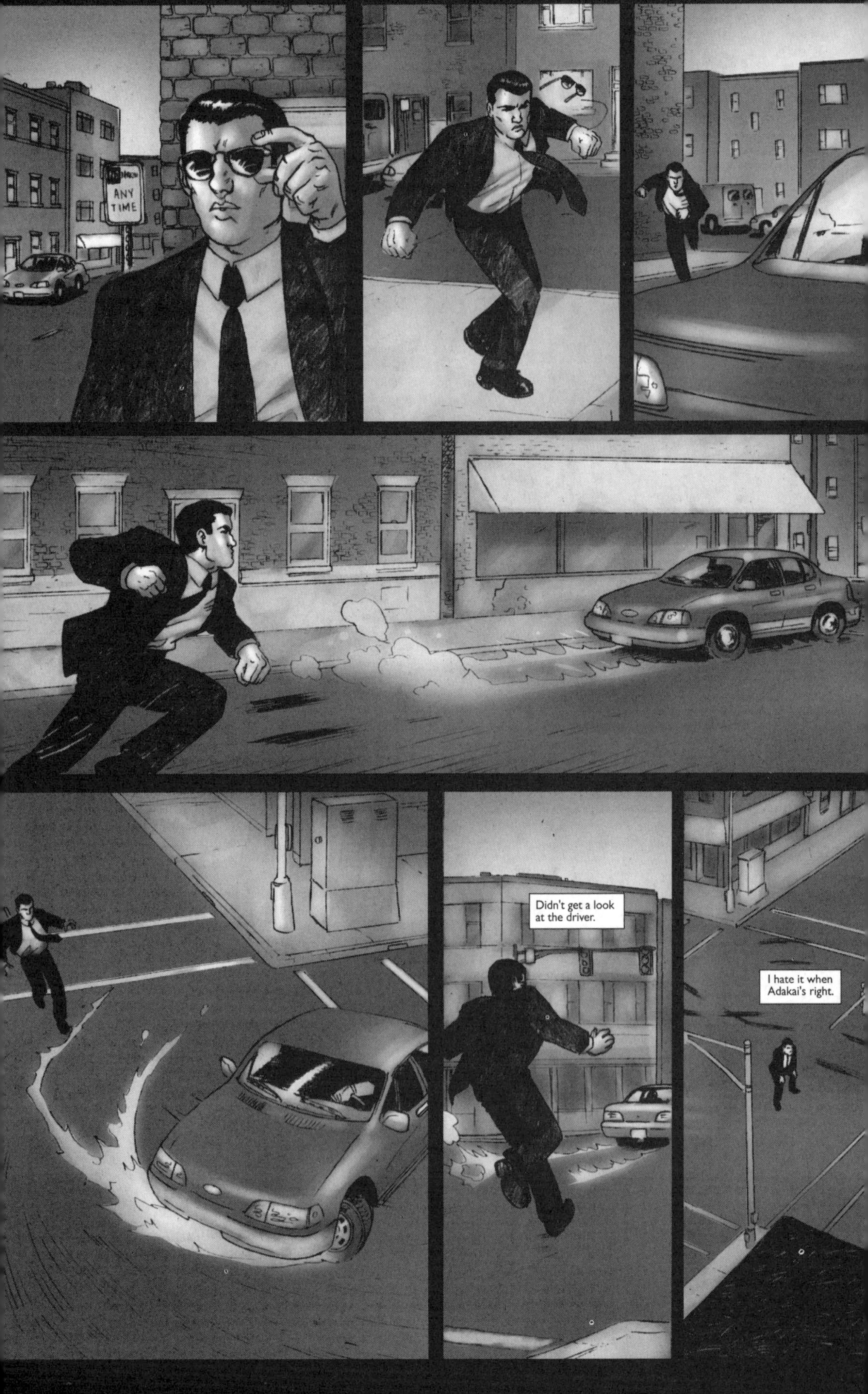
ANY
TIME
Didn't get a look at the driver.
I hate it when Adakai's right.

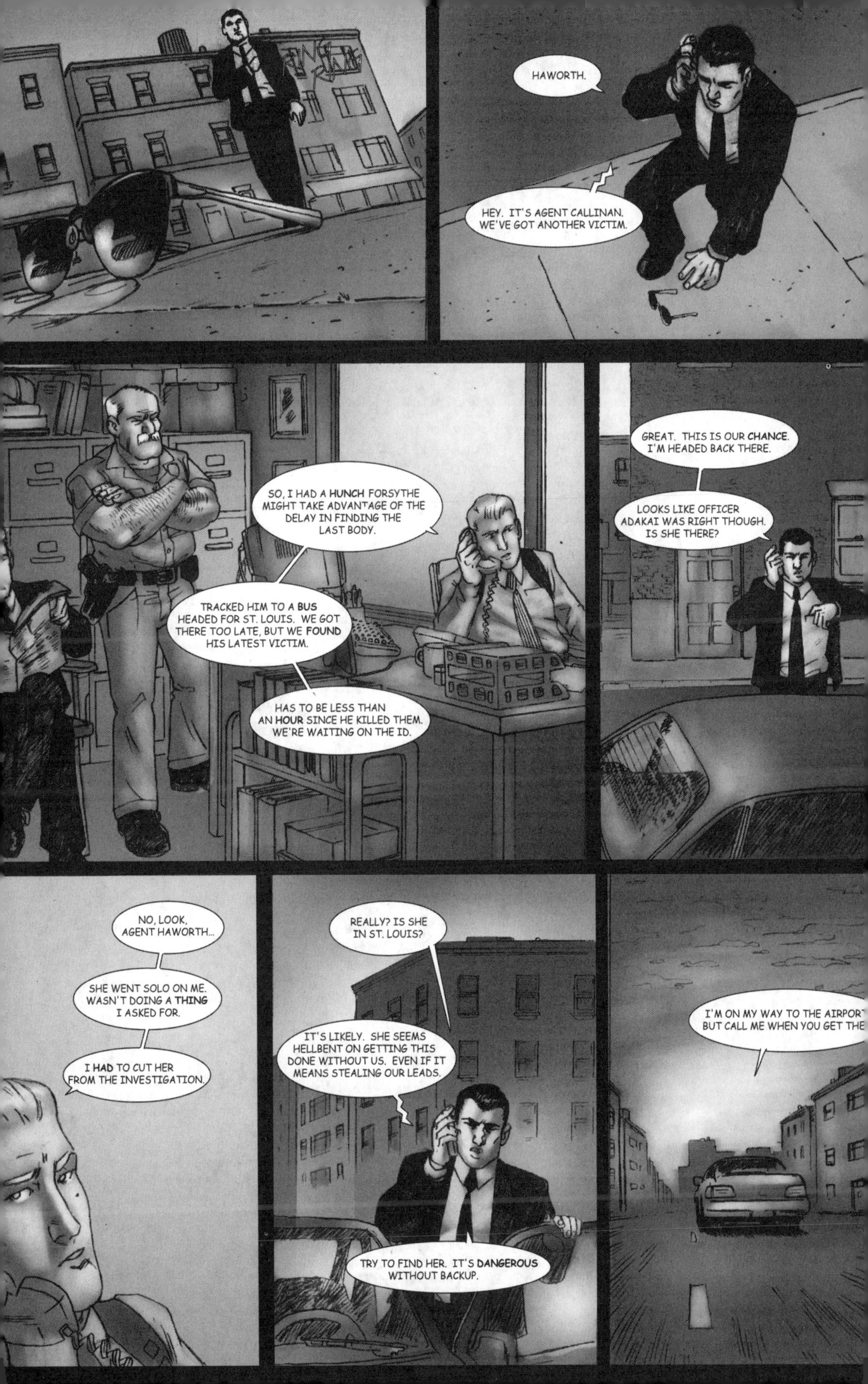
HAWORTH.
HEY. IT'S AGENT CALLINAN. WE'VE GOT ANOTHER VICTIM.
SO, I HAD A HUNCH FORSYTHE MIGHT TAKE ADVANTAGE OF THE DELAY IN FINDING THE LAST BODY.
TRACKED HIM TO A BUS HEADED FOR ST. LOUIS. WE GOT THERE TOO LATE, BUT WE FOUND HIS LATEST VICTIM.
HAS TO BE LESS THAN AN HOUR SINCE HE KILLED THEM. WE'RE WAITING ON THE ID.
GREAT. THIS IS OUR CHANCE. I'M HEADED BACK THERE.
LOOKS LIKE OFFICER ADAKAI WAS RIGHT THOUGH. IS SHE THERE?
NO, LOOK, AGENT HAWORTH...
SHE WENT SOLO ON ME. WASN'T DOING A THING I ASKED FOR.
I HAD TO CUT HER FROM THE INVESTIGATION.
REALLY? IS SHE IN ST. LOUIS?
IT'S LIKELY. SHE SEEMS HELLBENT ON GETTING THIS DONE WITHOUT US. EVEN IF IT MEANS STEALING OUR LEADS.
TRY TO FIND HER. IT'S DANGEROUS WITHOUT BACKUP.
I'M ON MY WAY TO THE AIRPORT BUT CALL ME WHEN YOU GET THE

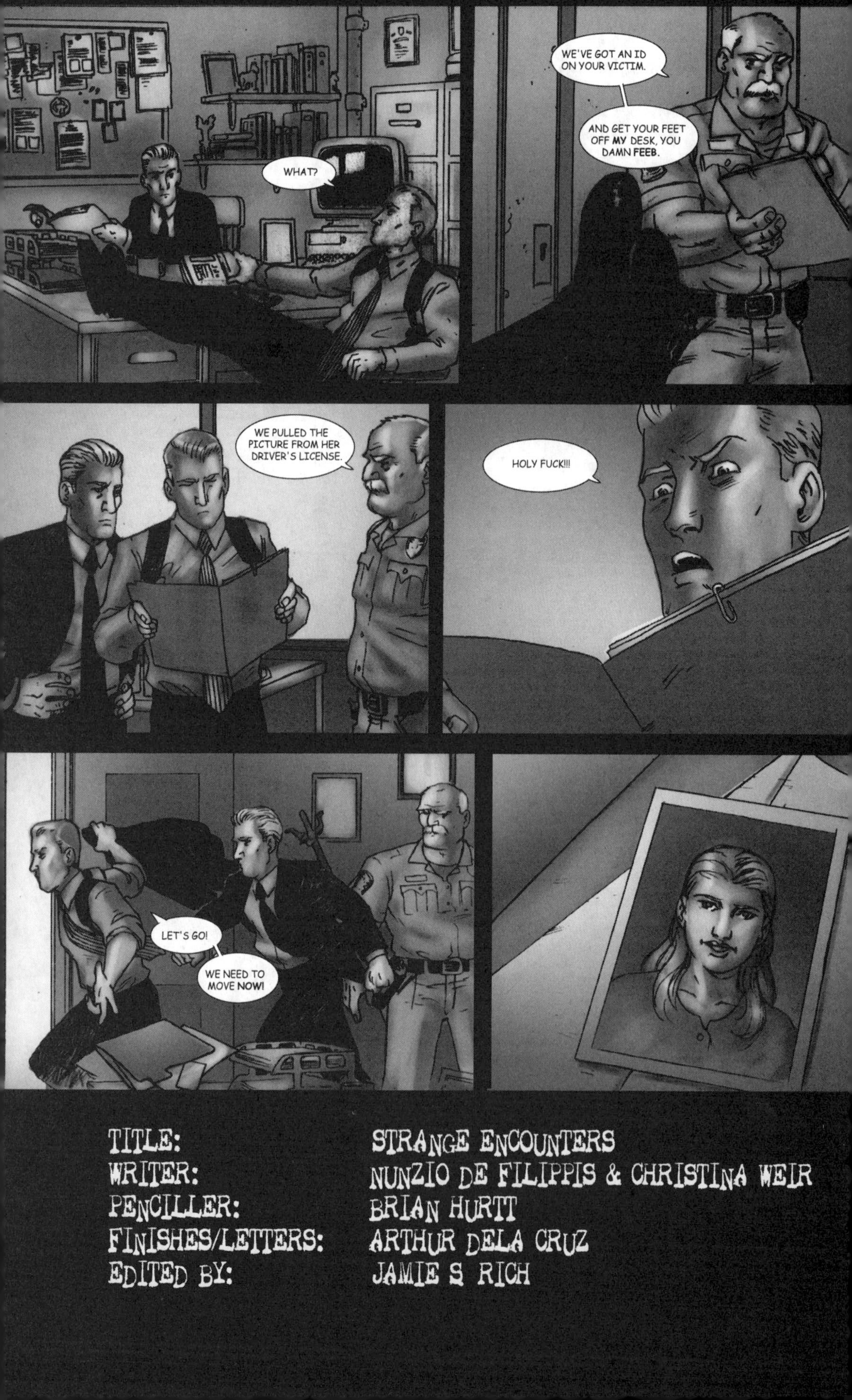
WHAT?
WE'VE GOT AN ID ON YOUR VICTIM.
AND GET YOUR FEET OFF MY DESK, YOU DAMN FEEB.
WE PULLED THE PICTURE FROM HER DRIVER'S LICENSE.
HOLY FUCK!!!
LET'S GO!
WE NEED TO MOVE NOW!

TITLE: STRANGE ENCOUNTERS
WRITER: NUNZIO DE FILIPPIS & CHRISTINA WEIR
PENCILLER: BRIAN HURTT
FINISHES/LETTERS: ARTHUR DELA CRUZ
EDITED BY: JAMIE S RICH

CHAPTER 4

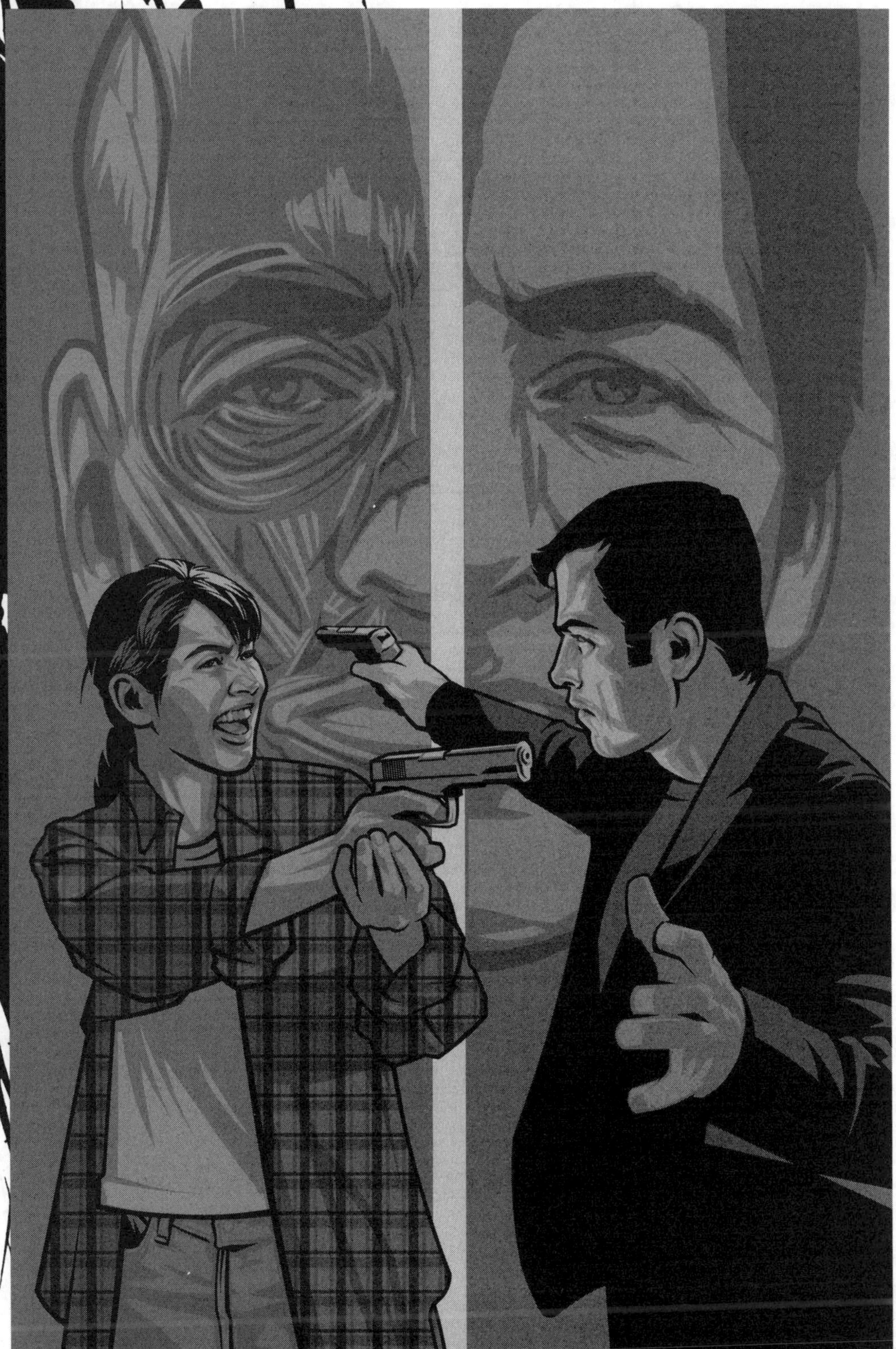
TALON · 02

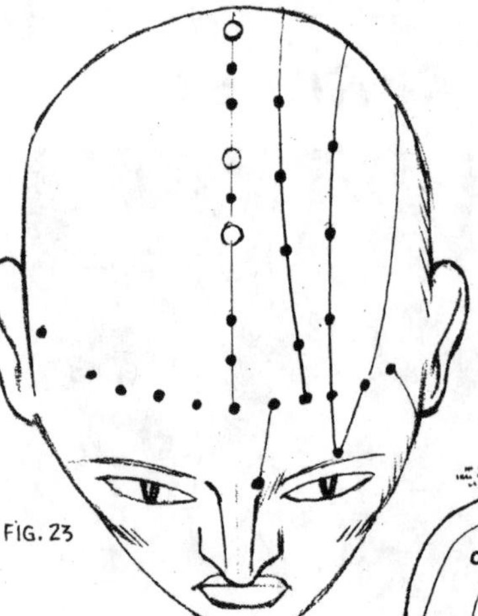

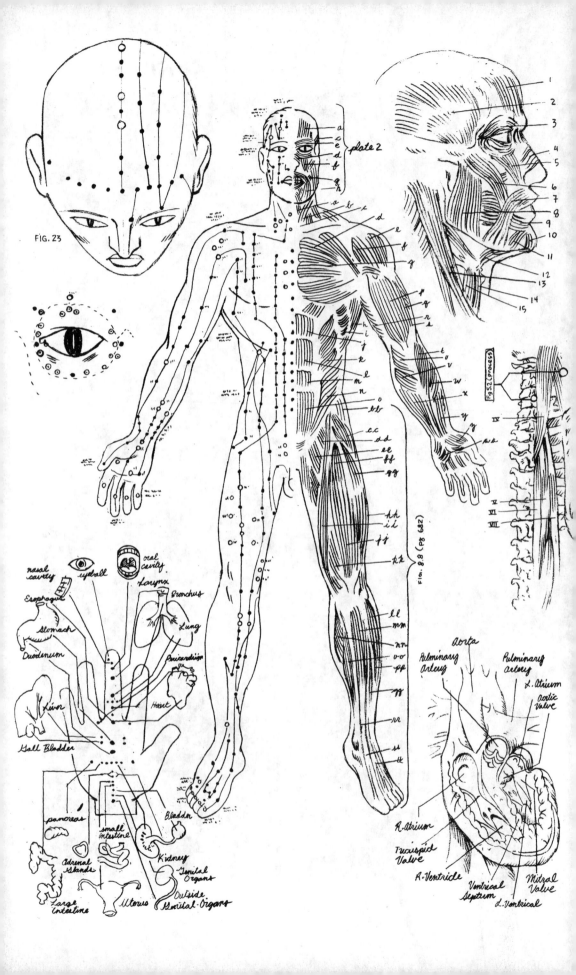

FIG. 23

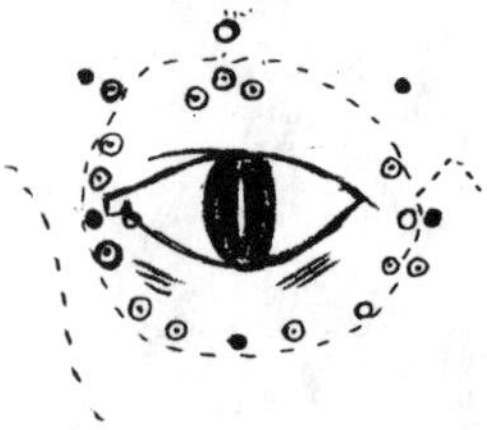

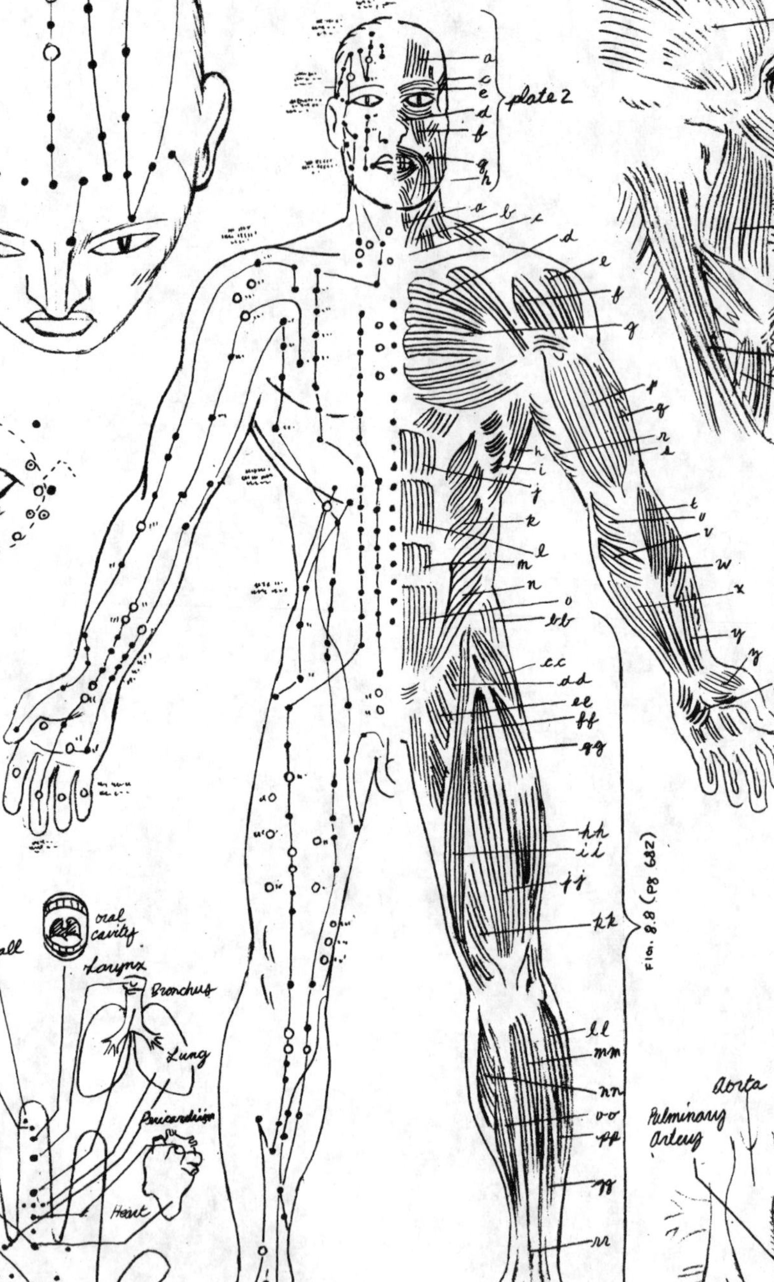
a
c
e
d
f
g
h
plate 2
a
b
c
d
e
f
g
p
q
r
s
h
i
j
k
l
m
n
o
bb
t
u
v
w
x
y
z
aa
cc
dd
ee
ff
gg
hh
ii
jj
kk
ll
mm
nn
oo
pp
qq
rr
ss
tt
Fig. 8.8 (pg 682)

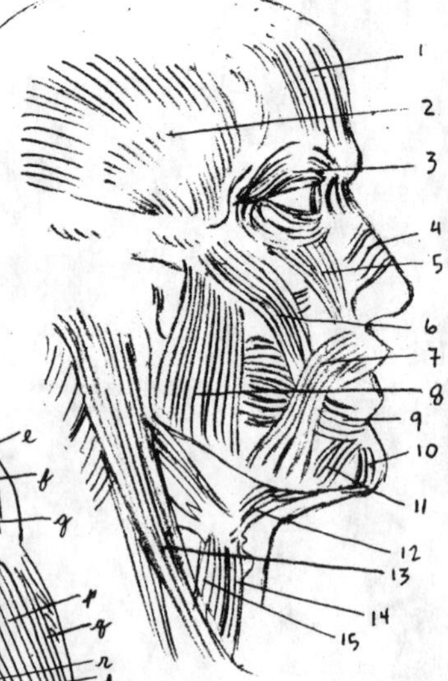
1
2
3
4
5
6
7
8
9
10
11
12
13
14
15

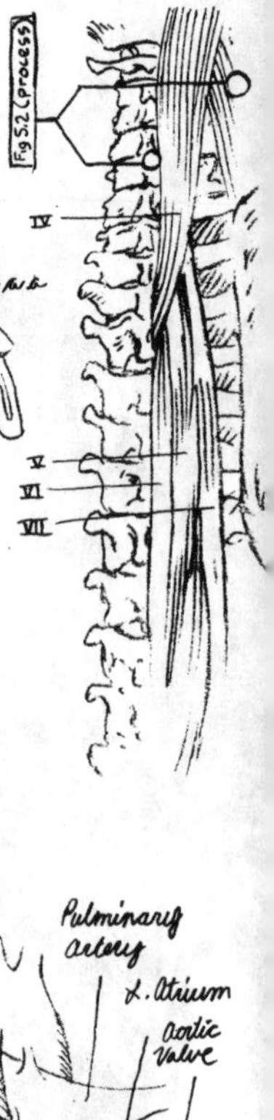
Fig 5.2 (process)
IV
V
VI
VII

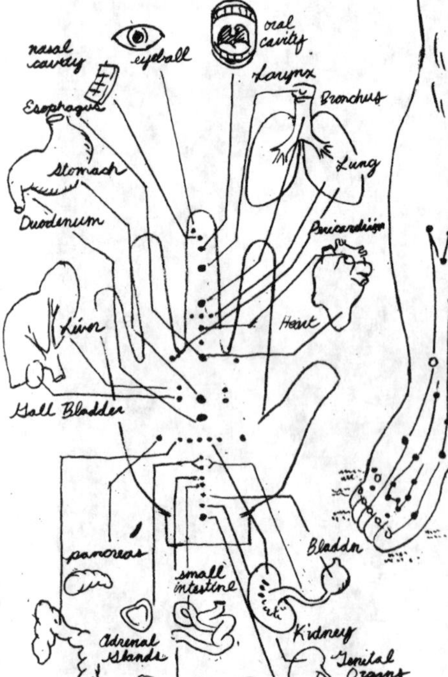
nasal cavity
eyeball
oral cavity
Larynx
Esophagus
Bronchus
Stomach
Lung
Duodenum
Pericardium
Heart
Liver
Gall Bladder
pancreas
small intestine
Bladder
Adrenal Glands
Kidney
Genital Organs
Large Intestine
Uterus
Outside Genital-Organs

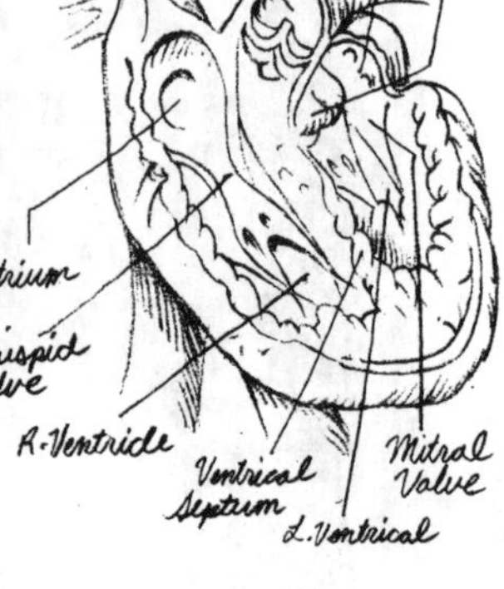
Aorta
Pulminary Artery
Pulminary artery
L. Atrium
Aortic Valve
R. Atrium
Tricuspid Valve
R. Ventricle
Ventrical Septum
L. Ventrical
Mitral Valve

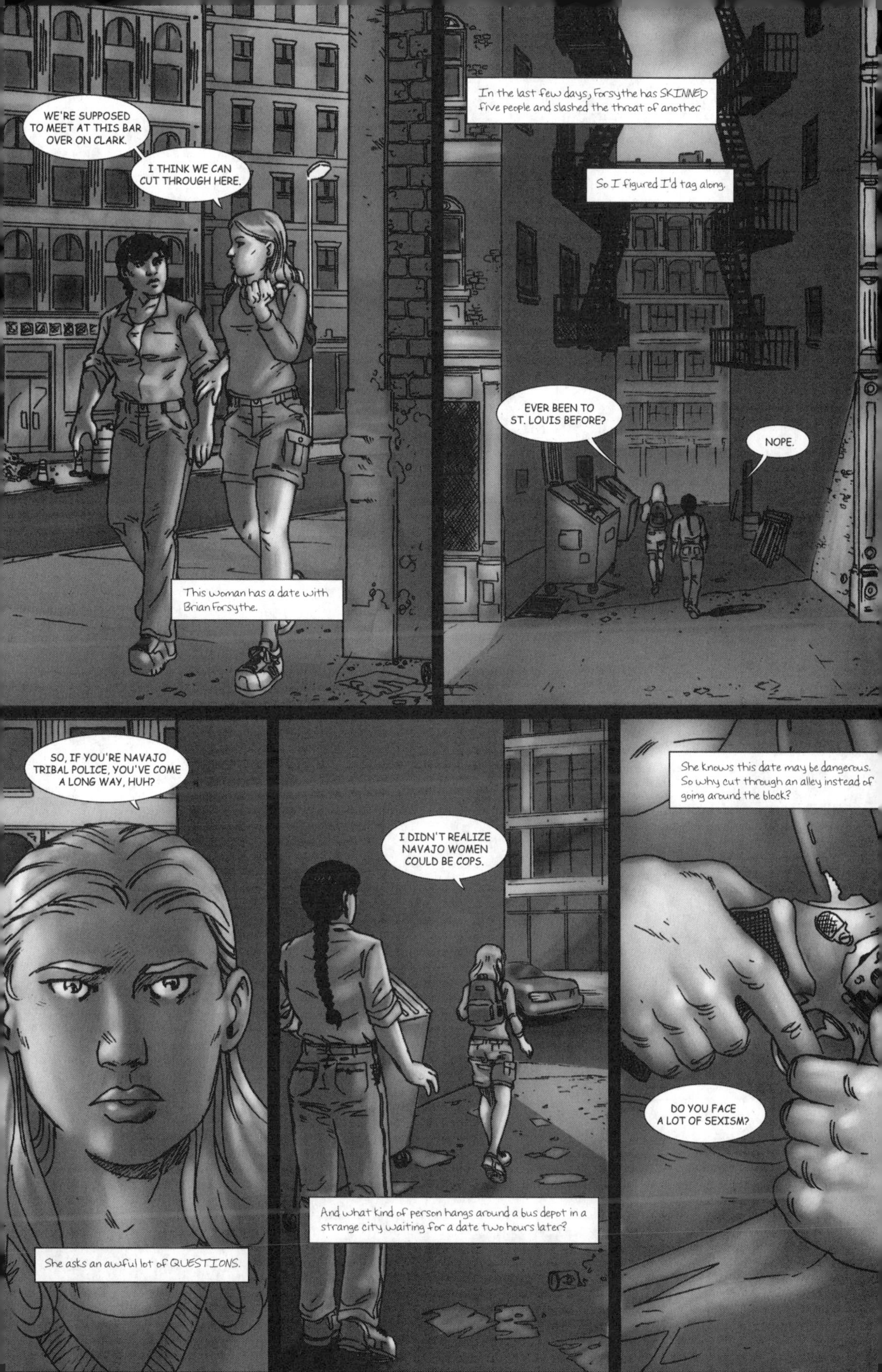
WE'RE SUPPOSED TO MEET AT THIS BAR OVER ON CLARK.
I THINK WE CAN CUT THROUGH HERE.
This woman has a date with Brian Forsythe.
In the last few days, Forsythe has SKINNED five people and slashed the throat of another.
So I figured I'd tag along.
EVER BEEN TO ST. LOUIS BEFORE?
NOPE.
SO, IF YOU'RE NAVAJO TRIBAL POLICE, YOU'VE COME A LONG WAY, HUH?
She asks an awful lot of QUESTIONS.
I DIDN'T REALIZE NAVAJO WOMEN COULD BE COPS.
And what kind of person hangs around a bus depot in a strange city waiting for a date two hours later?
She knows this date may be dangerous. So why cut through an alley instead of going around the block?
DO YOU FACE A LOT OF SEXISM?

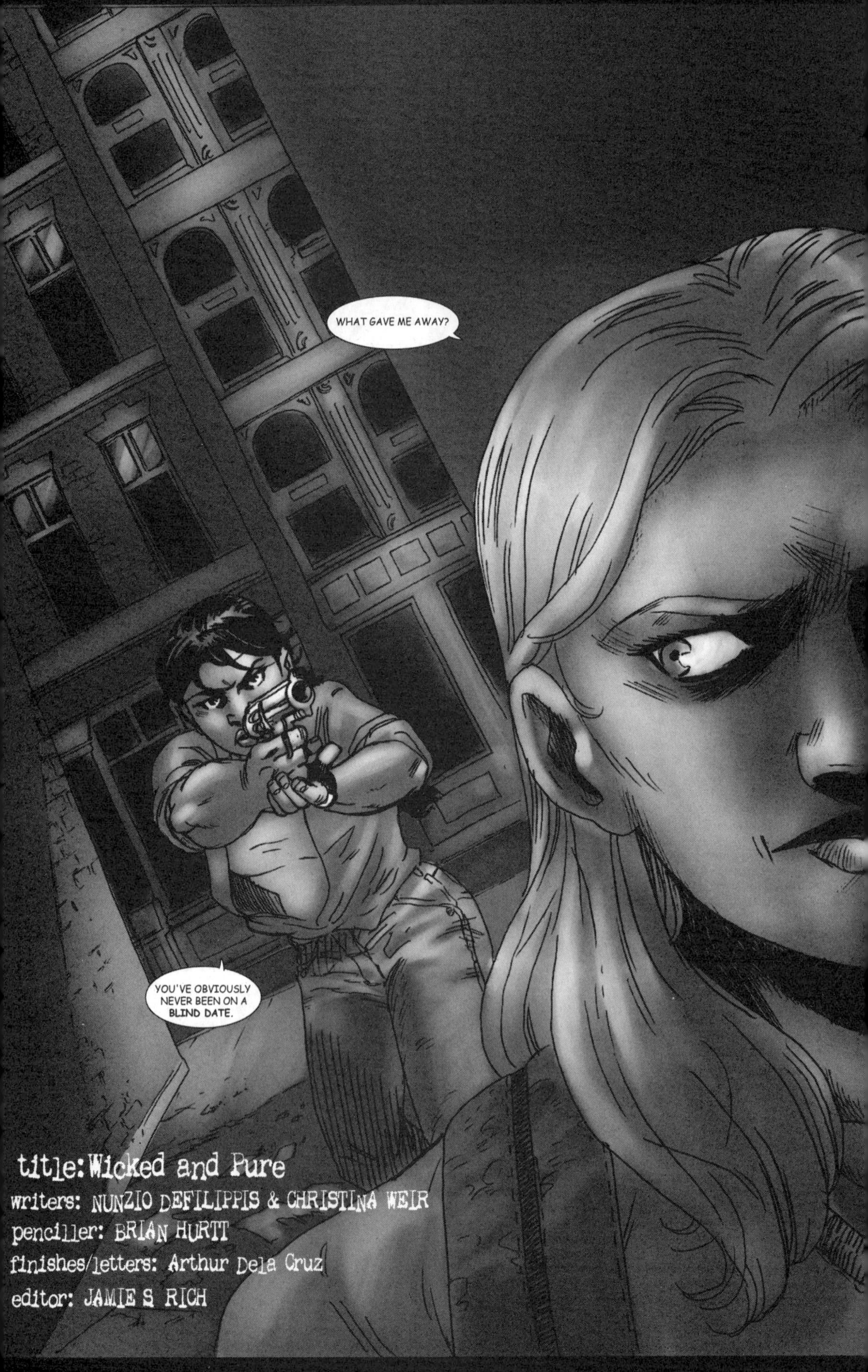
WHAT GAVE ME AWAY?
YOU'VE OBVIOUSLY NEVER BEEN ON A BLIND DATE.

title: Wicked and Pure
writers: NUNZIO DEFILIPPIS & CHRISTINA WEIR
penciller: BRIAN HURTT
finishes/letters: Arthur Dela Cruz
editor: JAMIE S. RICH

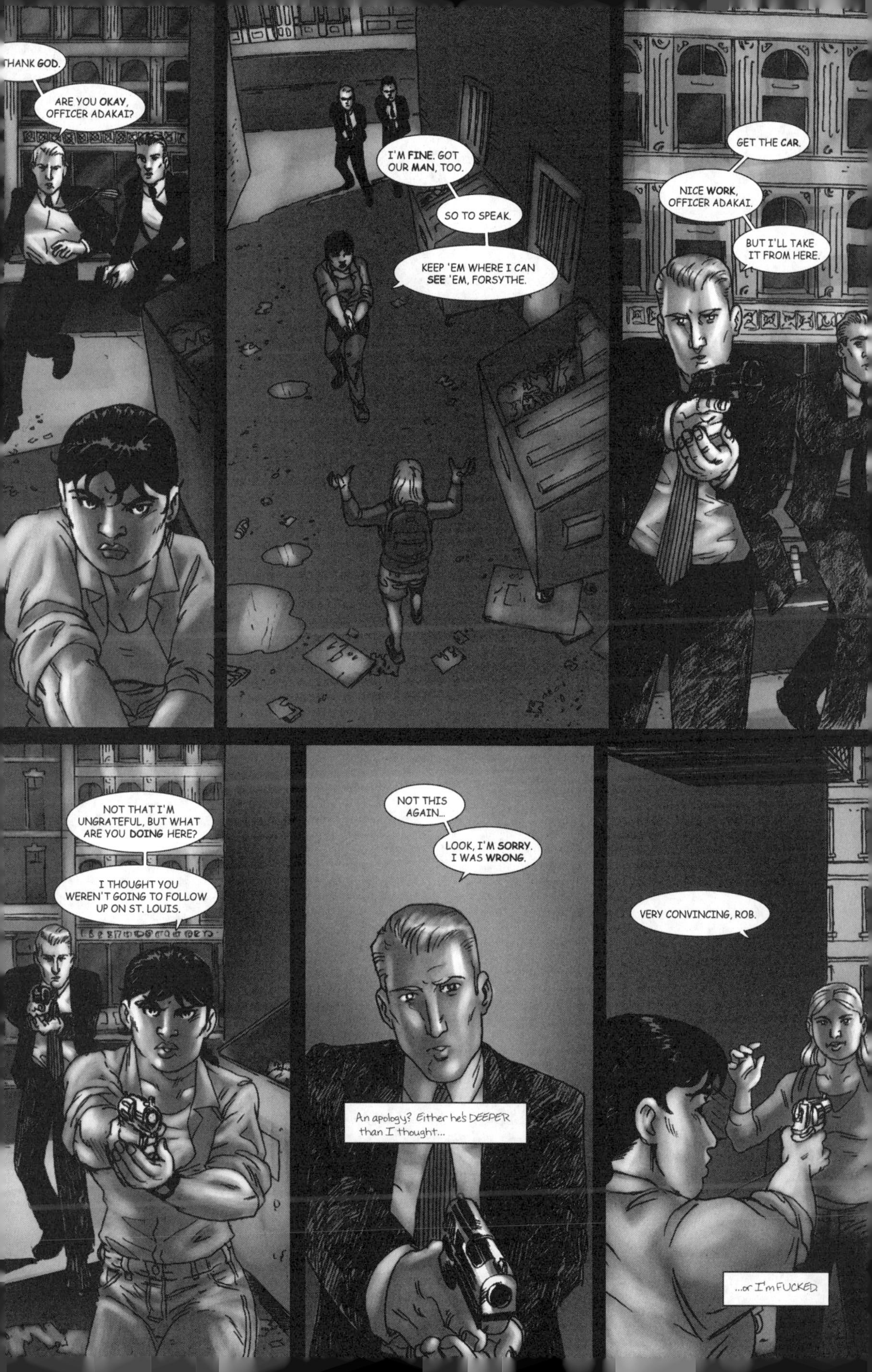
THANK GOD.
ARE YOU OKAY, OFFICER ADAKAI?
I'M FINE. GOT OUR MAN, TOO.
SO TO SPEAK.
KEEP 'EM WHERE I CAN SEE 'EM, FORSYTHE.
GET THE CAR.
NICE WORK, OFFICER ADAKAI.
BUT I'LL TAKE IT FROM HERE.
NOT THAT I'M UNGRATEFUL, BUT WHAT ARE YOU DOING HERE?
I THOUGHT YOU WEREN'T GOING TO FOLLOW UP ON ST. LOUIS.
NOT THIS AGAIN...
LOOK, I'M SORRY. I WAS WRONG.
An apology? Either he's DEEPER than I thought...
VERY CONVINCING, ROB.
...or I'm FUCKED.

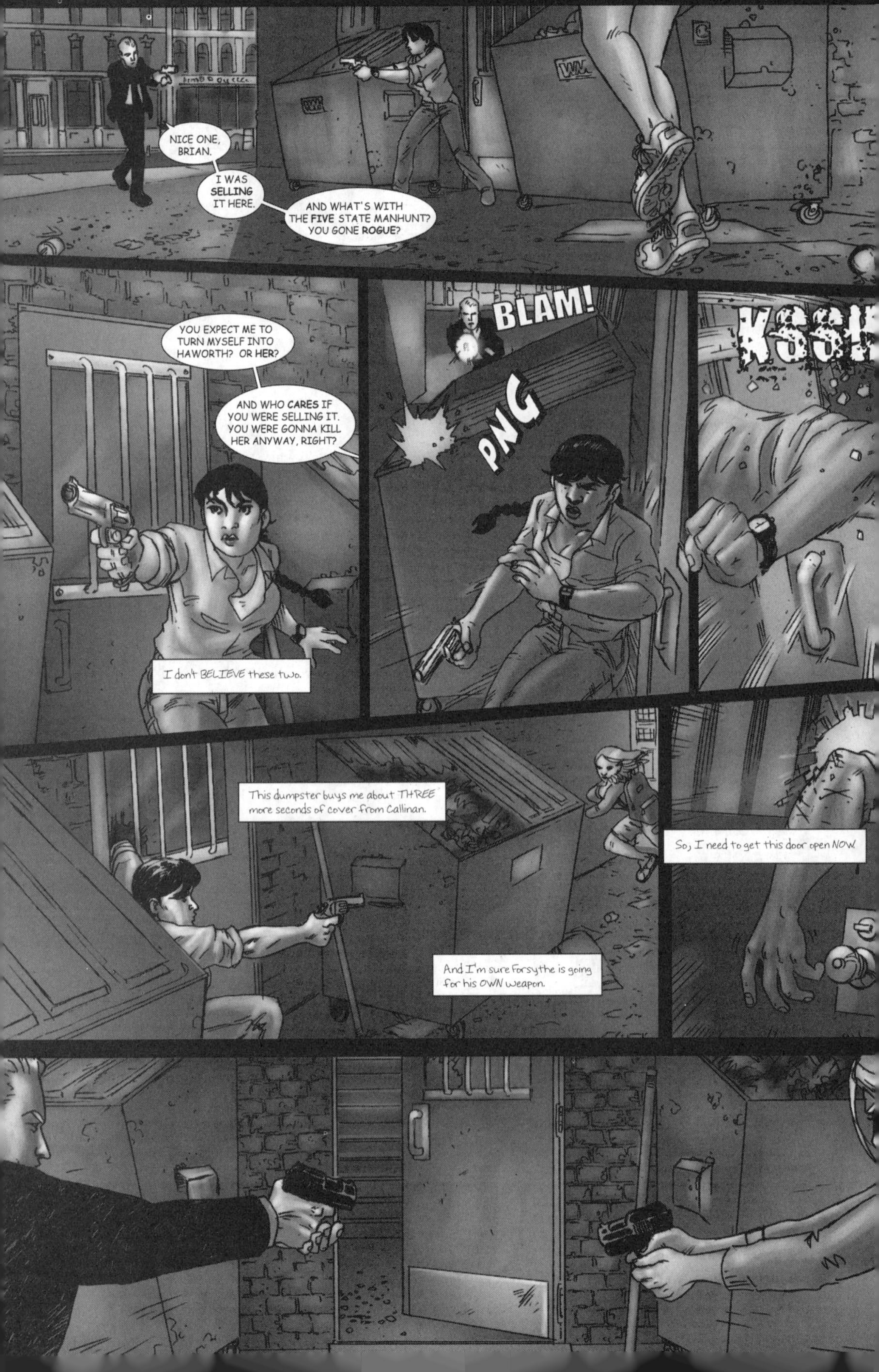
NICE ONE, BRIAN.
I WAS SELLING IT HERE.
AND WHAT'S WITH THE FIVE STATE MANHUNT? YOU GONE ROGUE?
YOU EXPECT ME TO TURN MYSELF INTO HAWORTH? OR HER?
AND WHO CARES IF YOU WERE SELLING IT. YOU WERE GONNA KILL HER ANYWAY, RIGHT?
I don't BELIEVE these two.
BLAM!
PNG
KSSH
This dumpster buys me about THREE more seconds of cover from Callinan.
And I'm sure Forsythe is going for his OWN weapon.
So, I need to get this door open NOW.

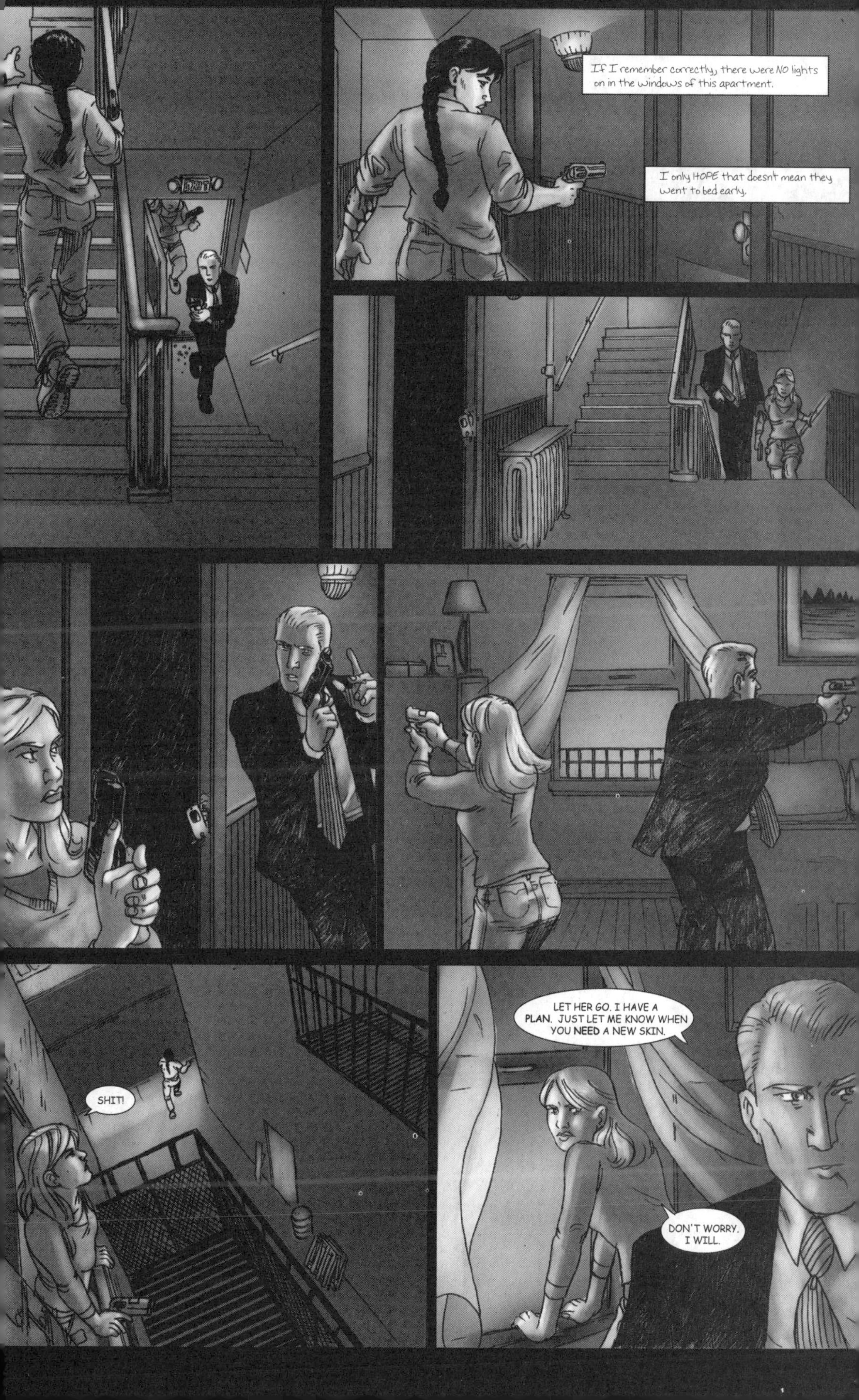

If I remember correctly, there were NO lights on in the windows of this apartment.
I only HOPE that doesn't mean they went to bed early.
SHIT!
LET HER GO. I HAVE A PLAN. JUST LET ME KNOW WHEN YOU NEED A NEW SKIN.
DON'T WORRY. I WILL.

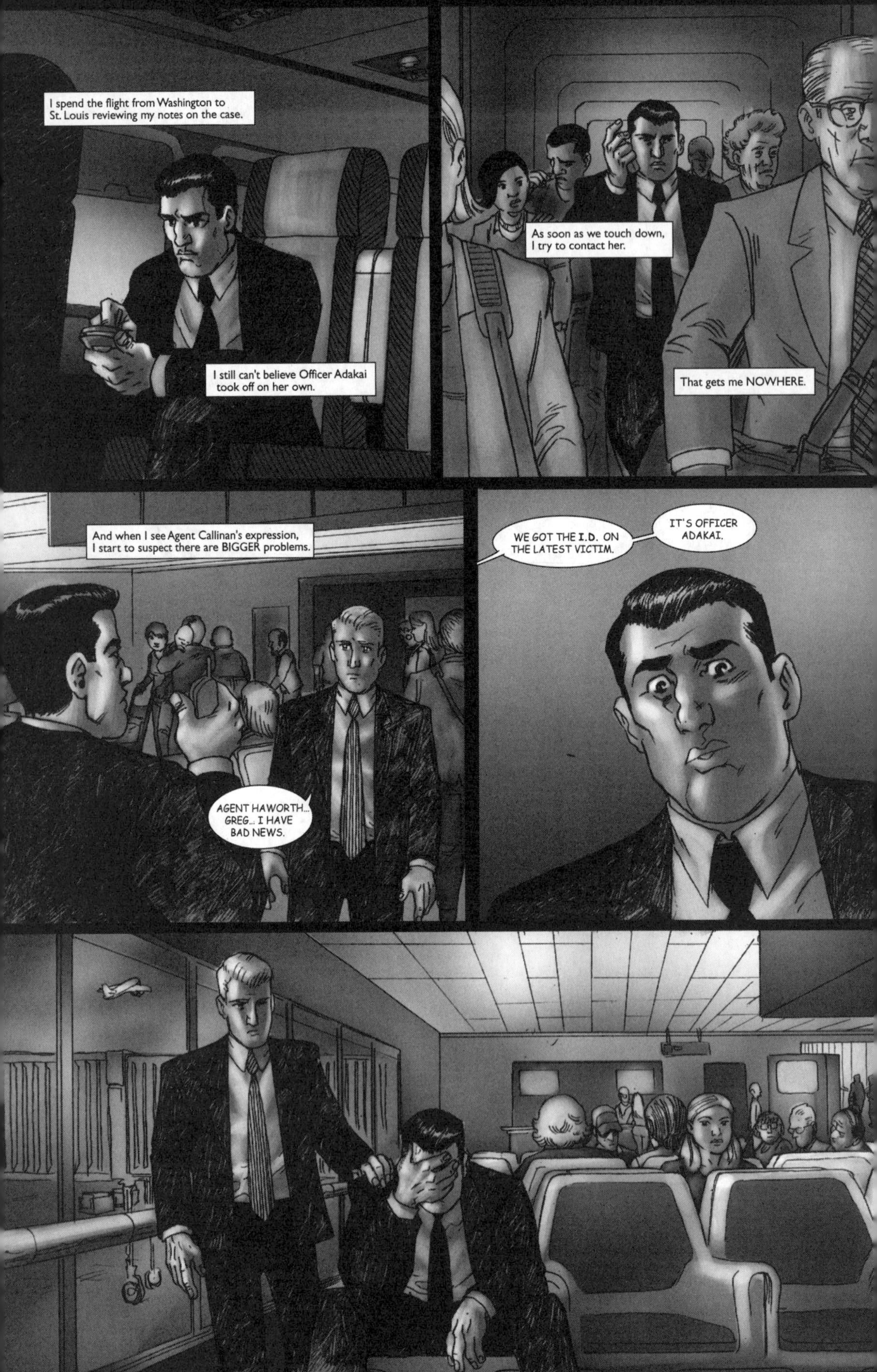
I spend the flight from Washington to St. Louis reviewing my notes on the case.
I still can't believe Officer Adakai took off on her own.
As soon as we touch down, I try to contact her.
That gets me NOWHERE.
And when I see Agent Callinan's expression, I start to suspect there are BIGGER problems.
AGENT HAWORTH... GREG... I HAVE BAD NEWS.
WE GOT THE I.D. ON THE LATEST VICTIM.
IT'S OFFICER ADAKAI.

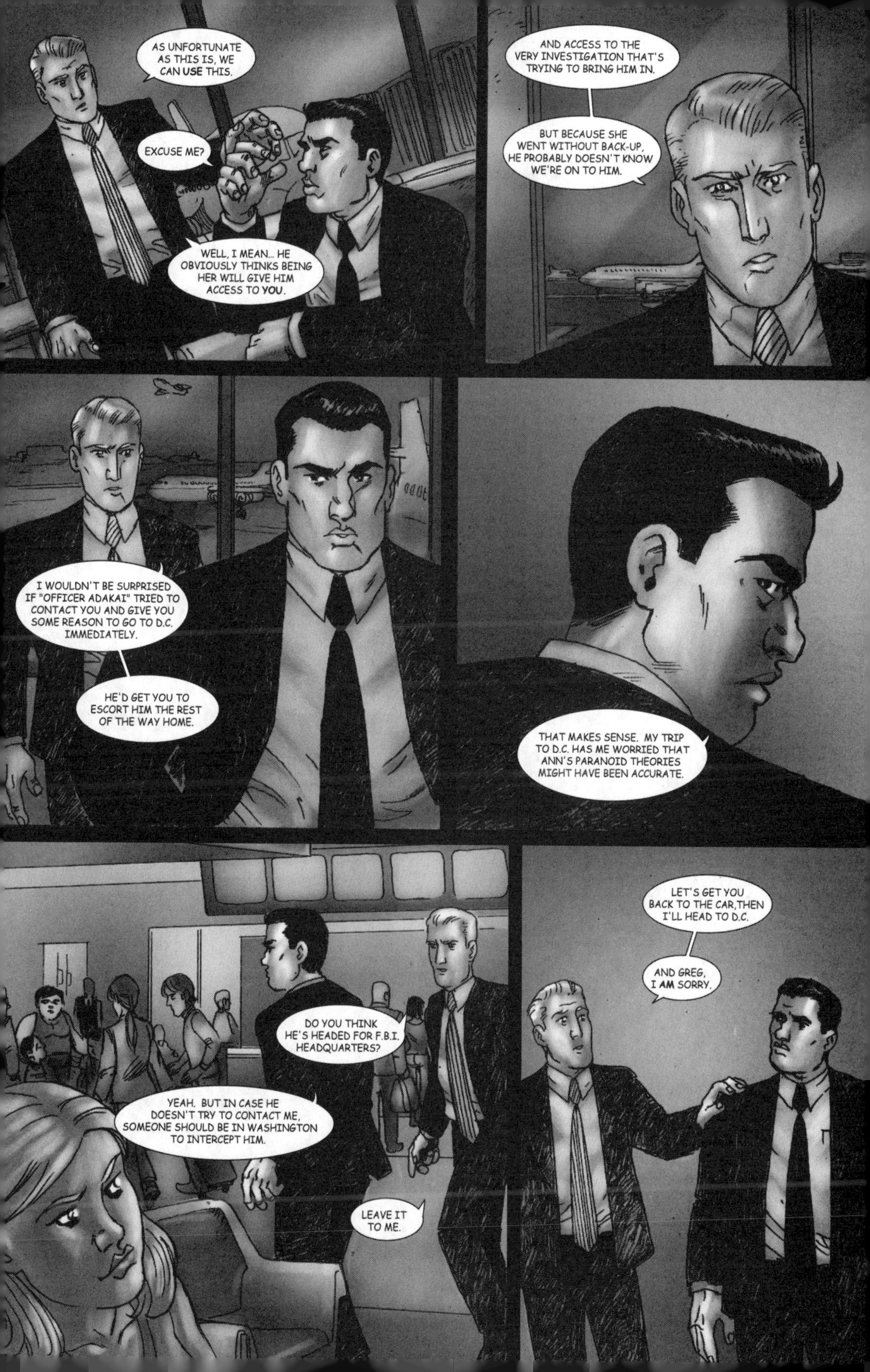
AS UNFORTUNATE AS THIS IS, WE CAN USE THIS.
EXCUSE ME?
WELL, I MEAN... HE OBVIOUSLY THINKS BEING HER WILL GIVE HIM ACCESS TO YOU.
AND ACCESS TO THE VERY INVESTIGATION THAT'S TRYING TO BRING HIM IN.
BUT BECAUSE SHE WENT WITHOUT BACK-UP, HE PROBABLY DOESN'T KNOW WE'RE ON TO HIM.
I WOULDN'T BE SURPRISED IF "OFFICER ADAKAI" TRIED TO CONTACT YOU AND GIVE YOU SOME REASON TO GO TO D.C. IMMEDIATELY.
HE'D GET YOU TO ESCORT HIM THE REST OF THE WAY HOME.
THAT MAKES SENSE. MY TRIP TO D.C. HAS ME WORRIED THAT ANN'S PARANOID THEORIES MIGHT HAVE BEEN ACCURATE.
DO YOU THINK HE'S HEADED FOR F.B.I. HEADQUARTERS?
YEAH. BUT IN CASE HE DOESN'T TRY TO CONTACT ME, SOMEONE SHOULD BE IN WASHINGTON TO INTERCEPT HIM.
LEAVE IT TO ME.
LET'S GET YOU BACK TO THE CAR,THEN I'LL HEAD TO D.C.
AND GREG, I AM SORRY.

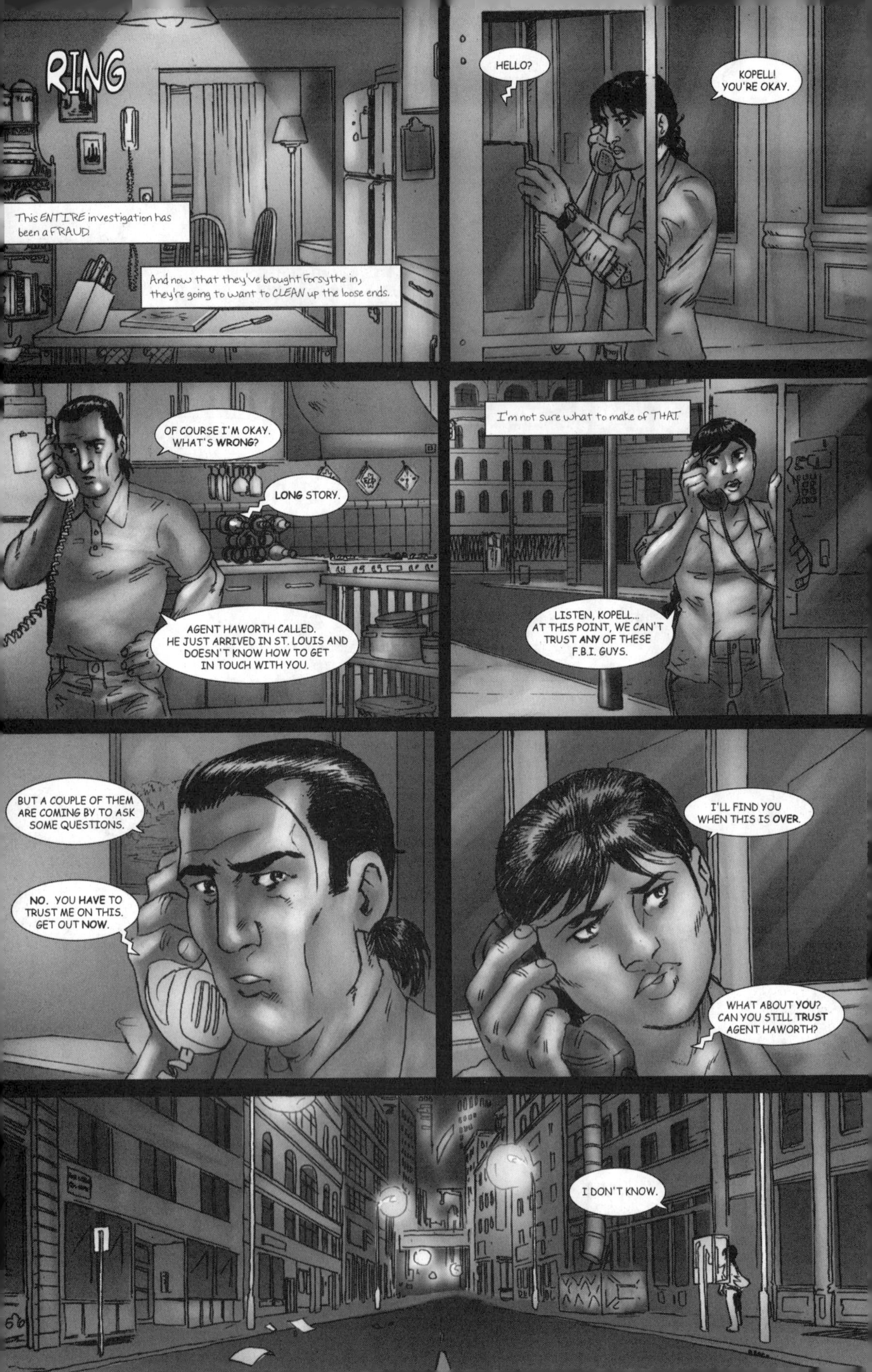
RING
This ENTIRE investigation has been a FRAUD.
And now that they've brought Forsythe in, they're going to want to CLEAN up the loose ends.
HELLO?
KOPELL! YOU'RE OKAY.
OF COURSE I'M OKAY. WHAT'S WRONG?
LONG STORY.
AGENT HAWORTH CALLED. HE JUST ARRIVED IN ST. LOUIS AND DOESN'T KNOW HOW TO GET IN TOUCH WITH YOU.
I'm not sure what to make of THAT.
LISTEN, KOPELL... AT THIS POINT, WE CAN'T TRUST ANY OF THESE F.B.I. GUYS.
BUT A COUPLE OF THEM ARE COMING BY TO ASK SOME QUESTIONS.
NO. YOU HAVE TO TRUST ME ON THIS. GET OUT NOW.
I'LL FIND YOU WHEN THIS IS OVER.
WHAT ABOUT YOU? CAN YOU STILL TRUST AGENT HAWORTH?
I DON'T KNOW.

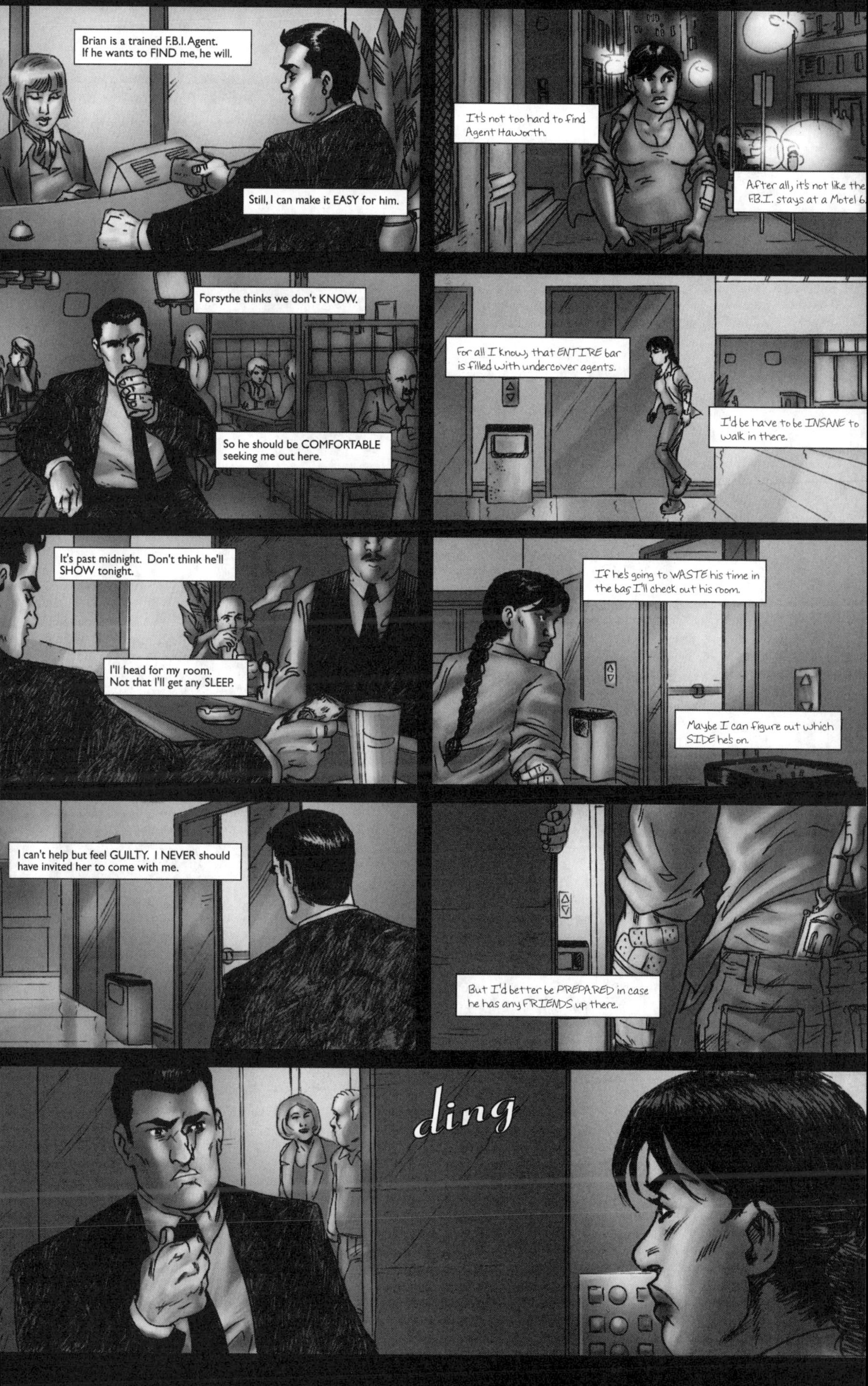
Brian is a trained F.B.I. Agent. If he wants to FIND me, he will.
Still, I can make it EASY for him.
It's not too hard to find Agent Haworth.
After all, it's not like the F.B.I. stays at a Motel 6.
Forsythe thinks we don't KNOW.
So he should be COMFORTABLE seeking me out here.
For all I know, that ENTIRE bar is filled with undercover agents.
I'd be have to be INSANE to walk in there.
It's past midnight. Don't think he'll SHOW tonight.
I'll head for my room. Not that I'll get any SLEEP.
If he's going to WASTE his time in the bas I'll check out his room.
Maybe I can figure out which SIDE he's on.
I can't help but feel GUILTY. I NEVER should have invited her to come with me.
But I'd better be PREPARED in case he has any FRIENDS up there.
ding

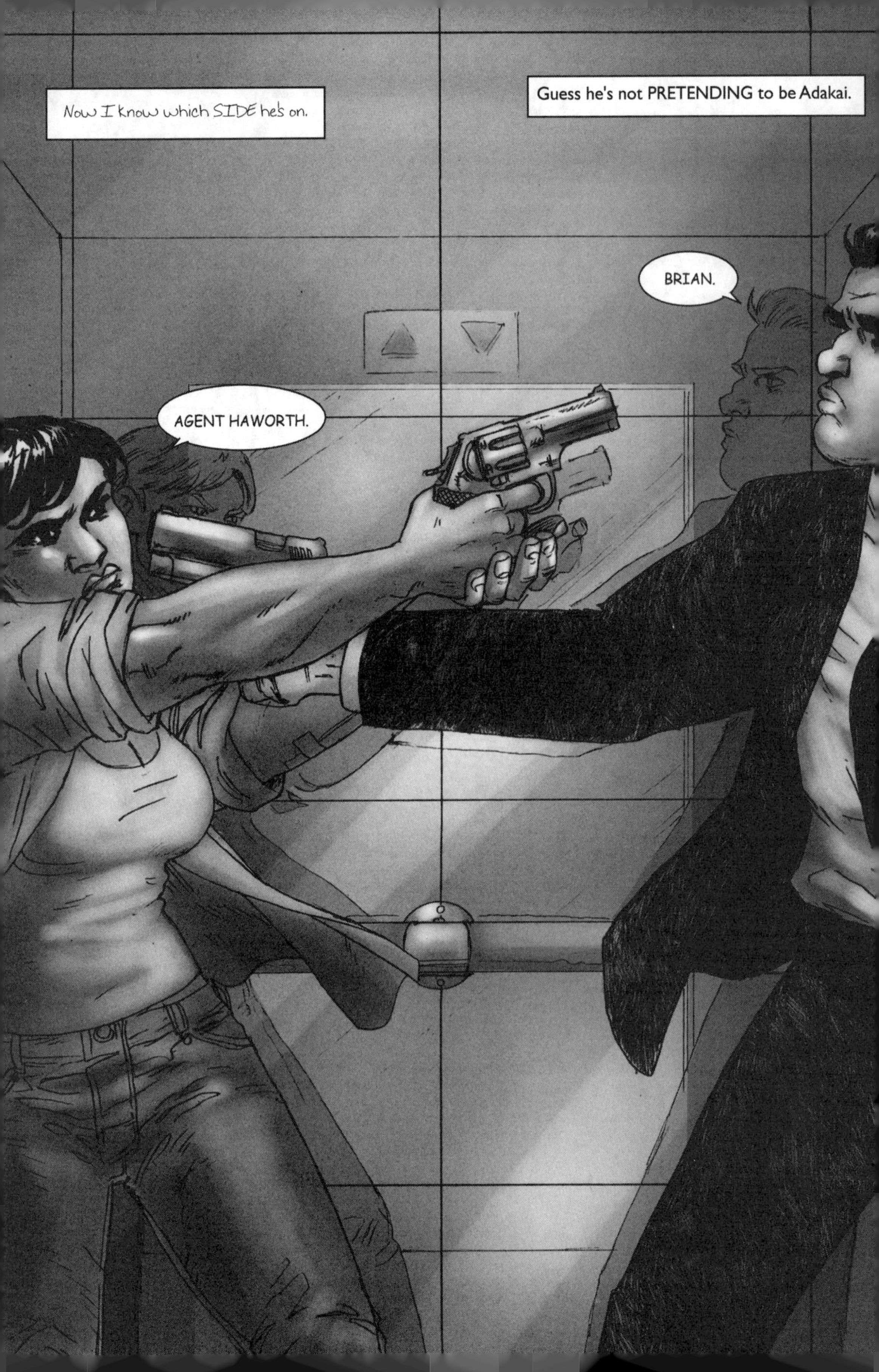
Now I know which SIDE he's on.
Guess he's not PRETENDING to be Adakai.
BRIAN.
AGENT HAWORTH.

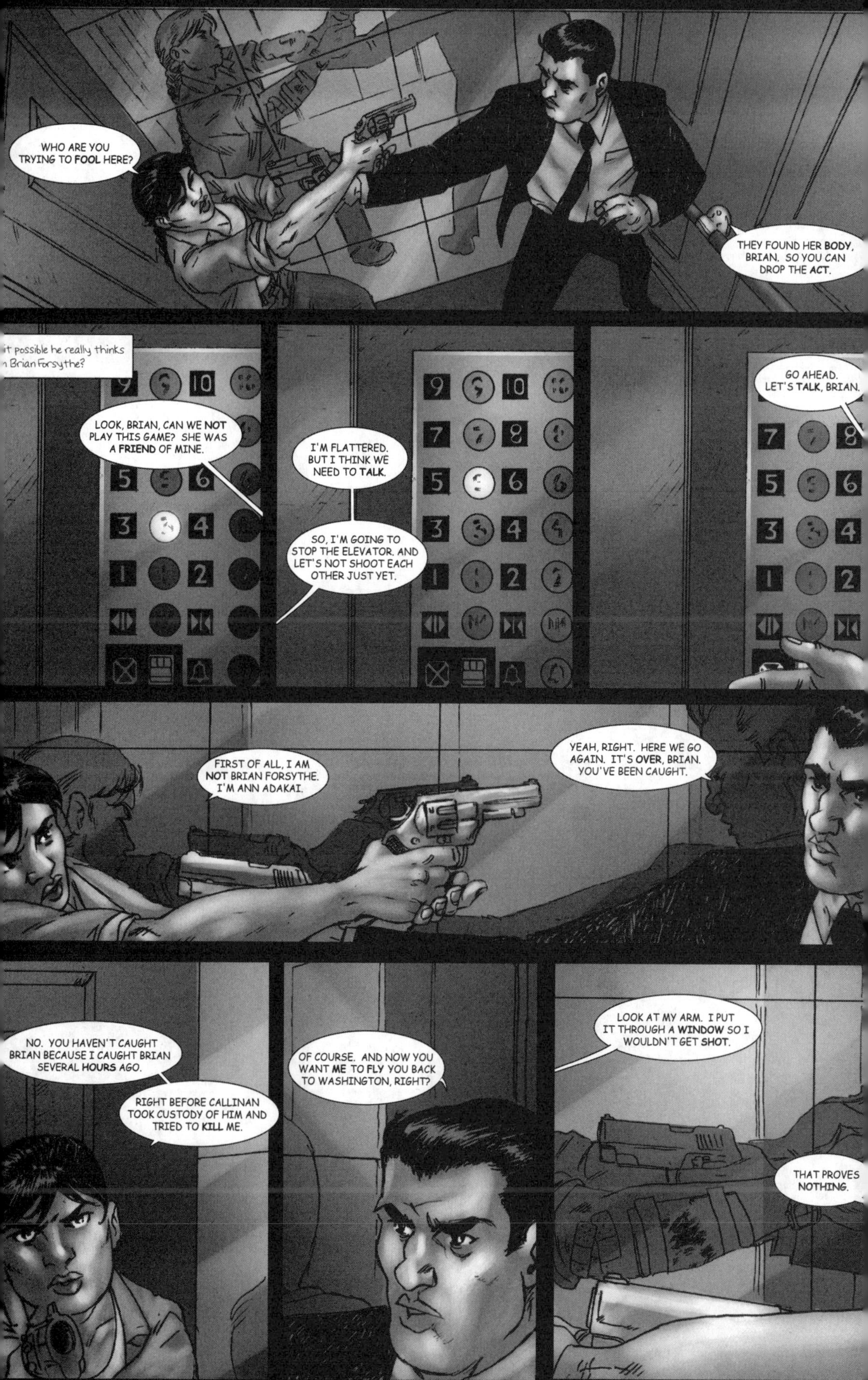

WHO ARE YOU TRYING TO FOOL HERE?
THEY FOUND HER BODY, BRIAN. SO YOU CAN DROP THE ACT.
it possible he really thinks n Brian Forsythe?
LOOK, BRIAN, CAN WE NOT PLAY THIS GAME? SHE WAS A FRIEND OF MINE.
I'M FLATTERED. BUT I THINK WE NEED TO TALK.
SO, I'M GOING TO STOP THE ELEVATOR. AND LET'S NOT SHOOT EACH OTHER JUST YET.
GO AHEAD. LET'S TALK, BRIAN.
FIRST OF ALL, I AM NOT BRIAN FORSYTHE. I'M ANN ADAKAI.
YEAH, RIGHT. HERE WE GO AGAIN. IT'S OVER, BRIAN. YOU'VE BEEN CAUGHT.
NO. YOU HAVEN'T CAUGHT BRIAN BECAUSE I CAUGHT BRIAN SEVERAL HOURS AGO.
RIGHT BEFORE CALLINAN TOOK CUSTODY OF HIM AND TRIED TO KILL ME.
OF COURSE. AND NOW YOU WANT ME TO FLY YOU BACK TO WASHINGTON, RIGHT?
LOOK AT MY ARM. I PUT IT THROUGH A WINDOW SO I WOULDN'T GET SHOT.
THAT PROVES NOTHING.

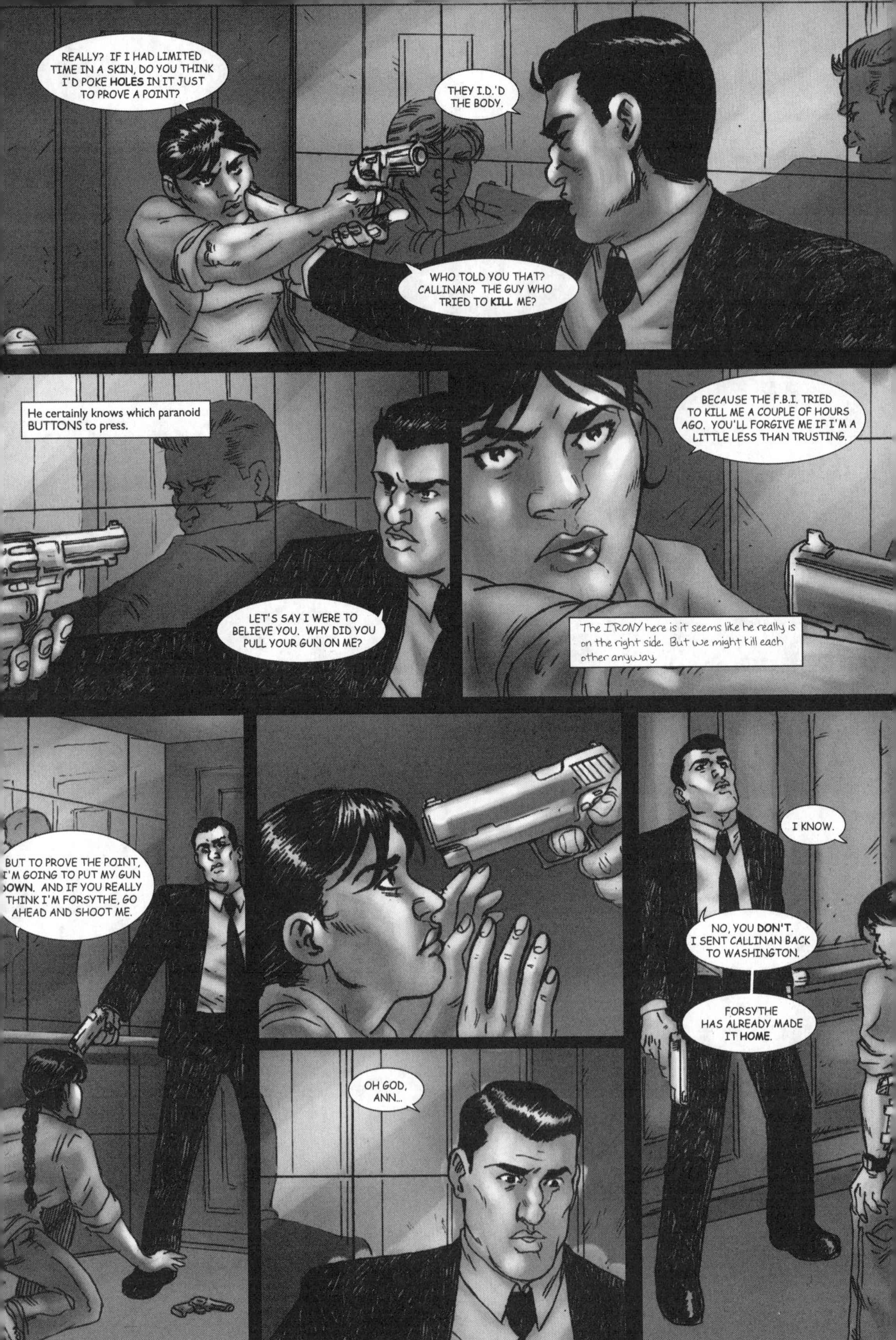

REALLY? IF I HAD LIMITED TIME IN A SKIN, DO YOU THINK I'D POKE HOLES IN IT JUST TO PROVE A POINT?
THEY I.D.'D THE BODY.
WHO TOLD YOU THAT? CALLINAN? THE GUY WHO TRIED TO KILL ME?
He certainly knows which paranoid BUTTONS to press.
LET'S SAY I WERE TO BELIEVE YOU. WHY DID YOU PULL YOUR GUN ON ME?
BECAUSE THE F.B.I. TRIED TO KILL ME A COUPLE OF HOURS AGO. YOU'LL FORGIVE ME IF I'M A LITTLE LESS THAN TRUSTING.
The IRONY here is it seems like he really is on the right side. But we might kill each other anyway.
BUT TO PROVE THE POINT, I'M GOING TO PUT MY GUN DOWN. AND IF YOU REALLY THINK I'M FORSYTHE, GO AHEAD AND SHOOT ME.
OH GOD, ANN...
I KNOW.
NO, YOU DON'T. I SENT CALLINAN BACK TO WASHINGTON.
FORSYTHE HAS ALREADY MADE IT HOME.

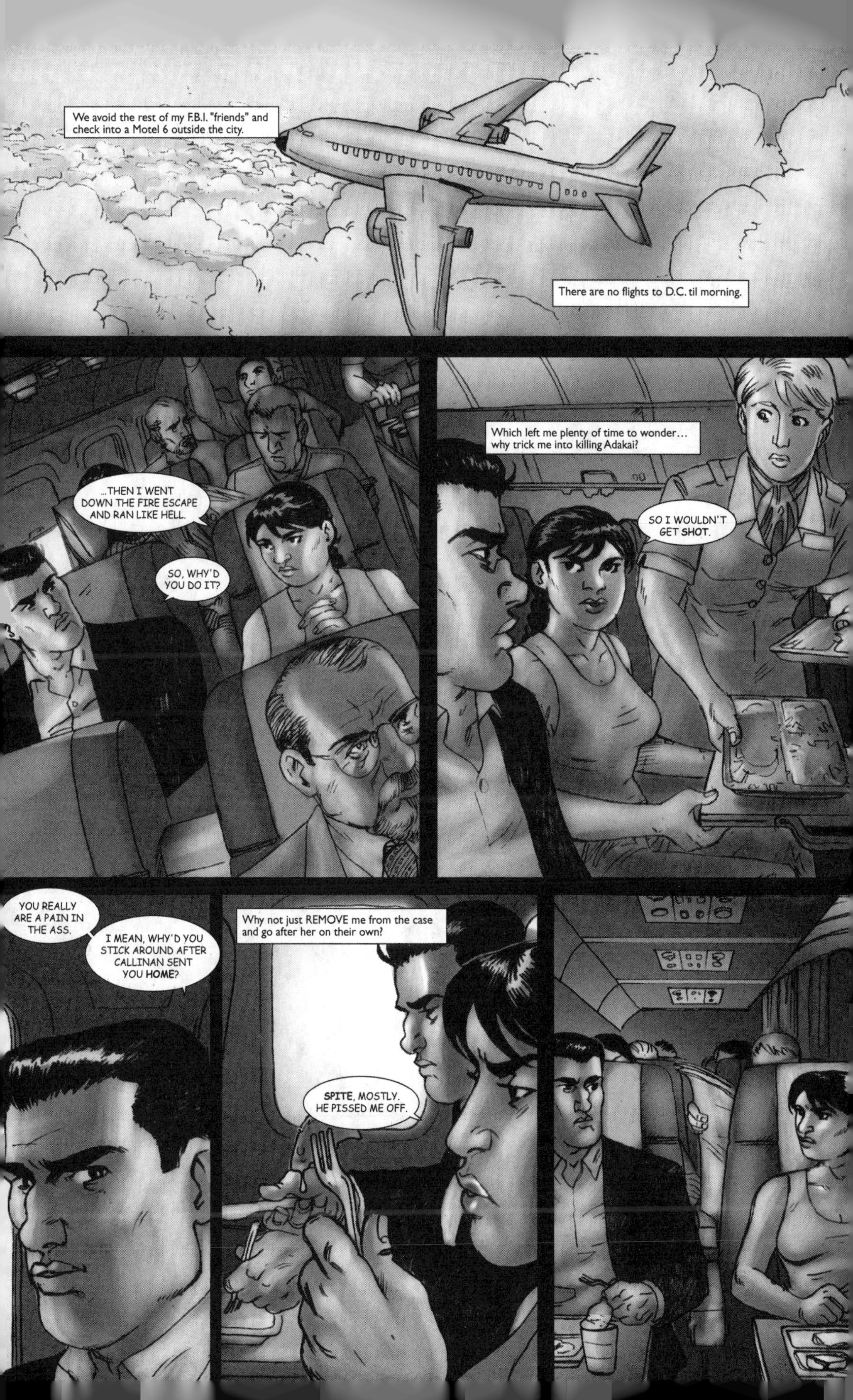
We avoid the rest of my F.B.I. "friends" and check into a Motel 6 outside the city.
There are no flights to D.C. til morning.
...THEN I WENT DOWN THE FIRE ESCAPE AND RAN LIKE HELL.
SO, WHY'D YOU DO IT?
Which left me plenty of time to wonder… why trick me into killing Adakai?
SO I WOULDN'T GET **SHOT**.
YOU REALLY ARE A PAIN IN THE ASS.
I MEAN, WHY'D YOU STICK AROUND AFTER CALLINAN SENT YOU **HOME**?
Why not just REMOVE me from the case and go after her on their own?
SPITE, MOSTLY. HE PISSED ME OFF.

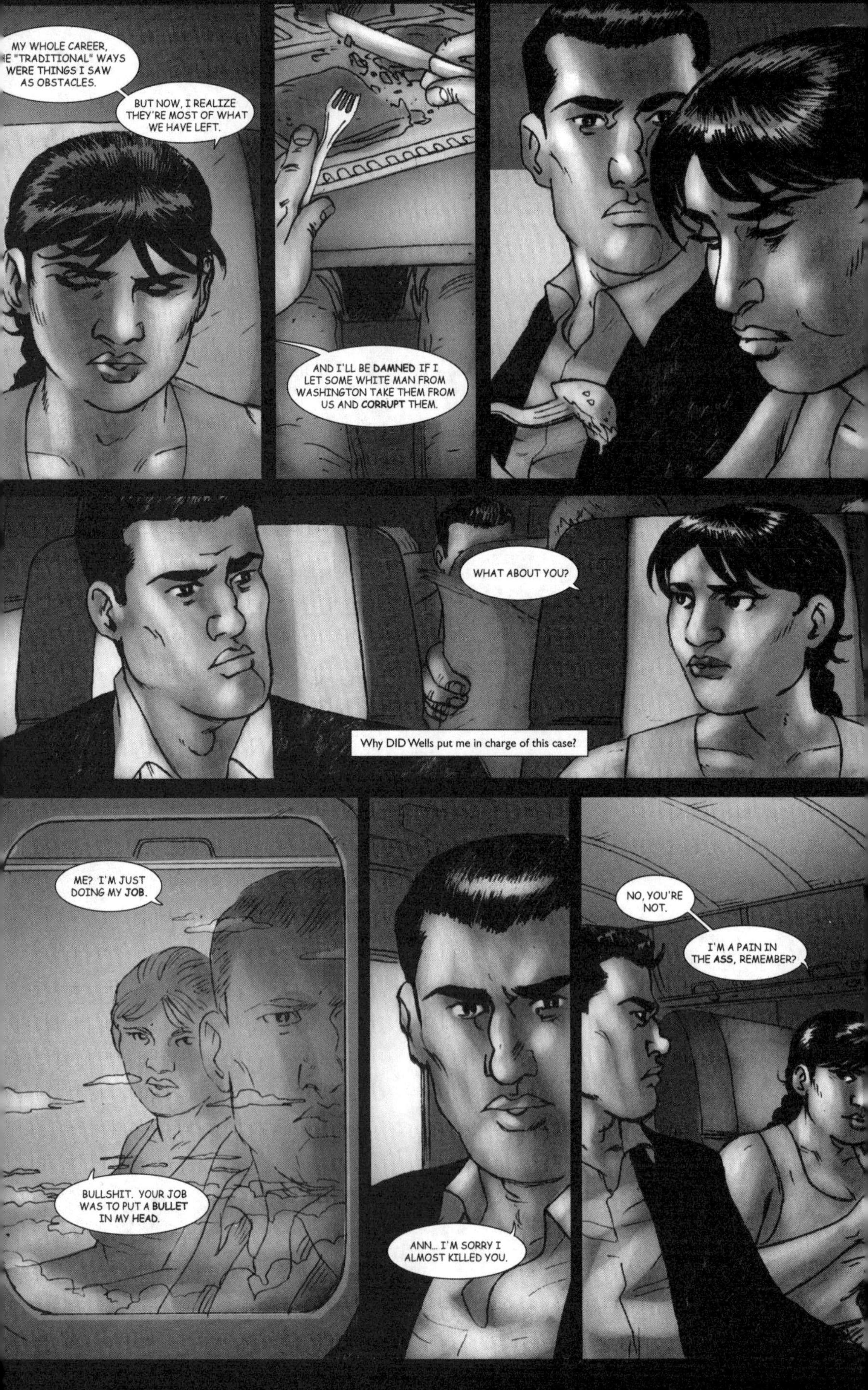
MY WHOLE CAREER, THE "TRADITIONAL" WAYS WERE THINGS I SAW AS OBSTACLES.
BUT NOW, I REALIZE THEY'RE MOST OF WHAT WE HAVE LEFT.
AND I'LL BE DAMNED IF I LET SOME WHITE MAN FROM WASHINGTON TAKE THEM FROM US AND CORRUPT THEM.
WHAT ABOUT YOU?
Why DID Wells put me in charge of this case?
ME? I'M JUST DOING MY JOB.
BULLSHIT. YOUR JOB WAS TO PUT A BULLET IN MY HEAD.
ANN... I'M SORRY I ALMOST KILLED YOU.
NO, YOU'RE NOT.
I'M A PAIN IN THE ASS, REMEMBER?

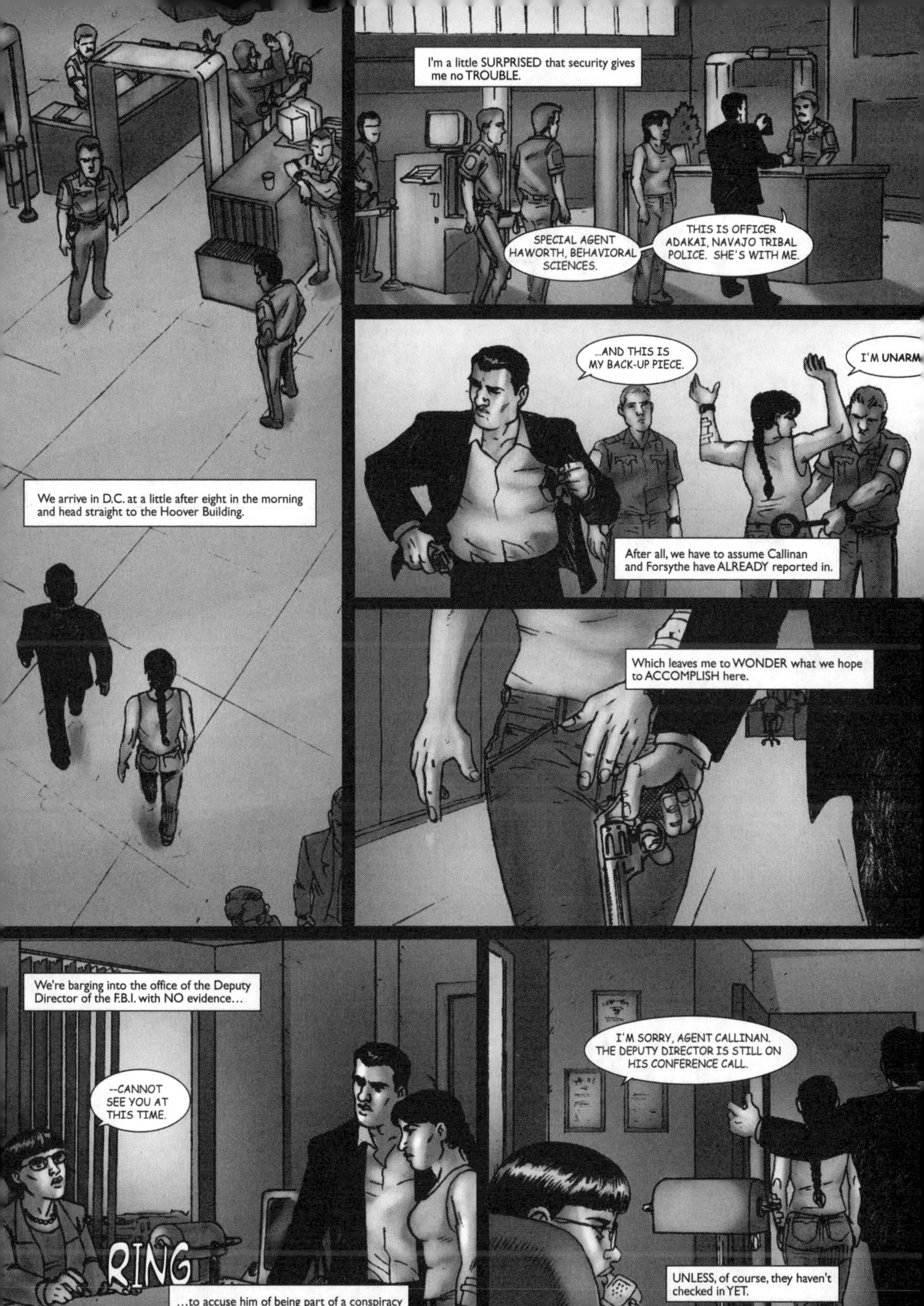
We arrive in D.C. at a little after eight in the morning and head straight to the Hoover Building.
I'm a little SURPRISED that security gives me no TROUBLE.
SPECIAL AGENT HAWORTH, BEHAVIORAL SCIENCES.
THIS IS OFFICER ADAKAI, NAVAJO TRIBAL POLICE. SHE'S WITH ME.
...AND THIS IS MY BACK-UP PIECE.
I'M UNARM
After all, we have to assume Callinan and Forsythe have ALREADY reported in.
Which leaves me to WONDER what we hope to ACCOMPLISH here.
We're barging into the office of the Deputy Director of the F.B.I. with NO evidence…
--CANNOT SEE YOU AT THIS TIME.
RING
…to accuse him of being part of a conspiracy which has already CLEANED itself up.
I'M SORRY, AGENT CALLINAN. THE DEPUTY DIRECTOR IS STILL ON HIS CONFERENCE CALL.
UNLESS, of course, they haven't checked in YET.

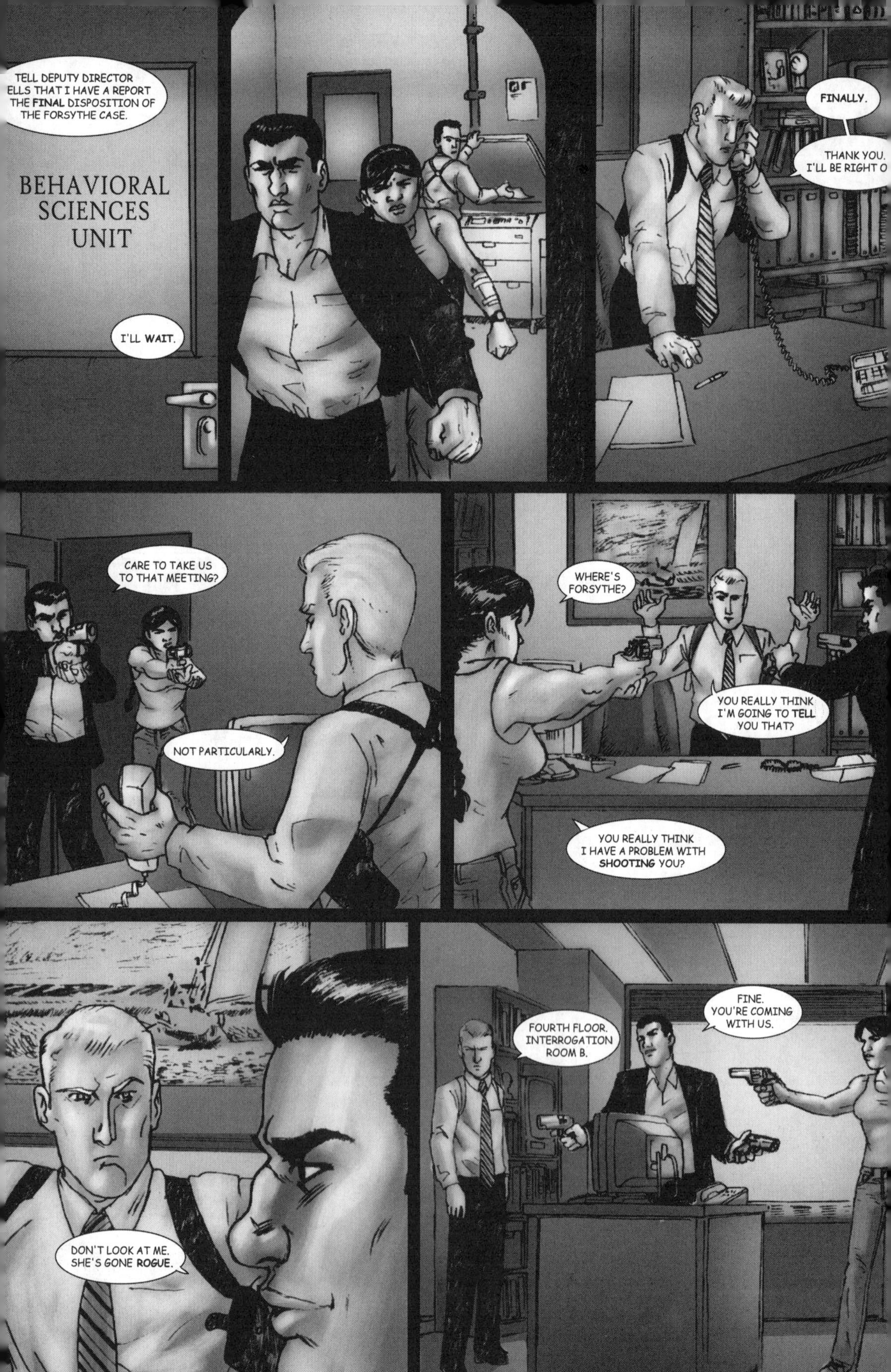

TELL DEPUTY DIRECTOR ELLS THAT I HAVE A REPORT THE FINAL DISPOSITION OF THE FORSYTHE CASE.
BEHAVIORAL SCIENCES UNIT
I'LL WAIT.
FINALLY.
THANK YOU. I'LL BE RIGHT O
CARE TO TAKE US TO THAT MEETING?
NOT PARTICULARLY.
WHERE'S FORSYTHE?
YOU REALLY THINK I'M GOING TO TELL YOU THAT?
YOU REALLY THINK I HAVE A PROBLEM WITH SHOOTING YOU?
DON'T LOOK AT ME. SHE'S GONE ROGUE.
FOURTH FLOOR. INTERROGATION ROOM B.
FINE. YOU'RE COMING WITH US.

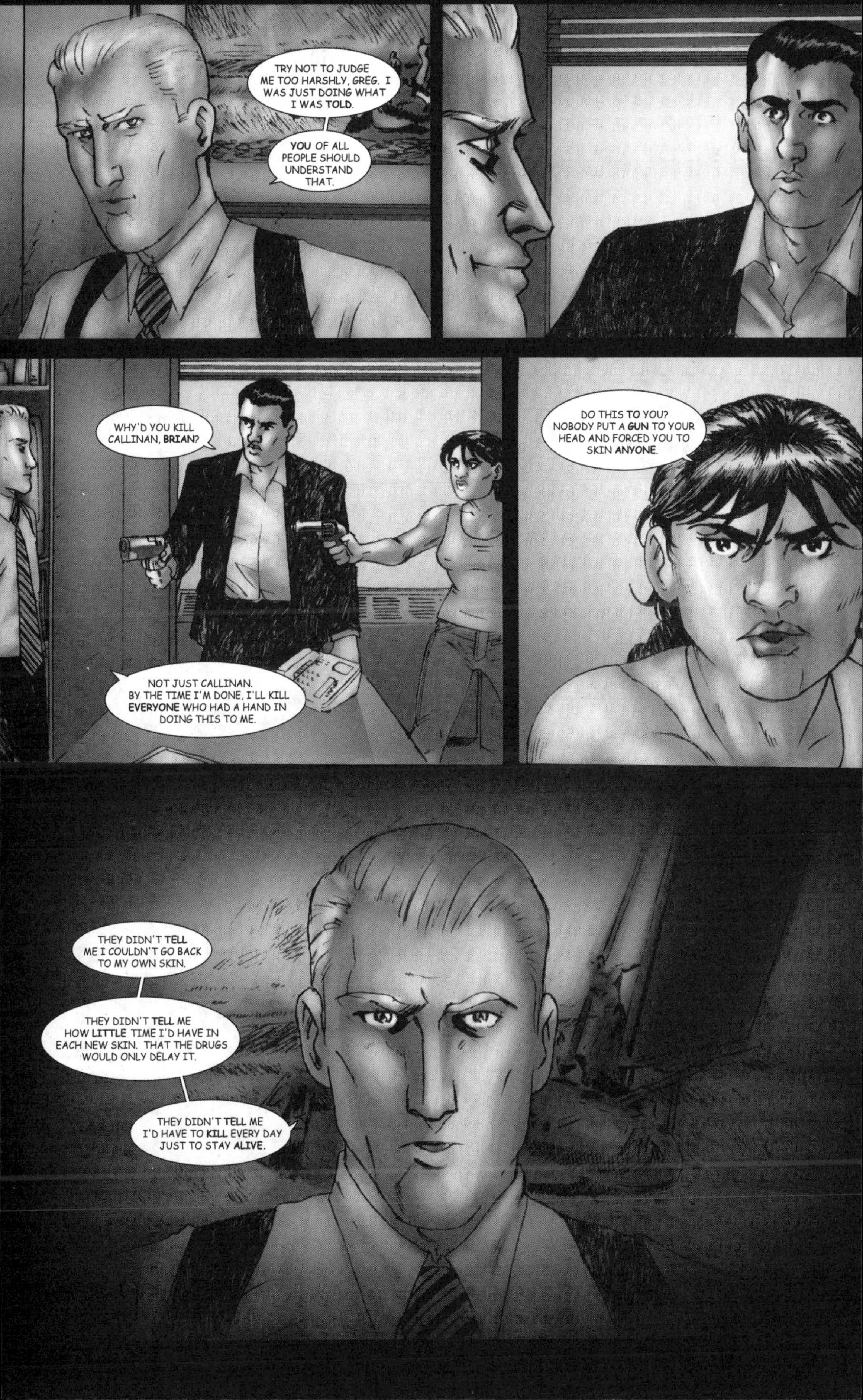
TRY NOT TO JUDGE ME TOO HARSHLY, GREG. I WAS JUST DOING WHAT I WAS TOLD.
YOU OF ALL PEOPLE SHOULD UNDERSTAND THAT.
WHY'D YOU KILL CALLINAN, BRIAN?
NOT JUST CALLINAN. BY THE TIME I'M DONE, I'LL KILL EVERYONE WHO HAD A HAND IN DOING THIS TO ME.
DO THIS TO YOU? NOBODY PUT A GUN TO YOUR HEAD AND FORCED YOU TO SKIN ANYONE.
THEY DIDN'T TELL ME I COULDN'T GO BACK TO MY OWN SKIN.
THEY DIDN'T TELL ME HOW LITTLE TIME I'D HAVE IN EACH NEW SKIN. THAT THE DRUGS WOULD ONLY DELAY IT.
THEY DIDN'T TELL ME I'D HAVE TO KILL EVERY DAY JUST TO STAY ALIVE.

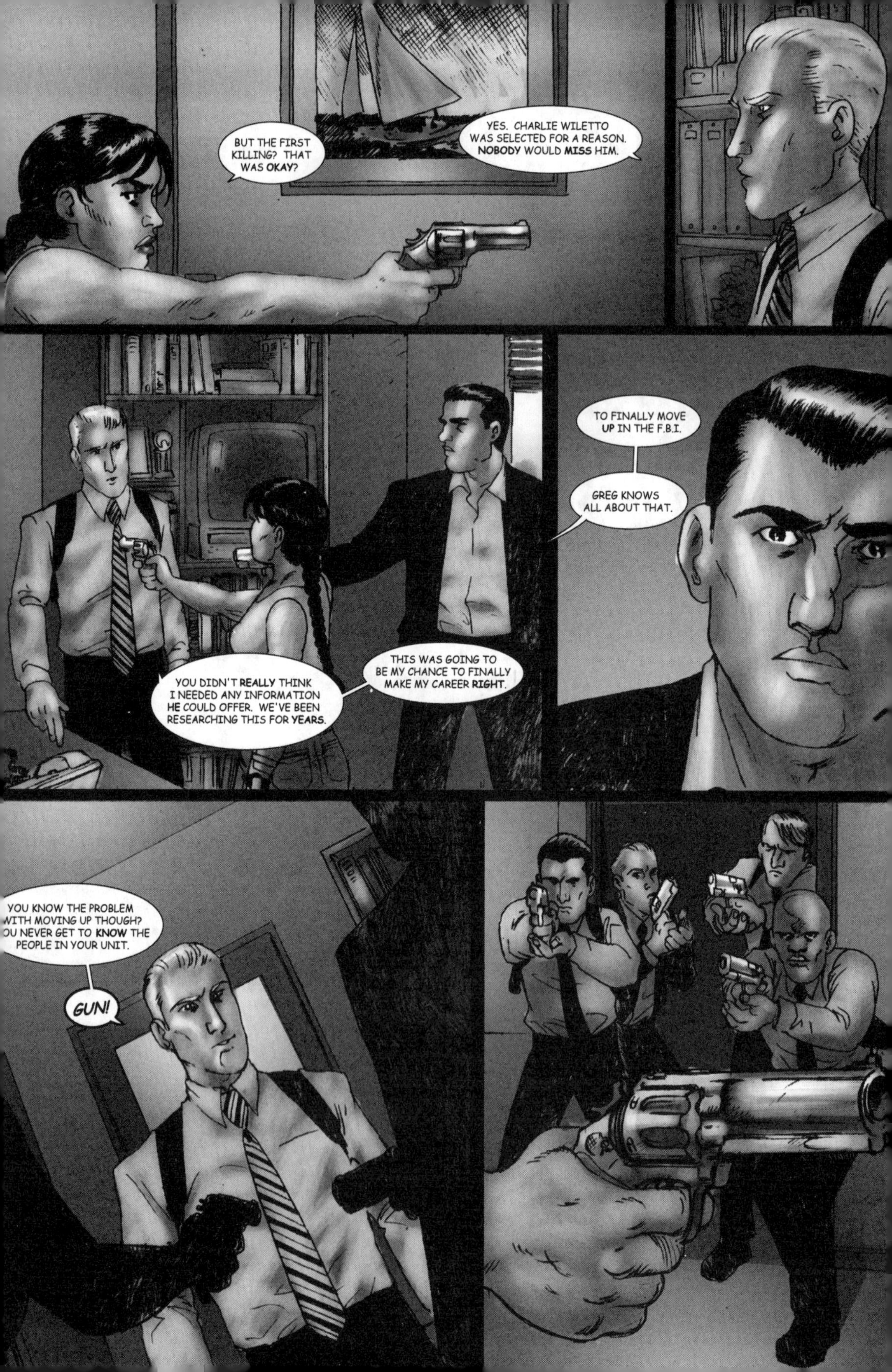
BUT THE FIRST KILLING? THAT WAS OKAY?
YES. CHARLIE WILETTO WAS SELECTED FOR A REASON. NOBODY WOULD MISS HIM.
YOU DIDN'T REALLY THINK I NEEDED ANY INFORMATION HE COULD OFFER. WE'VE BEEN RESEARCHING THIS FOR YEARS.
THIS WAS GOING TO BE MY CHANCE TO FINALLY MAKE MY CAREER RIGHT.
TO FINALLY MOVE UP IN THE F.B.I.
GREG KNOWS ALL ABOUT THAT.
YOU KNOW THE PROBLEM WITH MOVING UP THOUGH? OU NEVER GET TO KNOW THE PEOPLE IN YOUR UNIT.
GUN!

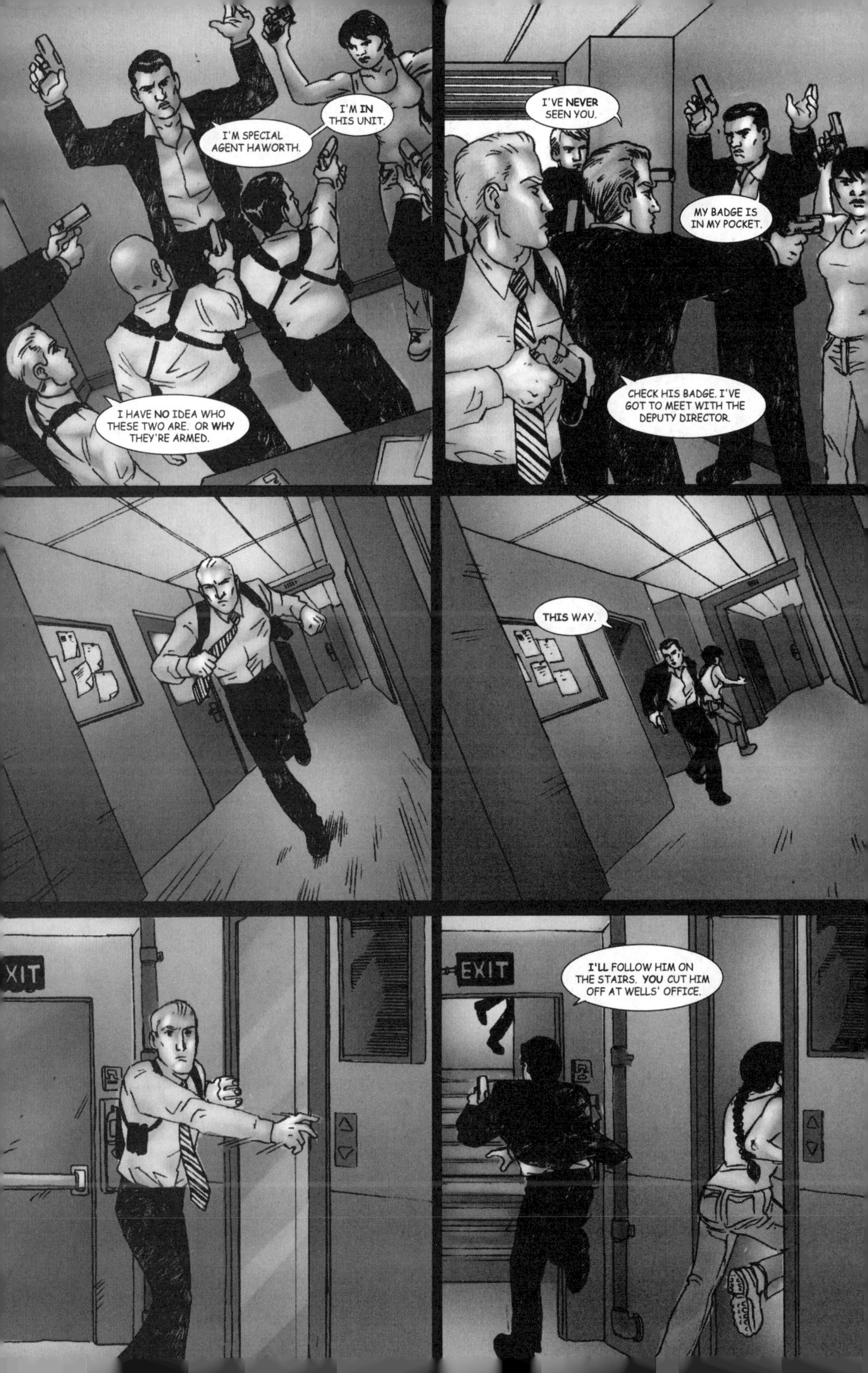
I'M SPECIAL AGENT HAWORTH.
I'M IN THIS UNIT.
I HAVE NO IDEA WHO THESE TWO ARE. OR WHY THEY'RE ARMED.
I'VE NEVER SEEN YOU.
MY BADGE IS IN MY POCKET.
CHECK HIS BADGE. I'VE GOT TO MEET WITH THE DEPUTY DIRECTOR.
THIS WAY.
EXIT
EXIT
I'LL FOLLOW HIM ON THE STAIRS. YOU CUT HIM OFF AT WELLS' OFFICE.

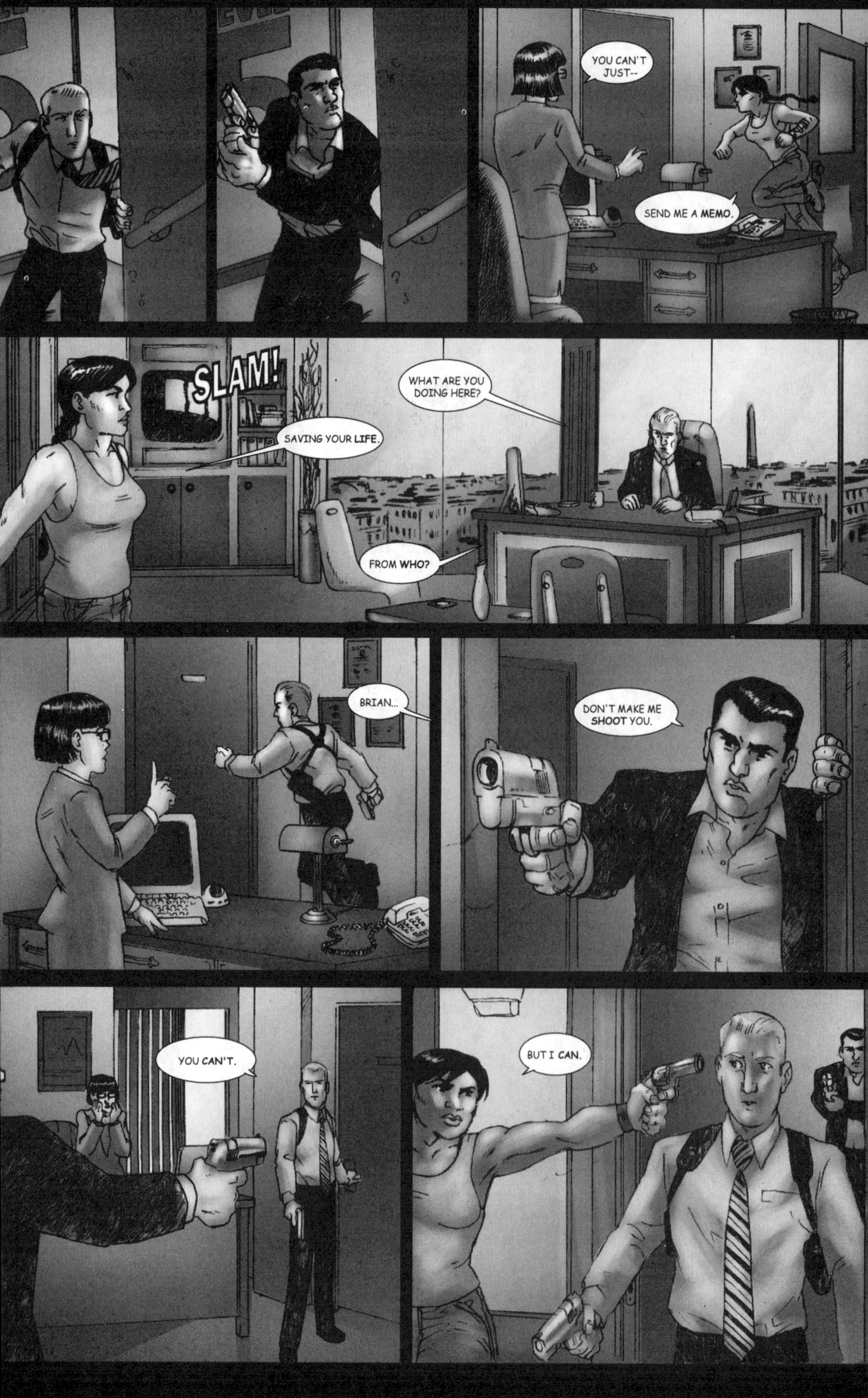
YOU CAN'T JUST--
SEND ME A MEMO.
SLAM!
WHAT ARE YOU DOING HERE?
SAVING YOUR LIFE.
FROM WHO?
BRIAN...
DON'T MAKE ME SHOOT YOU.
YOU CAN'T.
BUT I CAN.

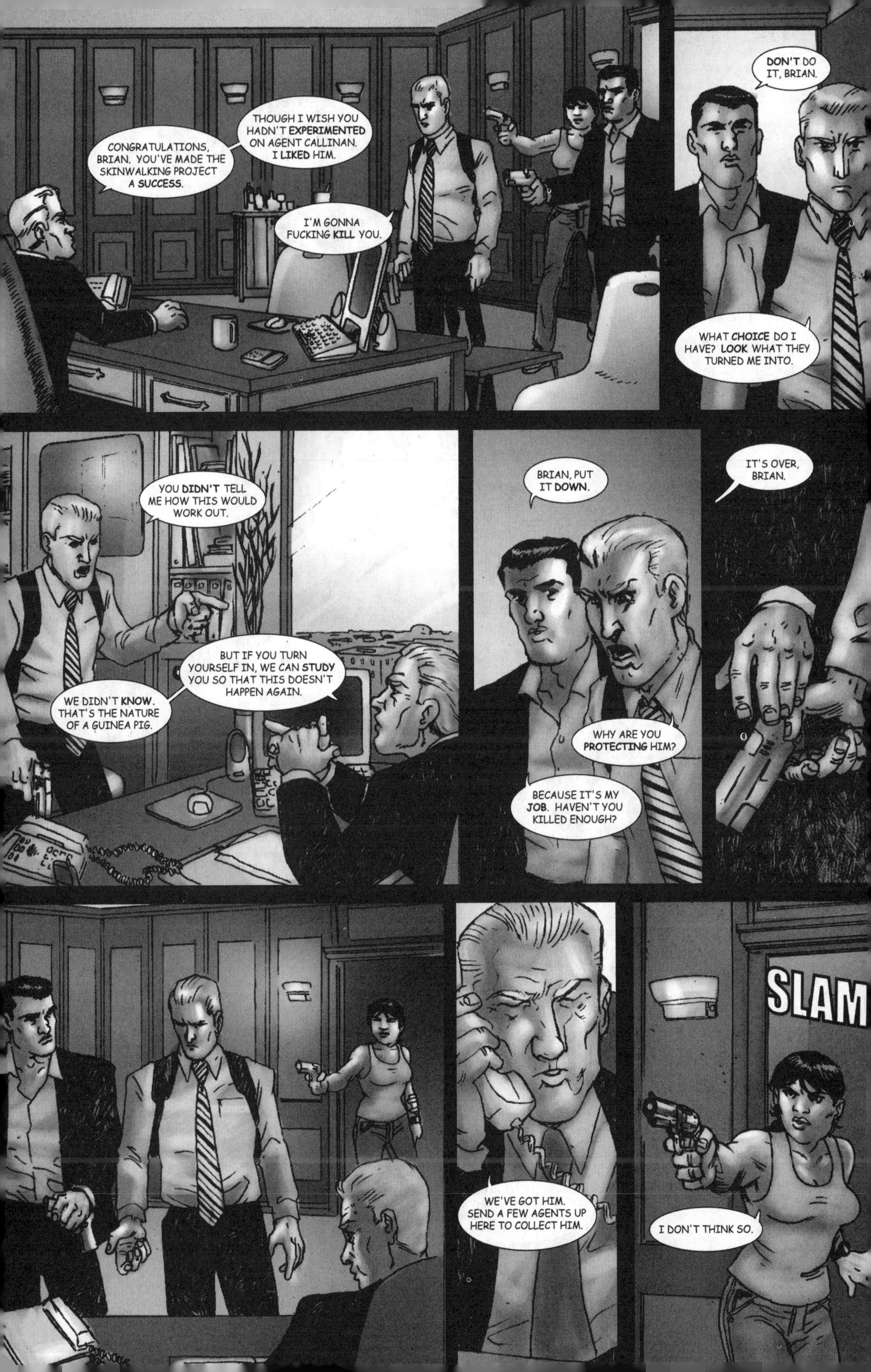
CONGRATULATIONS, BRIAN. YOU'VE MADE THE SKINWALKING PROJECT A SUCCESS.
THOUGH I WISH YOU HADN'T EXPERIMENTED ON AGENT CALLINAN. I LIKED HIM.
I'M GONNA FUCKING KILL YOU.
DON'T DO IT, BRIAN.
WHAT CHOICE DO I HAVE? LOOK WHAT THEY TURNED ME INTO.
YOU DIDN'T TELL ME HOW THIS WOULD WORK OUT.
WE DIDN'T KNOW. THAT'S THE NATURE OF A GUINEA PIG.
BUT IF YOU TURN YOURSELF IN, WE CAN STUDY YOU SO THAT THIS DOESN'T HAPPEN AGAIN.
BRIAN, PUT IT DOWN.
WHY ARE YOU PROTECTING HIM?
BECAUSE IT'S MY JOB. HAVEN'T YOU KILLED ENOUGH?
IT'S OVER, BRIAN.
WE'VE GOT HIM. SEND A FEW AGENTS UP HERE TO COLLECT HIM.
SLAM
I DON'T THINK SO.

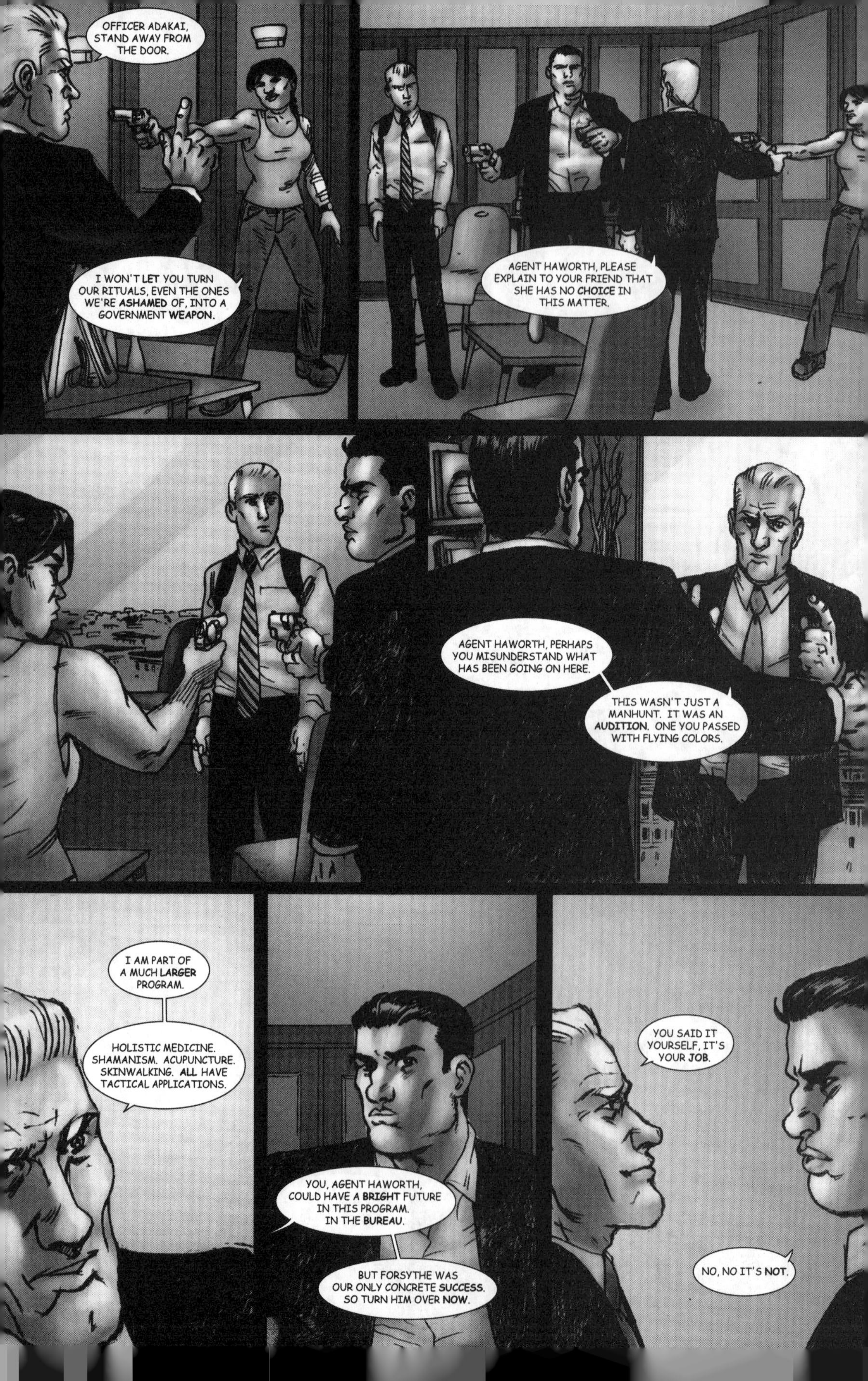

OFFICER ADAKAI, STAND AWAY FROM THE DOOR.
I WON'T LET YOU TURN OUR RITUALS, EVEN THE ONES WE'RE ASHAMED OF, INTO A GOVERNMENT WEAPON.
AGENT HAWORTH, PLEASE EXPLAIN TO YOUR FRIEND THAT SHE HAS NO CHOICE IN THIS MATTER.
AGENT HAWORTH, PERHAPS YOU MISUNDERSTAND WHAT HAS BEEN GOING ON HERE.
THIS WASN'T JUST A MANHUNT. IT WAS AN AUDITION. ONE YOU PASSED WITH FLYING COLORS.
I AM PART OF A MUCH LARGER PROGRAM.
HOLISTIC MEDICINE. SHAMANISM. ACUPUNCTURE. SKINWALKING. ALL HAVE TACTICAL APPLICATIONS.
YOU, AGENT HAWORTH, COULD HAVE A BRIGHT FUTURE IN THIS PROGRAM. IN THE BUREAU.
BUT FORSYTHE WAS OUR ONLY CONCRETE SUCCESS. SO TURN HIM OVER NOW.
YOU SAID IT YOURSELF, IT'S YOUR JOB.
NO, NO IT'S NOT.

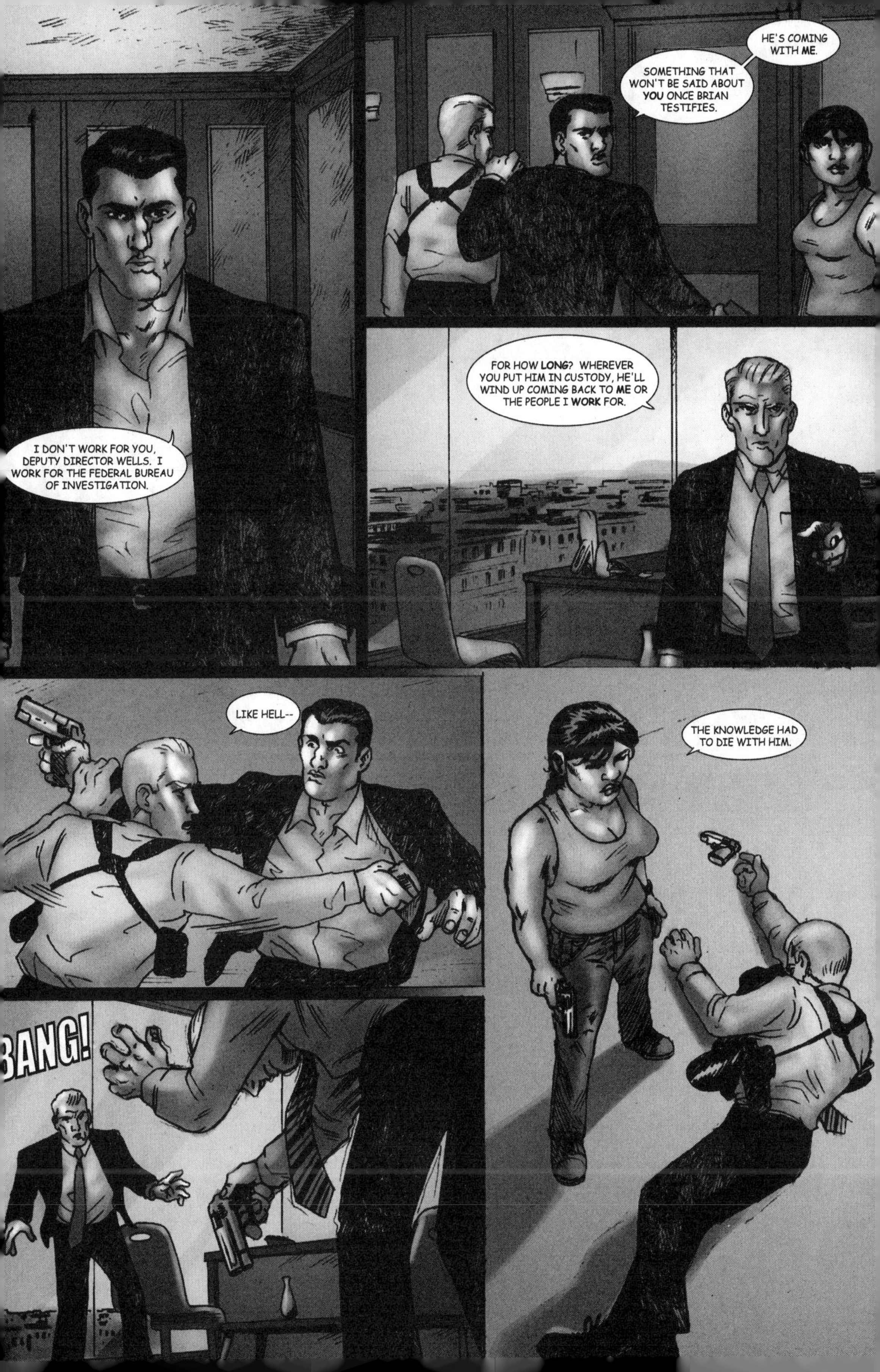
I DON'T WORK FOR YOU, DEPUTY DIRECTOR WELLS. I WORK FOR THE FEDERAL BUREAU OF INVESTIGATION.
HE'S COMING WITH ME.
SOMETHING THAT WON'T BE SAID ABOUT YOU ONCE BRIAN TESTIFIES.
FOR HOW LONG? WHEREVER YOU PUT HIM IN CUSTODY, HE'LL WIND UP COMING BACK TO ME OR THE PEOPLE I WORK FOR.
LIKE HELL--
BANG!
THE KNOWLEDGE HAD TO DIE WITH HIM.

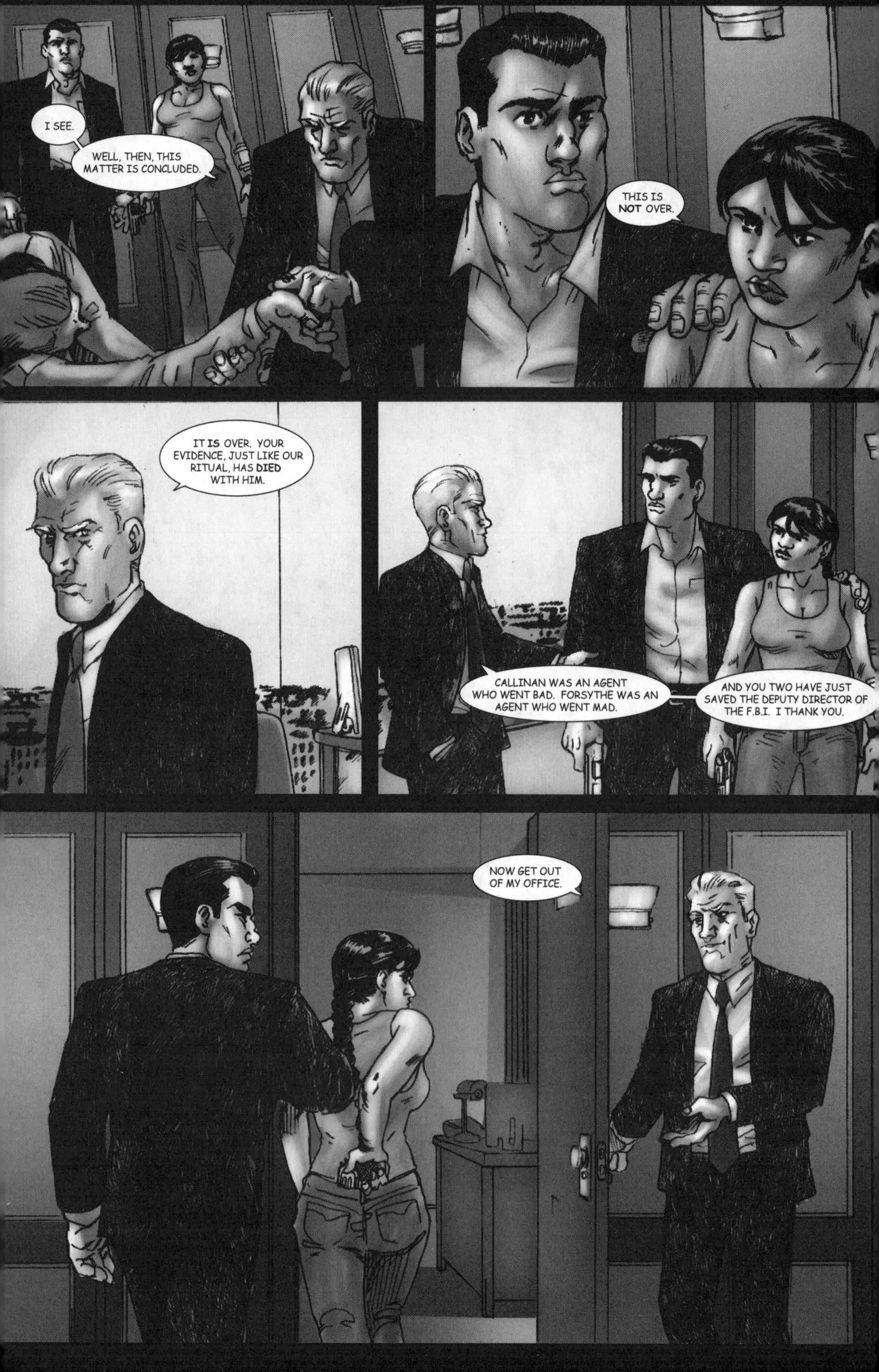
I SEE.
WELL, THEN, THIS MATTER IS CONCLUDED.
THIS IS **NOT** OVER.
IT **IS** OVER. YOUR EVIDENCE, JUST LIKE OUR RITUAL, HAS **DIED** WITH HIM.
CALLINAN WAS AN AGENT WHO WENT BAD. FORSYTHE WAS AN AGENT WHO WENT MAD.
AND YOU TWO HAVE JUST SAVED THE DEPUTY DIRECTOR OF THE F.B.I. I THANK YOU.
NOW GET OUT OF MY OFFICE.

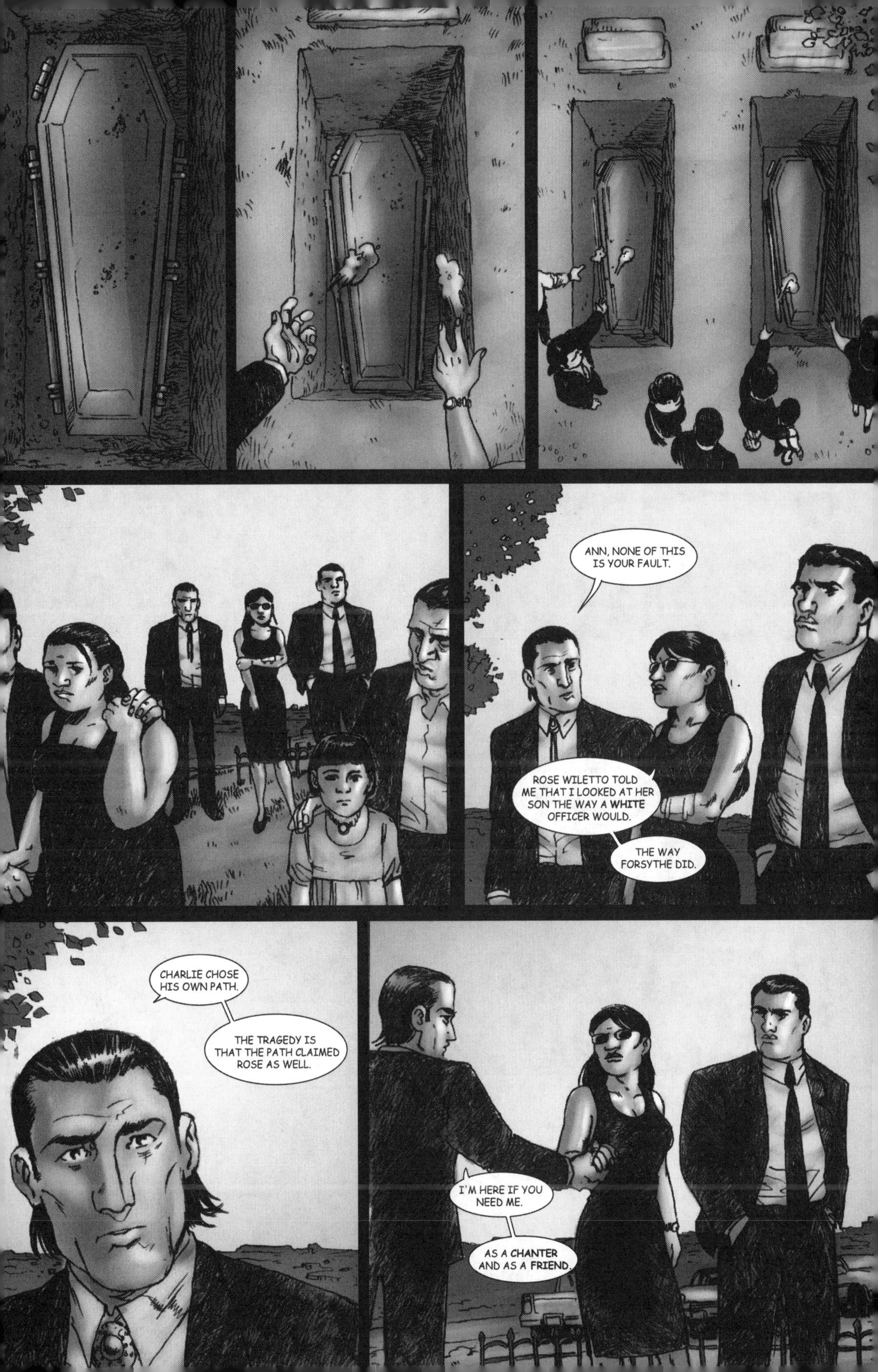
ANN, NONE OF THIS IS YOUR FAULT.
ROSE WILETTO TOLD ME THAT I LOOKED AT HER SON THE WAY A **WHITE** OFFICER WOULD.
THE WAY FORSYTHE DID.
CHARLIE CHOSE HIS OWN PATH.
THE TRAGEDY IS THAT THE PATH CLAIMED ROSE AS WELL.
I'M HERE IF YOU NEED ME.
AS A **CHANTER** AND AS A **FRIEND**.

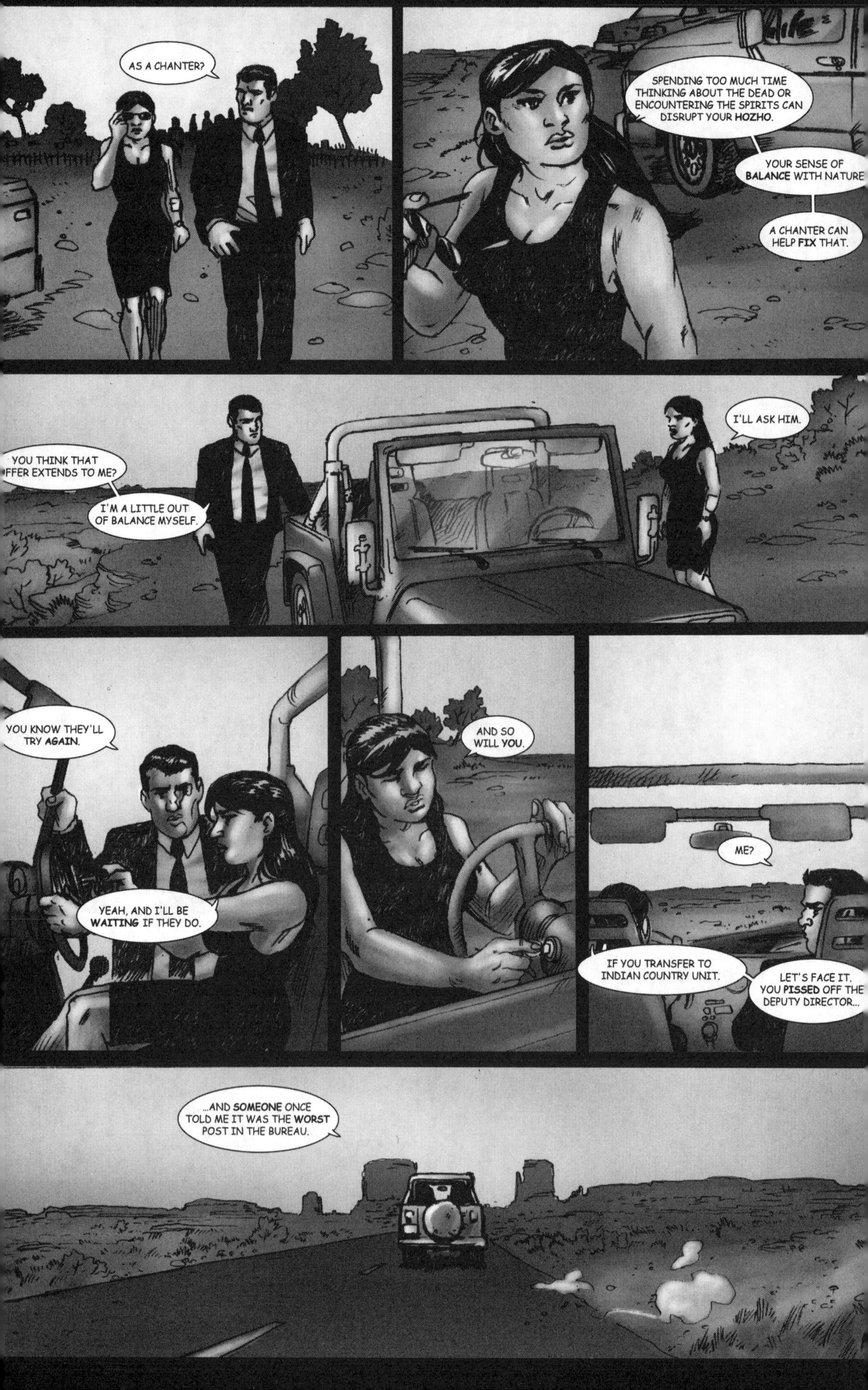

AS A CHANTER?
SPENDING TOO MUCH TIME THINKING ABOUT THE DEAD OR ENCOUNTERING THE SPIRITS CAN DISRUPT YOUR HOZHO.
YOUR SENSE OF BALANCE WITH NATURE
A CHANTER CAN HELP FIX THAT.
YOU THINK THAT FFER EXTENDS TO ME?
I'M A LITTLE OUT OF BALANCE MYSELF.
I'LL ASK HIM.
YOU KNOW THEY'LL TRY AGAIN.
YEAH, AND I'LL BE WAITING IF THEY DO.
AND SO WILL YOU.
ME?
IF YOU TRANSFER TO INDIAN COUNTRY UNIT.
LET'S FACE IT. YOU PISSED OFF THE DEPUTY DIRECTOR...
...AND SOMEONE ONCE TOLD ME IT WAS THE WORST POST IN THE BUREAU.

BOnuS SEction

Previously Unpublished Material

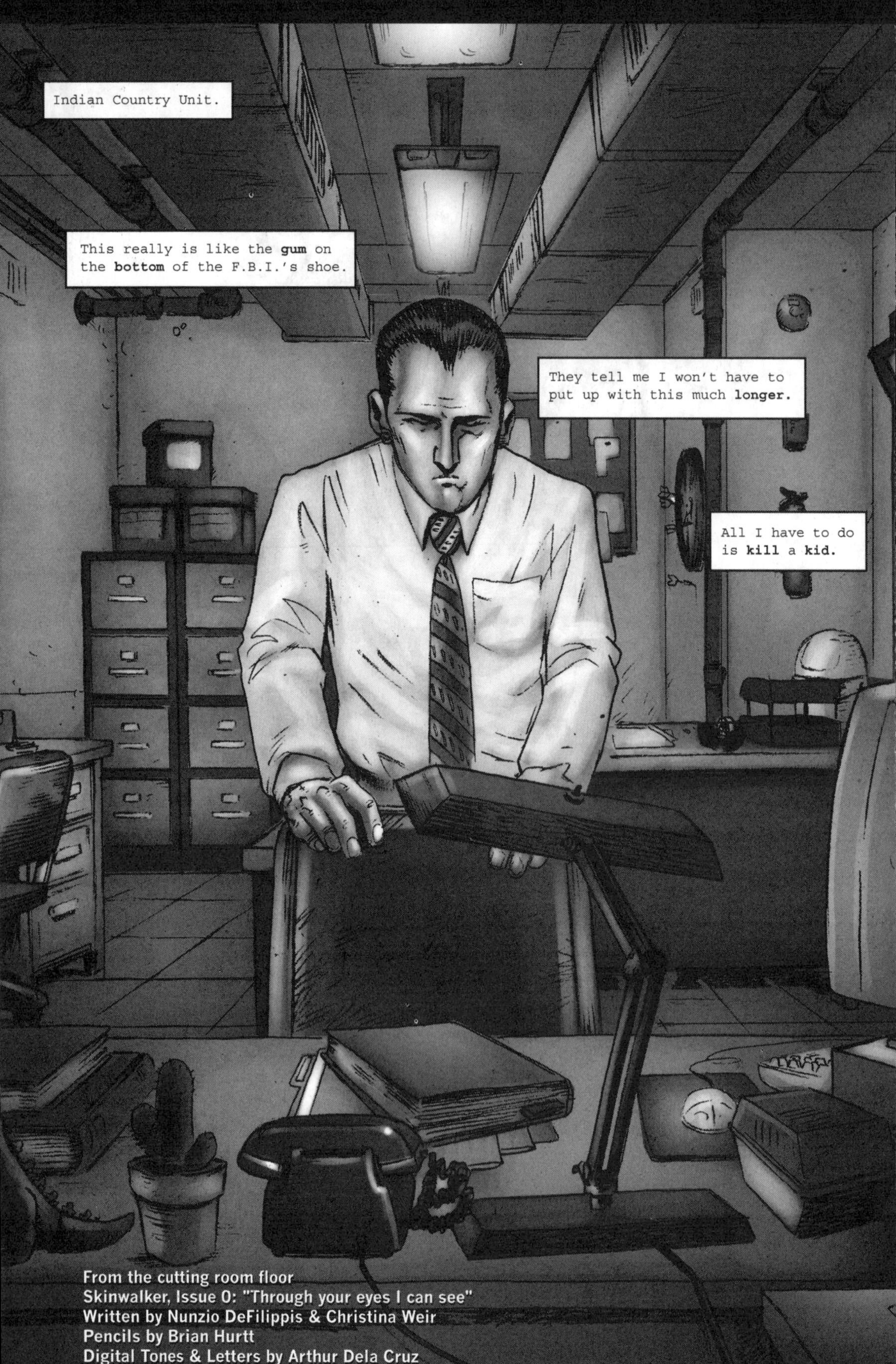
Indian Country Unit.
This really is like the **gum** on the **bottom** of the F.B.I.'s shoe.
They tell me I won't have to put up with this much **longer.**
All I have to do is **kill** a **kid.**

From the cutting room floor
Skinwalker, Issue 0: "Through your eyes I can see"
Written by Nunzio DeFilippis & Christina Weir
Pencils by Brian Hurtt
Digital Tones & Letters by Arthur Dela Cruz
Edited by Jamie S. Rich

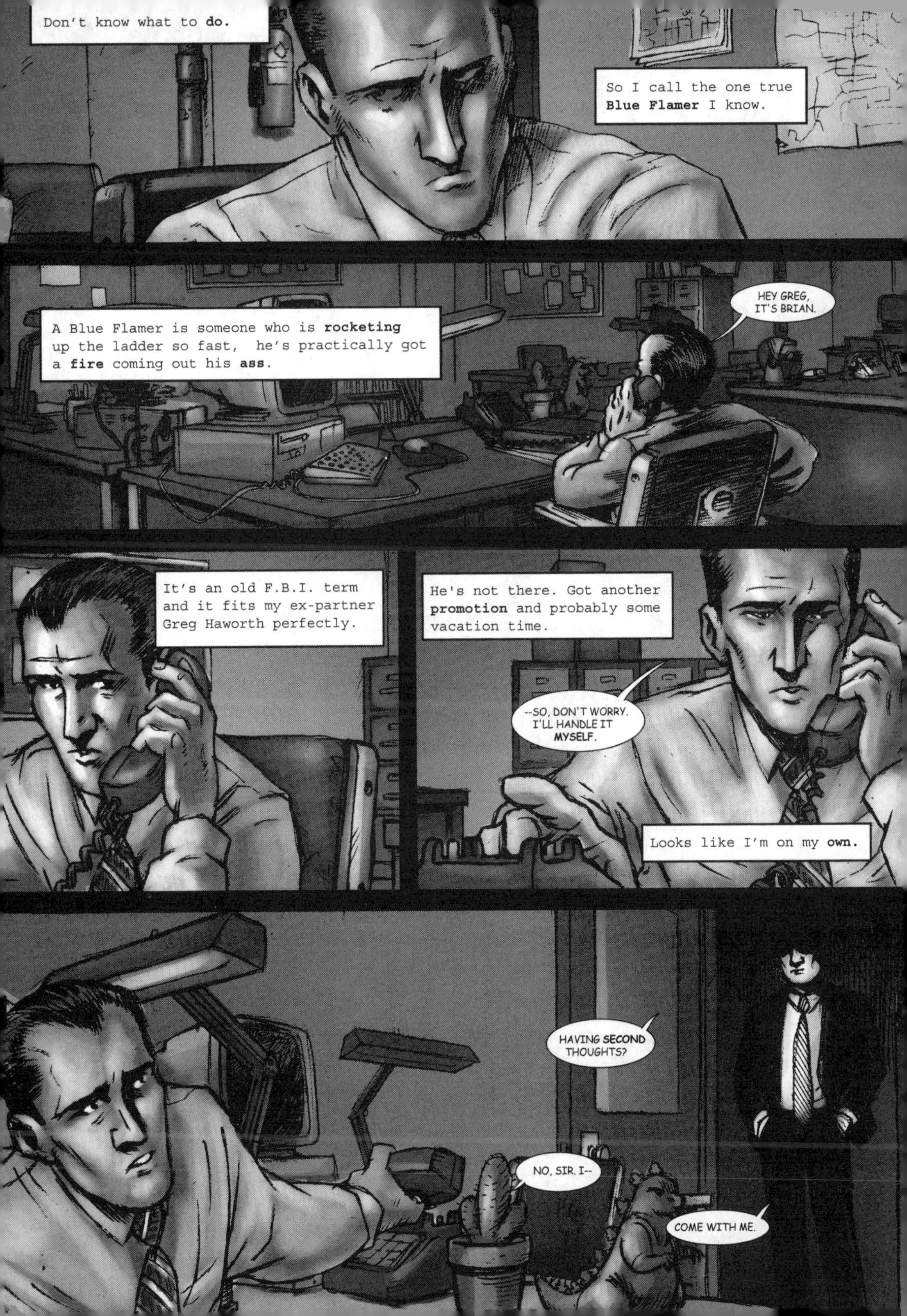

Don't know what to **do.**
So I call the one true **Blue Flamer** I know.
A Blue Flamer is someone who is **rocketing** up the ladder so fast, he's practically got a **fire** coming out his **ass**.
HEY GREG, IT'S BRIAN.
It's an old F.B.I. term and it fits my ex-partner Greg Haworth perfectly.
He's not there. Got another **promotion** and probably some vacation time.
--SO, DON'T WORRY. I'LL HANDLE IT **MYSELF**.
Looks like I'm on my **own.**
HAVING **SECOND** THOUGHTS?
NO, SIR. I--
COME WITH ME.

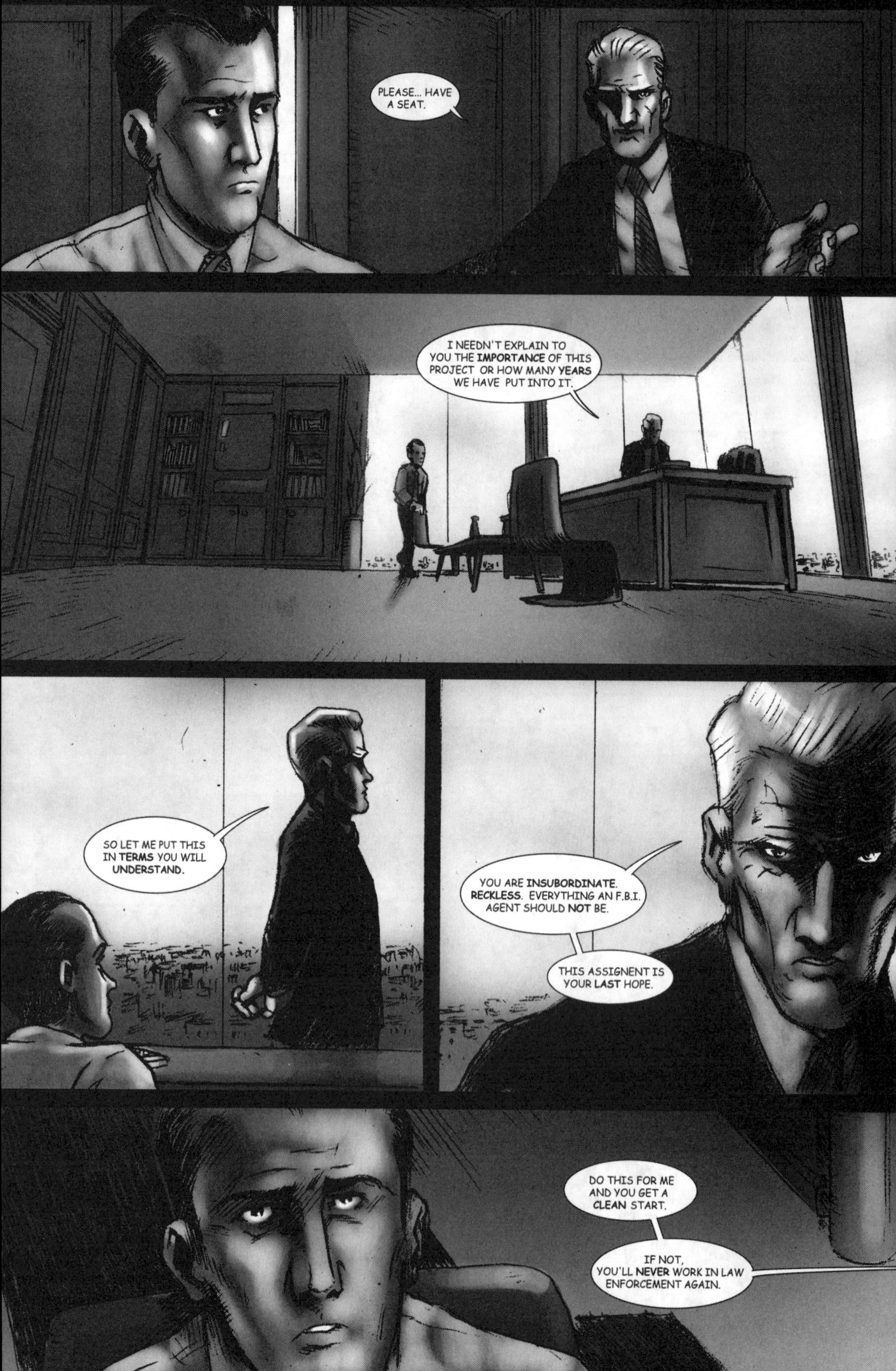

PLEASE... HAVE A SEAT.
I NEEDN'T EXPLAIN TO YOU THE IMPORTANCE OF THIS PROJECT OR HOW MANY YEARS WE HAVE PUT INTO IT.
SO LET ME PUT THIS IN TERMS YOU WILL UNDERSTAND.
YOU ARE INSUBORDINATE. RECKLESS. EVERYTHING AN F.B.I. AGENT SHOULD NOT BE.
THIS ASSIGNENT IS YOUR LAST HOPE.
DO THIS FOR ME AND YOU GET A CLEAN START.
IF NOT, YOU'LL NEVER WORK IN LAW ENFORCEMENT AGAIN.

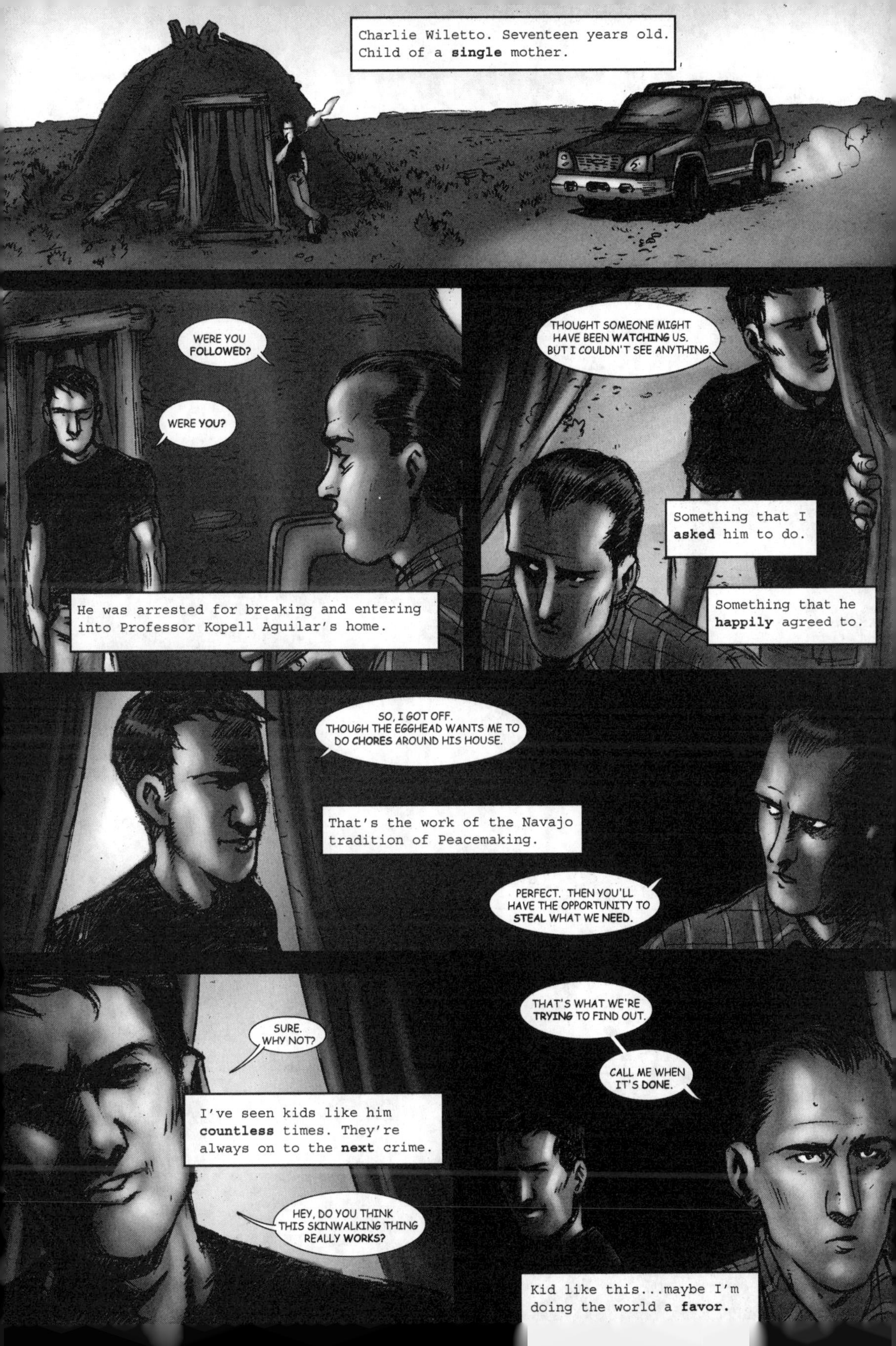
Charlie Wiletto. Seventeen years old. Child of a **single** mother.
WERE YOU FOLLOWED?
WERE YOU?
He was arrested for breaking and entering into Professor Kopell Aguilar's home.
THOUGHT SOMEONE MIGHT HAVE BEEN WATCHING US. BUT I COULDN'T SEE ANYTHING.
Something that I **asked** him to do.
Something that he **happily** agreed to.
SO, I GOT OFF. THOUGH THE EGGHEAD WANTS ME TO DO CHORES AROUND HIS HOUSE.
That's the work of the Navajo tradition of Peacemaking.
PERFECT. THEN YOU'LL HAVE THE OPPORTUNITY TO STEAL WHAT WE NEED.
SURE. WHY NOT?
I've seen kids like him **countless** times. They're always on to the **next** crime.
HEY, DO YOU THINK THIS SKINWALKING THING REALLY WORKS?
THAT'S WHAT WE'RE TRYING TO FIND OUT.
CALL ME WHEN IT'S DONE.
Kid like this...maybe I'm doing the world a **favor.**

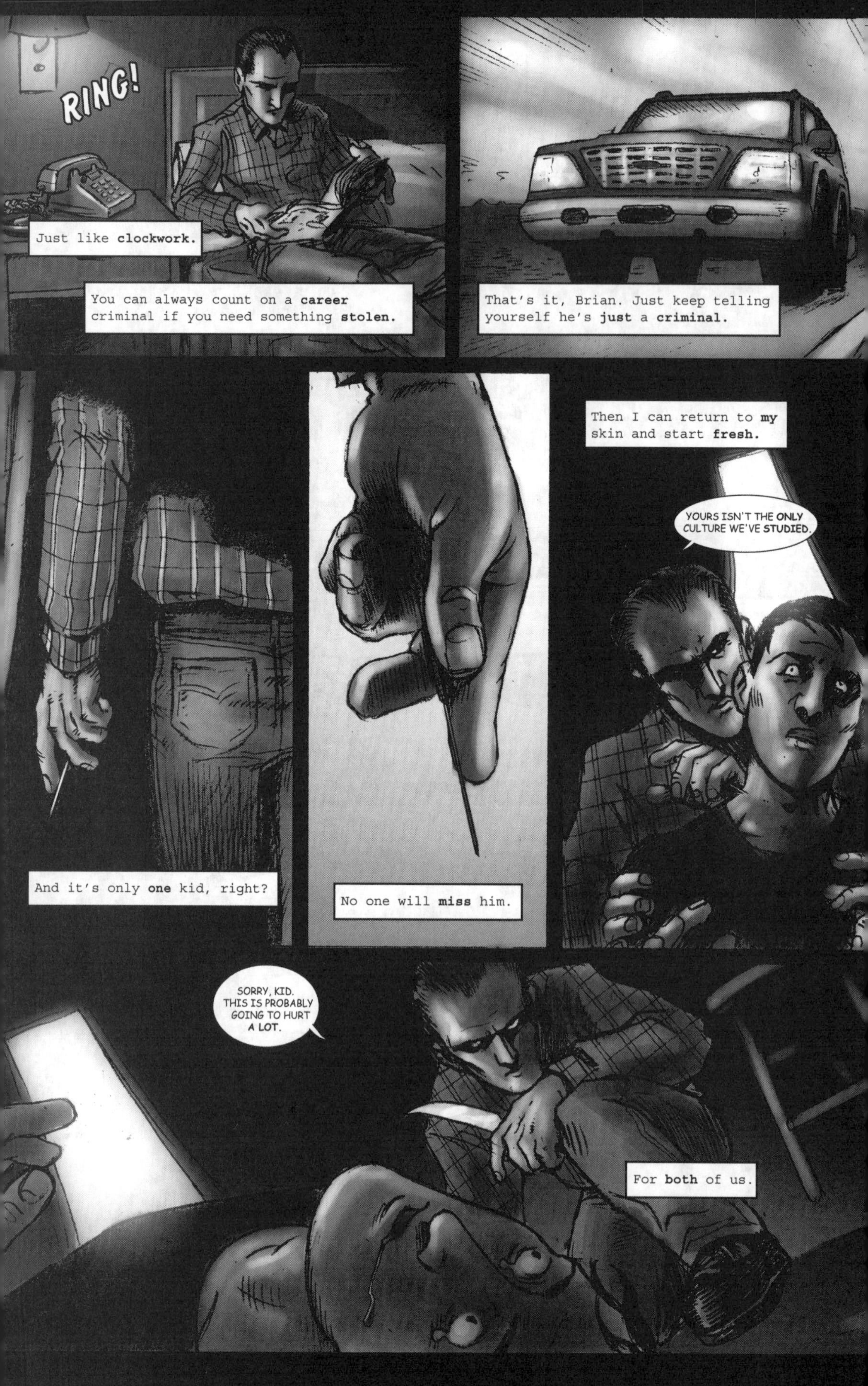
RING!
Just like clockwork.
You can always count on a career criminal if you need something stolen.
That's it, Brian. Just keep telling yourself he's just a criminal.
And it's only one kid, right?
No one will miss him.
Then I can return to my skin and start fresh.
YOURS ISN'T THE ONLY CULTURE WE'VE STUDIED.
SORRY, KID. THIS IS PROBABLY GOING TO HURT A LOT.
For both of us.

From Script To Final Art

The following layout is an example of the process that a standard page of Skinwalker went through to reach what you saw in the actual printed comic book. Using page 2 of the new story on the preceding pages, you will see the original script; notes between Nunzio, Christina, & Brian; and then how Brian's art goes from pencils to being imbued with the Arthur Dela Cruz magic.

* Script, version 1

Page 2

ONE:
BRIAN sits at his desk, phone cradled up to his ear. His eyes scan the room to make sure no one else is there.

1 CAPTION/Brian:	Don't know what to DO.
2 CAPTION/Brian:	So I call the one true BLUE FLAMER I know.
3 BRIAN:	Hey Greg, it's Brian.

TWO:
BRIAN talks on the phone, leaving his message, but we don't hear what he is saying (or more accurately, see his dialogue balloons). Brian's expression shows a bit of nervousness.

4 CAPTION/Brian:	A Blue Flamer is someone who is ROCKETING up the ladder so fast, he's practically got a FIRE coming out his ASS.
5 CAPTION/Brian:	It's an old F.B.I. term and it fits my ex-partner Greg Haworth perfectly.

THREE:
BRIAN still talks on the phone, but now has his other hand on the cradle, about to click down and hang up. There's a sad resolution on his face. He can't get the advice he needed.

6 CAPTION/Brian:	He's not there. Got another PROMOTION and probably some vacation time.
7 BRIAN:	...So, don't worry. I'll handle it MYSELF.
8 CAPTION/Brian:	Looks like I'm on my OWN.

FOUR:
A different angle on the desk. This time showing the door to the office. DEPUTY DIRECTOR WELLS stands in the doorway, smug as ever. BRIAN has turned to look at him, startled, but trying to recover.

9 WELLS:	Having SECOND thoughts?
10 BRIAN:	No... sir. I—
11 WELLS:	Come with me.

FIVE:
In WELLS' office. It's the same power office we saw in the original Skinwalker. Wells closes the door as BRIAN walks into the center of the office. Brian seems a bit hesitant. After all, Wells' office can be pretty damn intimidating. Wells has something of a disingenuous smile on his face.

12 WELLS:	Please... have a seat.
13 WELLS/linked:	I needn't explain to you the IMPORTANCE of this project or how many YEARS we have put into it.

SIX:
WELLS has moved to stand behind his desk. He looks down at BRIAN who now sits in a chair in front of the desk. Wells' expression has turned serious, mildly threatening.

14 WELLS:	So let me put this in TERMS you will UNDERSTAND.

SEVEN:
Close on WELLS. He's in full intimidation mode, laying down the law, cutting straight to the chase.

15 WELLS: You are INSUBORDINATE. RECKLESS. Everything an F.B.I. Agent should NOT be.

16 WELLS/linked: This assignment is your LAST hope.

EIGHT:
Close on BRIAN. He's cornered. His face shows that he knows he has no way out.

17 WELLS/off panel: Do this for me and you get a CLEAN start.

18 WELLS/o.p., linked: **If not, you'll NEVER work in law enforcement again.**

* Script notes

From: Nunzio DeFilippis & Christina Weir
Date: Sun Jan 12, 2003 6:05:57 PM US/Pacific
To: Brian Hurtt
Cc: Jamie Rich
Subject: Skinwalker Extra #1: 4 Page Story
Attachments: There is 1 attachment

Hey there,

So here's the first extra for the trade paperback. As you requested, we did the 4 page story first. It covers pretty much from Forsythe calling Haworth to Forsythe making up his mind and killing Charlie. It's mostly about Forsythe convincing himself to do this.

Feel free to muck around with the layout. We have one super crowded page and one splash so go figure...

- N & C

From: Brian Hurtt
Date: Sat Jan 18, 2003 9:54:56 AM US/Pacific
To: Nunzio DeFilippis & Christina Weir
Subject: skinwalker extras

I wanted to start drawing the new SKINWALKER story as soon as possible but I have some questions first.

First of all, do you mind if I split page 2 into two seperate pages? It's a difficult one pager but I can make it pretty comfortable by adding a panel to each page. My proposal: Have panels one through four (the scene in the Indian Country Unit) on one page and panels five through eight (scene in Wells' office) on a separate page. On the first page I would keep the first panel the same--showing Brian's face--his eyes scanning the room. In the second panel I'd go wide and show a reverse from behind Brian of the empty office. Then I'd add a new panel right after that of Brian talking on the phone, looking nervous (as described in panel two). On the next page I'd have the first panel showing Brian and Wells entering the office (as described) then I'd add a panel after that--a wide shot of the office as they make their way across it (this would help instill that sort of intimidation that Brian feels being in this office).

What do you think? Any of this not going to work for you? Let me know!

talk to you two shortly,

bri

From: Nunzio DeFilippis & Christina Weir
Date: Sat Jan 18, 2003 10:32:21 AM US/Pacific
To: Brian Hurtt
Subject: Re: skinwalker extras

Brian,

We think we understand all the changes you're suggesting. We wanted to field test them
in the script with regard to text placement so we typed up the script as a five pager with
all the changes. The split into two pages seems to work with the text, but we wondered if
four panels of Brian on the phone was too many so we thought maybe in the first one he
hadn't picked up the phone yet. We juggled the text and we think we got it right. The Wells'
office scene works fine with the change - we tweaked text placement to fill the new panel.

Our main concern is making sure Jamie is down with making it five pages. Do you want to run
it by him or shall we? Since we're looking to fill pages, it seems like he'll go for it, but we
don't know if he likes to keep these things at even numbers.

Here's the text of the new script. Let us know if it's what you're looking for or if there's
anything else you want to play with.

- N & C

From: Brian Hurtt
Date: Sat Jan 18, 2003 11:16:54 AM US/Pacific
To: Nunzio DeFilippis & Christina Weir
Subject: Re: skinwalker extras

It reads great! I think I'm all set so I'll get cracking! Hopefully I'll have the full pencils
to show you in the next few days. As far as the page count goes I'm sure that Jamie won't
have a problem with it but I'll contact him to make sure.

-bri

----

* Script, version 2

<u>Page 2</u>

<u>ONE:</u>
BRIAN sits at his desk. His eyes scan the room to make sure no one else is there. If his
hand is visible, it is on the phone, touching the handset, about to pick it up.

1 CAPTION/Brian: Don't know what to DO.
2 CAPTION/Brian: So I call the one true BLUE FLAMER I know.

<u>TWO:</u>
A wide shot – a reverse, behind BRIAN, showing the office. He now has the handset up to
his ear and talks on the phone.

3 CAPTION/Brian: A Blue Flamer is someone who is ROCKETING up the ladder so fast,
                          he's practically got a FIRE coming out his ASS.
4 BRIAN: Hey Greg, it's Brian.

<u>THREE:</u>
BRIAN continues to talk on the phone, his expression shows a bit of nervousness. We don't
hear what he is saying (or more accurately, see his dialogue balloons).

5 CAPTION/Brian: It's an old F.B.I. term and it fits my ex-partner Greg
                                  Haworth perfectly.

FOUR:
BRIAN still talks on the phone, but now has his other hand on the cradle, about to click down and hang up. There's a sad resolution on his face. He can't get the advice he needed.

6 CAPTION/Brian:	He's not there. Got another PROMOTION and probably some vacation time.
7 BRIAN:	...So, don't worry. I'll handle it MYSELF.
8 CAPTION/Brian:	Looks like I'm on my OWN.

FIVE:
A different angle on the desk. This time showing the door to the office. DEPUTY DIRECTOR WELLS stands in the doorway, smug as ever. BRIAN has turned to look at him, startled, but trying to recover.

9 WELLS:	Having SECOND thoughts?
10 BRIAN:	No... sir. I—
11 WELLS:	Come with me.

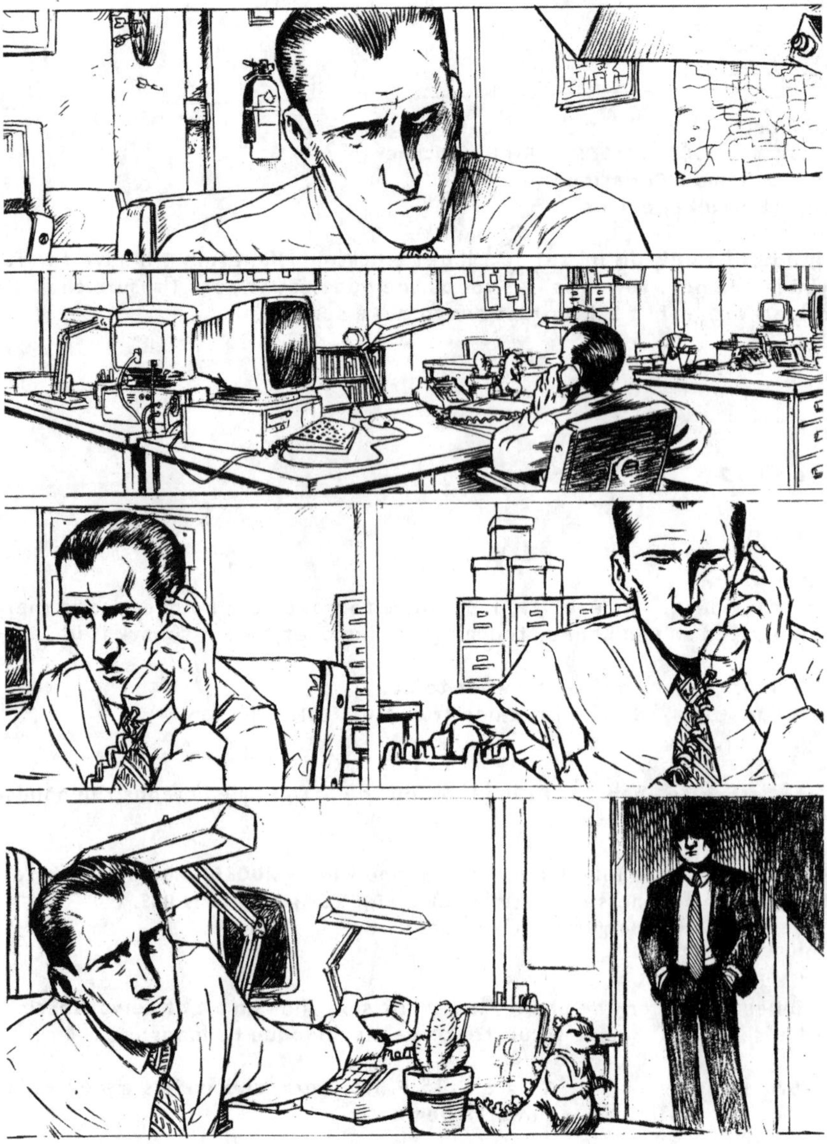

(1) After Brian's pencils are scanned into the computer, all the foreground elements and the main characters are rendered first.

(2) The background then gets rendered separately, on a different layer than the foreground.

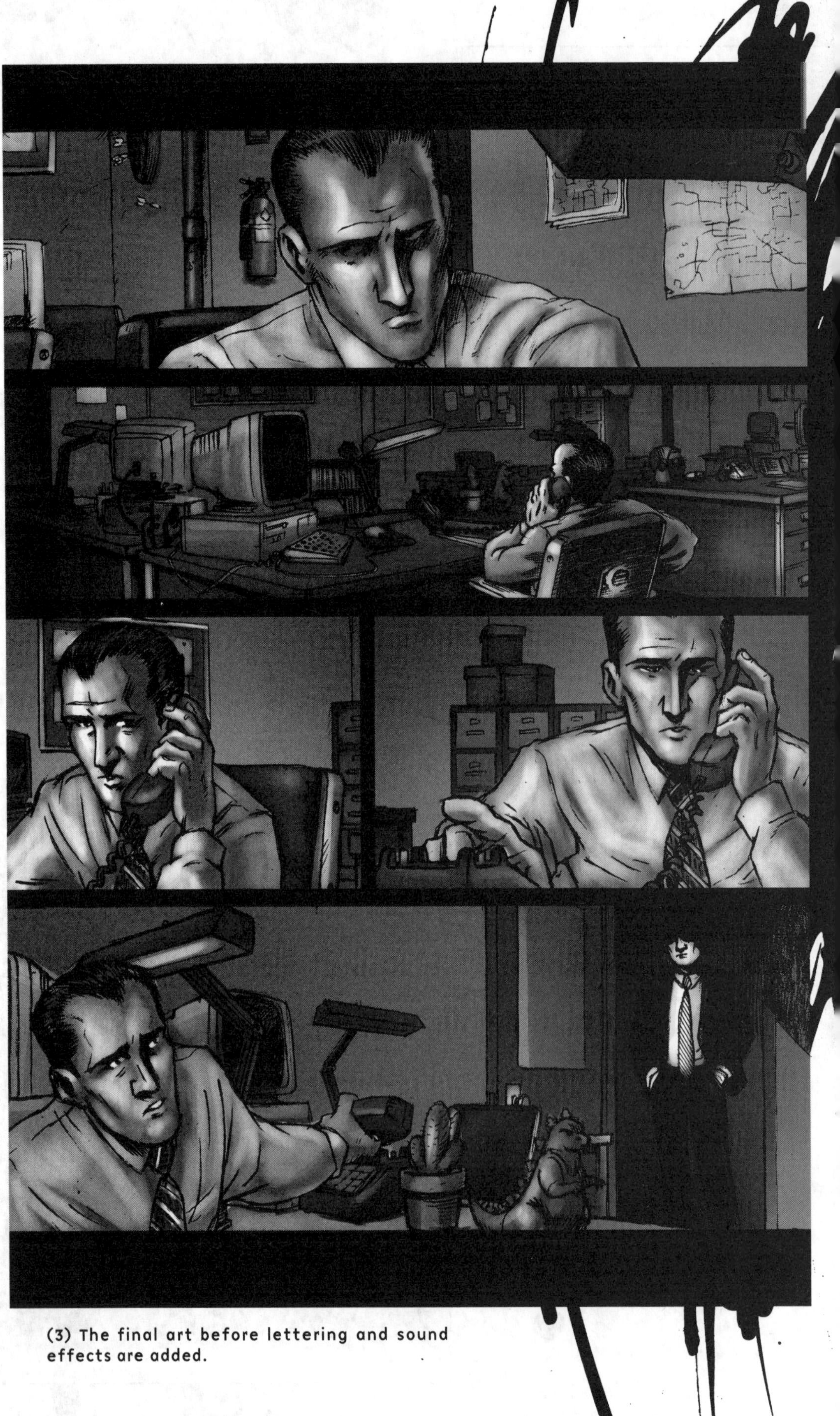

(3) The final art before lettering and sound effects are added.

The Process Of Durwin Talon

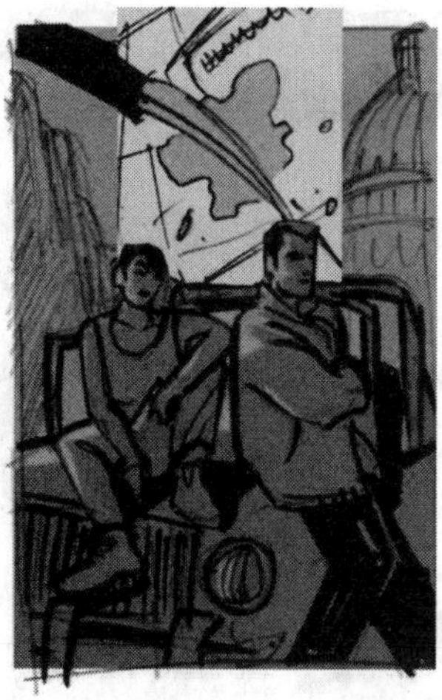

(1) Durwin starts off with numerous thumbnail drawings to determine all cover elements needed to tell the story.

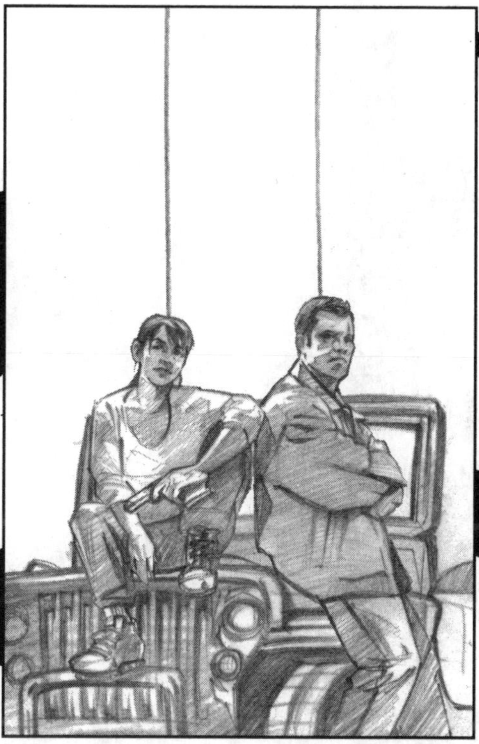

(2) Once the concept has been approved, a tighter sketch is created with an emphasis on light and shadow.

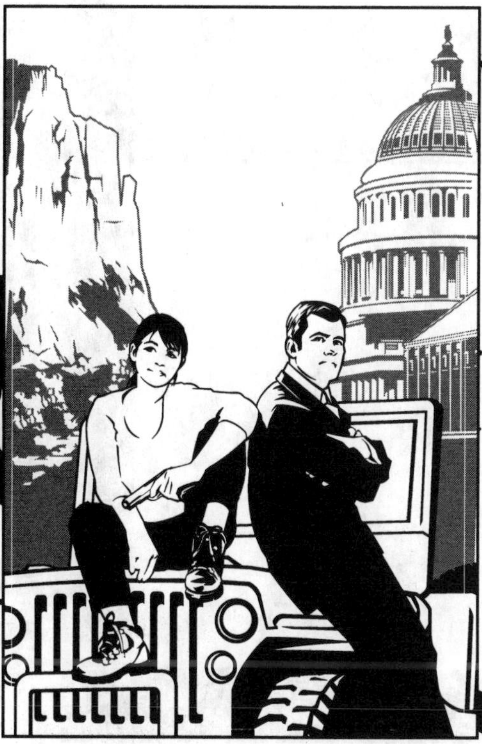

(3) The tight sketch is scanned in and the linework is inked in the computer. Shapes are then flattened and assigned colors.

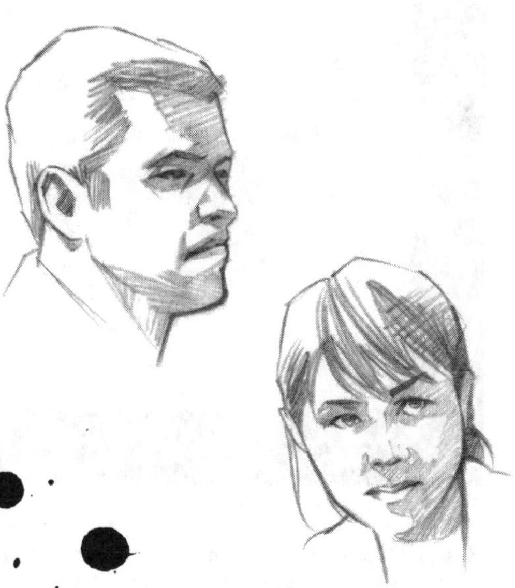

(4) The initial sketches of Greg and Ann.

Convention sketches by Brian Hurtt.

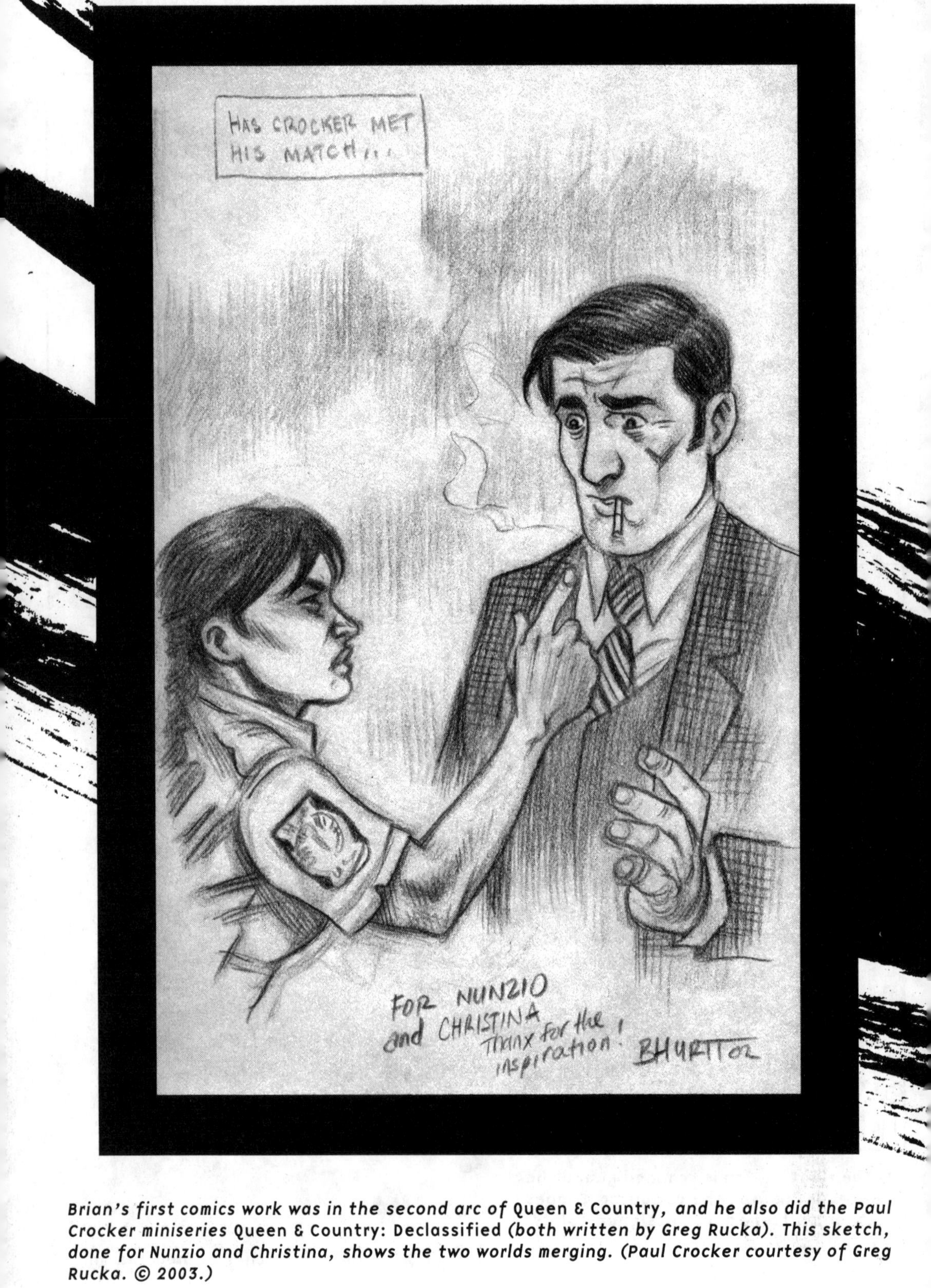
HAS CROCKER MET HIS MATCH...
FOR NUNZIO and CHRISTINA Thanx for the inspiration!
BHURTT02

Brian's first comics work was in the second arc of Queen & Country, *and he also did the Paul Crocker miniseries* Queen & Country: Declassified *(both written by Greg Rucka). This sketch, done for Nunzio and Christina, shows the two worlds merging. (Paul Crocker courtesy of Greg Rucka. © 2003.)*

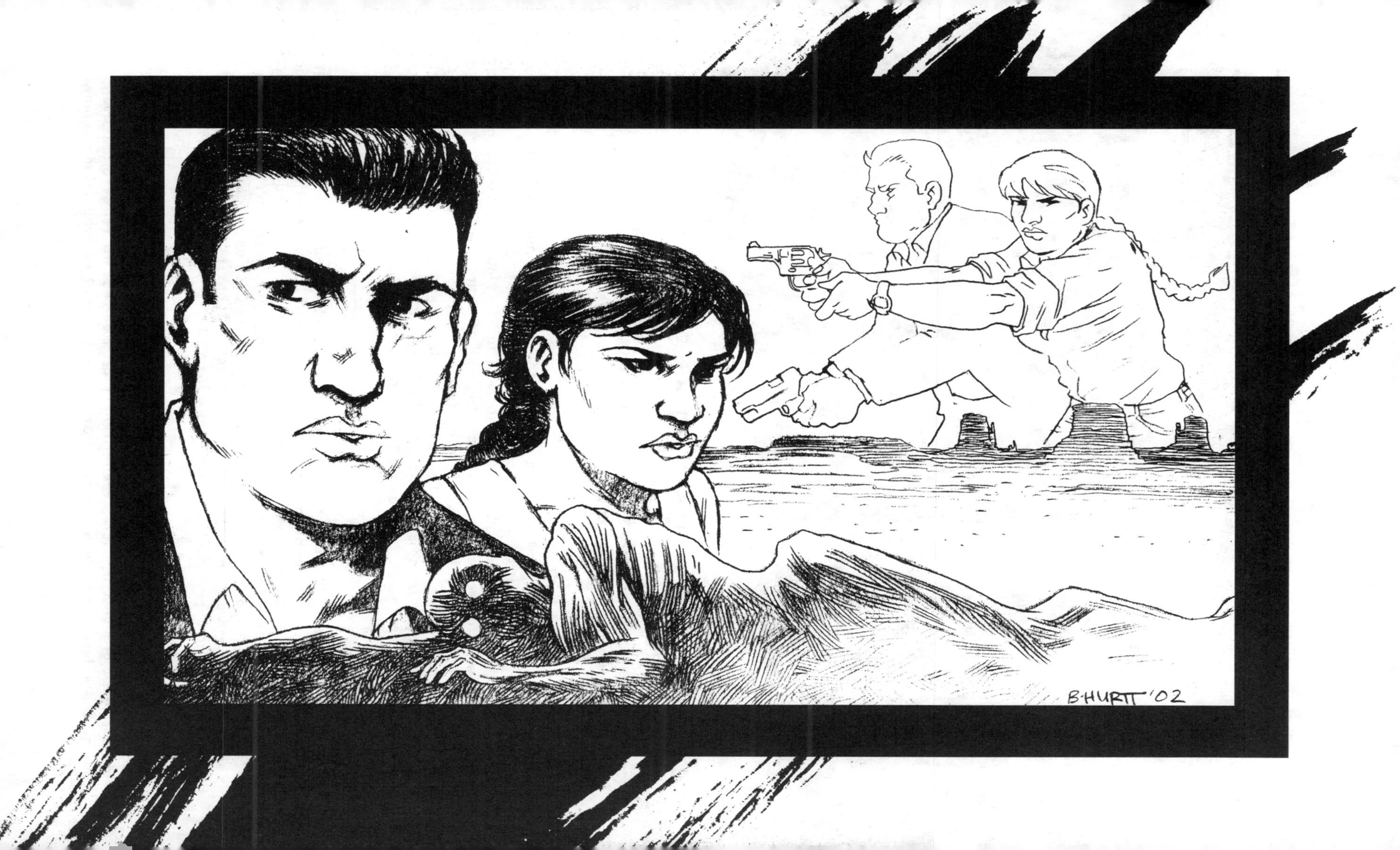
B·HURTT '02

ABOUT THE CREATORS...

Reader's note: The order of the biographies corresponds to the placement of each creator in the photo, running from left to right.

Arthur Dela Cruz

Though he was always picked last in gym class, Arthur Dela Cruz harbors little resentment. Even though he was conditioned since birth to "look out for #1," he likes to keep an eye out for everyone and thinks *everybody* should share in his "last laugh." Dela Cruz is sometimes seen smiling, when he feels like a blurry photograph of a girl standing in the rain. Other times he's a creep, and he sleeps just fine. His first comic book series, *Kissing Chaos*, earned him an Eisner nomination and was collected into trade paperback by Oni Press. He recently completed its sequel, *Kissing Chaos: Nonstop Beauty*, and plans more in the saga of youth and conspiracies in the future, as well as many other projects of graphic literature.

Brian Hurtt

Brian Hurtt was born in Wichita, KS, and since then has traveled the world, only recently settling in St. Louis, MO. He began his career in comics in 2001, debuting as the second penciller of *Queen & Country*. He has since worked with Jen Van Meter and Jim Mahfood on a story for *Captain America #50* before jumping on *Skinwalker*. Hurtt recently finished the *Queen & Country: Declassified* miniseries, set for a July release as a trade paperback, and is currently hard at work on *Three Strikes*, his latest collaboration with Nunzio DeFilippis, Christine Weir, and Oni Press. He also watches a lot of *Buffy The Vampire Slayer*.

Nunzio DeFilippis & Christina Weir

Nunzio DeFilippis was born in New York, grew up in New York, loves New York, and lives in Los Angeles. He is a graduate of USC's screenwriting program and has written several feature films that no one will ever see, including one that was purchased by a production company that

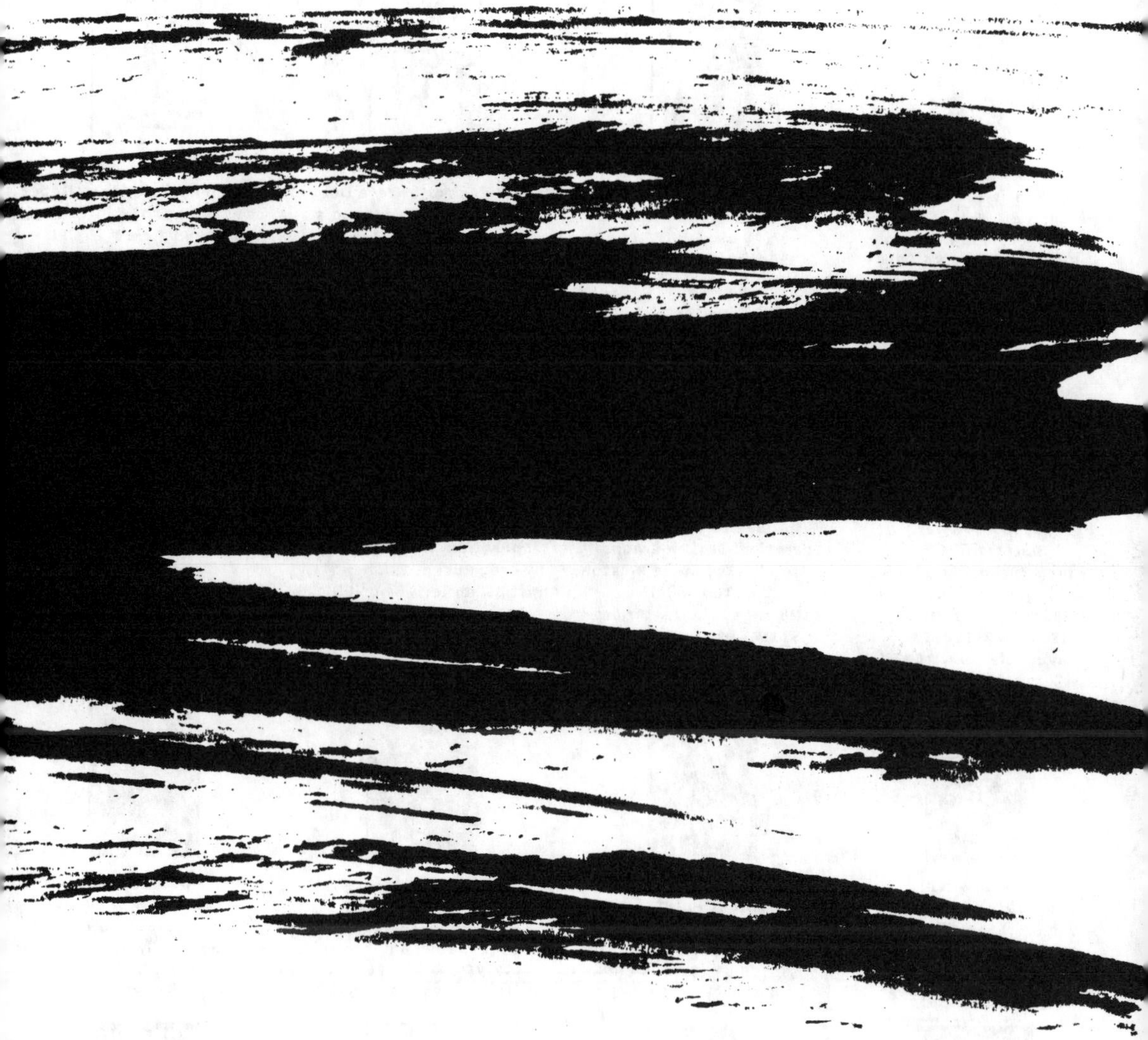

went out of business mere weeks later. After that, he started writing with Christina Weir.

Christina Weir was born in New York but spent her formative years in Boston. She has a Master's Degree in Television Production (for all the good that does) from Emerson College. She has lived in Los Angeles for the past nine years.

As a team, they have spent several years writing for television. They were on the writing staff of HBO's *Arliss* for two seasons, and have worked on Disney's *Kim Possible*. In addition, they have written several feature films, none of which have been produced. This led them to explore the comics medium, collaborating on *Skinwalker* for Oni Press, as well as the forthcoming *Three Strikes* and *Maria's Wedding*. Nunzio has also scripted an issue of *Detective Comics* as a solo writer.

Durwin Talon

Since the dream of becoming a nuclear physicist never panned out for this Canadian boy, Durwin Talon decided that the pursuit of art should be a sufficiently challenging career move. Of course, this would prove to be a classic, if not wildly ironic understatement. He has been an illustrator, graphic designer, art director, lecturer, and educator (he currently teaches in the New Media Program at Indiana University, Indianapolis), but he still maintains that the 124-page graphic novel he collaborated on in high school was his toughest gig. In comics, Talon has written *Panel Discussions*, an overview of the design trends in sequential art storytelling, and has illustrated covers for *Batman: Officer Down*, *Queen and Country*, and of course *Skinwalker*. His goal is to complete the great American Graphic Novel before his 80th birthday.

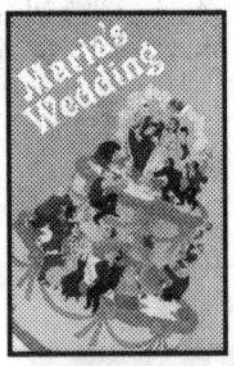
Maria's Wedding

Maria's Wedding™
By Nunzio DeFilippis,
Christina Weir, & Jose Garibaldi
88 pages, b&W interiors
$10.95 US, $15.95 CAN
ISBN: 1-929998-57-0
Available July, 2003

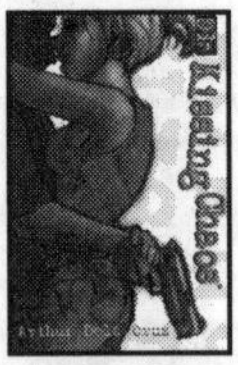
Kissing Chaos

Kissing Chaos™
by Arthur Dela Cruz
196 pages, b&W interiors
$17.95 US, $28.95 CAN
ISBN: 1-929998-32-5

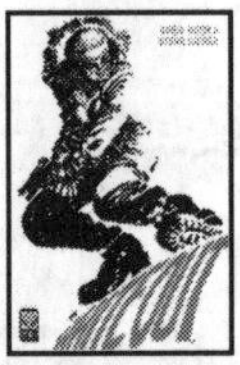

Whiteout™
by Greg Rucka & Steve Lieber
128 pages, b&W interiors
$11.95 US, $16.95 CAB
ISBN 0-9667127-1-4

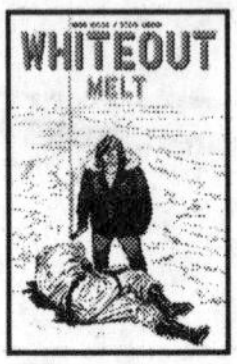
WHITEOUT
MELT

Whiteout: Melt™
by Greg Rucka & Steve Lieber
128 pages, b&W interiors
$11.95 US, $16.95 CAN
ISBN 1-929998-03-1

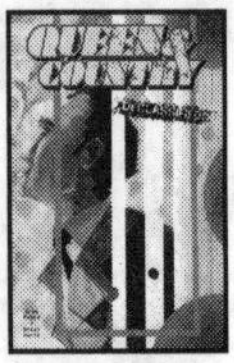

Queen & Country: Declassified™
by Greg Rucka & Brian Hurtt
88 pages, b&W interiors
$8.95 US, $12.95 CAN
ISBN 1-929998-58-9
Available July, 2003

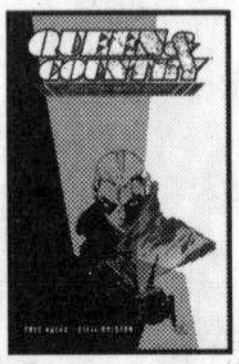

Queen & Country: Operation: Broken Ground™
by Greg Rucka, Steve Rolston, & Stan Sakai
128 pages, b&W interiors
$11.95 US, $16.95 CAN
ISBN 1-929998-21-X

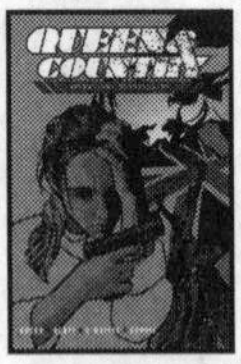

Queen & Country: Operation: Morningstar™
By Greg Rucka, Brian Hurtt, Christine Norrie, & Bryan O'Malley
88 pages, b&W interiors
$8.95 US, $12.95 CAN
ISBN: 1-929998-35-X

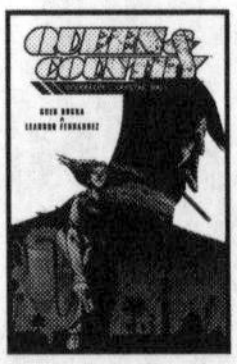

Queen & Country: Operation: Crystal Ball™
By Greg Rucka & Leandro Fernandez
152 pages, b&W interiors
$14.95 US, $22.50 CAN
ISBN: 1-929998-49-X

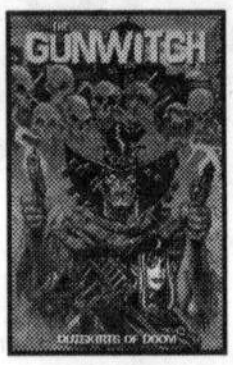
GUNWITCH

The Gunwitch: Outskirts of Doom™
by Dan Brereton & Ted Naifeh
88 pages, b&W interiors
$9.95 US, $13.95 CAN
ISBN: 1-929998-22-8

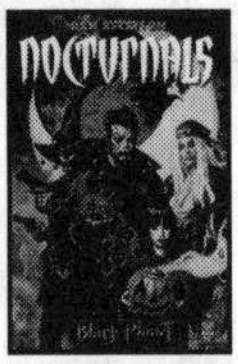
NOCTURNALS

Nocturnals®: BLACK PLANET
by Dan Brereton
184 pages, fully painted color
$19.95 US, $27.95 CAN
ISBN: 0-9667127-0-6

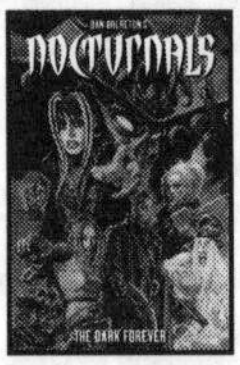
NOCTURNALS

Nocturnals®: The Dark Forever
by Dan Brereton
96 pages, fully painted color
$9.95 US, $13.95 CAN
ISBN: 1-929998-23-6

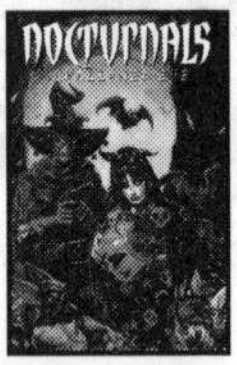
NOCTURNALS

Nocturnals®: Unhallowed Eve
by Dan Brereton & various
96 pages, fully painted color
$9.95 US, $13.95 CAN
ISBN: 1-929998-43-0

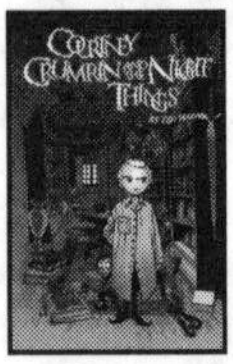

Courtney Crumrin & The Night Things™
by Ted Naifeh
128 pages, b&W interiors
$11.95 US, $17.95 CAN
ISBN: 1-929998-42-2

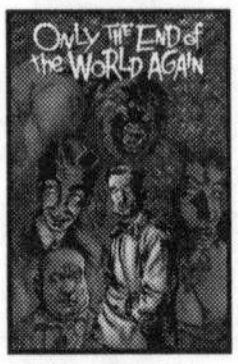
Only the End of the World Again

Only The End of the World Again™
by Neil Gaiman, P. Craig Russell, Troy Nixey, & Matthew Hollingsworth
48 pages, full color interiors
$6.95 US, $10.95 CAN
ISBN: 1-929998-09-0

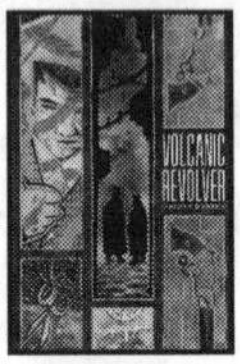
VOLCANIC
REVOLVER

Volcanic Revolver™
by Scott Morse
120 pages,
sepia-and-white interiors
$9.95 US, $15.95 CAN
ISBN 0-9667127-5-7

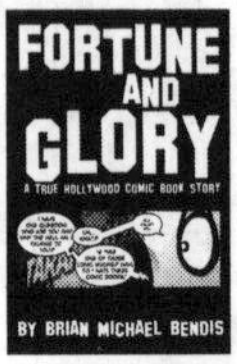
FORTUNE AND GLORY
A TRUE HOLLYWOOD COMIC BOOK STORY
BY BRIAN MICHAEL BENDIS

FORTUNE & GLORY: A TRUE HOLLYWOOD COMIC BOOK STORY™
by Brian Michael Bendis
136 pages, b&W interiors
$14.95 US, $22.50 CAN
ISBN 1-929998-06-6

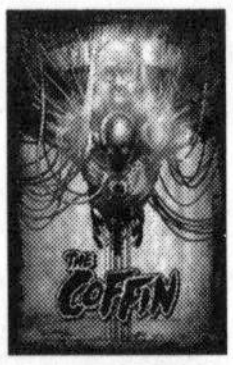
THE COFFIN

The Coffin™
by Phil Hester & Mike Huddleston
120 pages, b&W interiors
$11.95 US, $17.95 CAN
ISBN: 1-929998-16-3

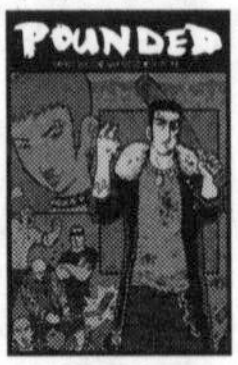
POUNDED

Pounded™
by Brian Wood & Steve Rolston
88 pages, b&W interiors
$8.95 U.S., $12.95 CAN
ISBN: 1-929998-37-6

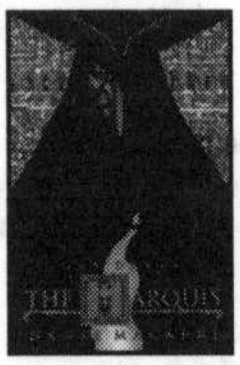

The Marquis: Danse Macabre™
by Guy Davis
192 pages, b&W interiors
$18.95 US, $27.95 CAN
ISBN: 1-929998-15-5

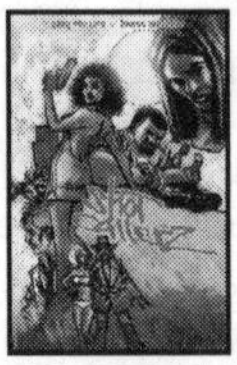

Shot Callerz™
by Gary Phillips & Brett Weldele
128 pages, b&W interiors
$11.95 US, $16.95 CAN
ISBN 1-929998-46-5

Available at finer bookstores everywhere.

For a comics store near you, call 1-888-COMIC-BOOK or visit www.the-master-list.com..
For more information on more Oni Press books go to: www.onipress.com